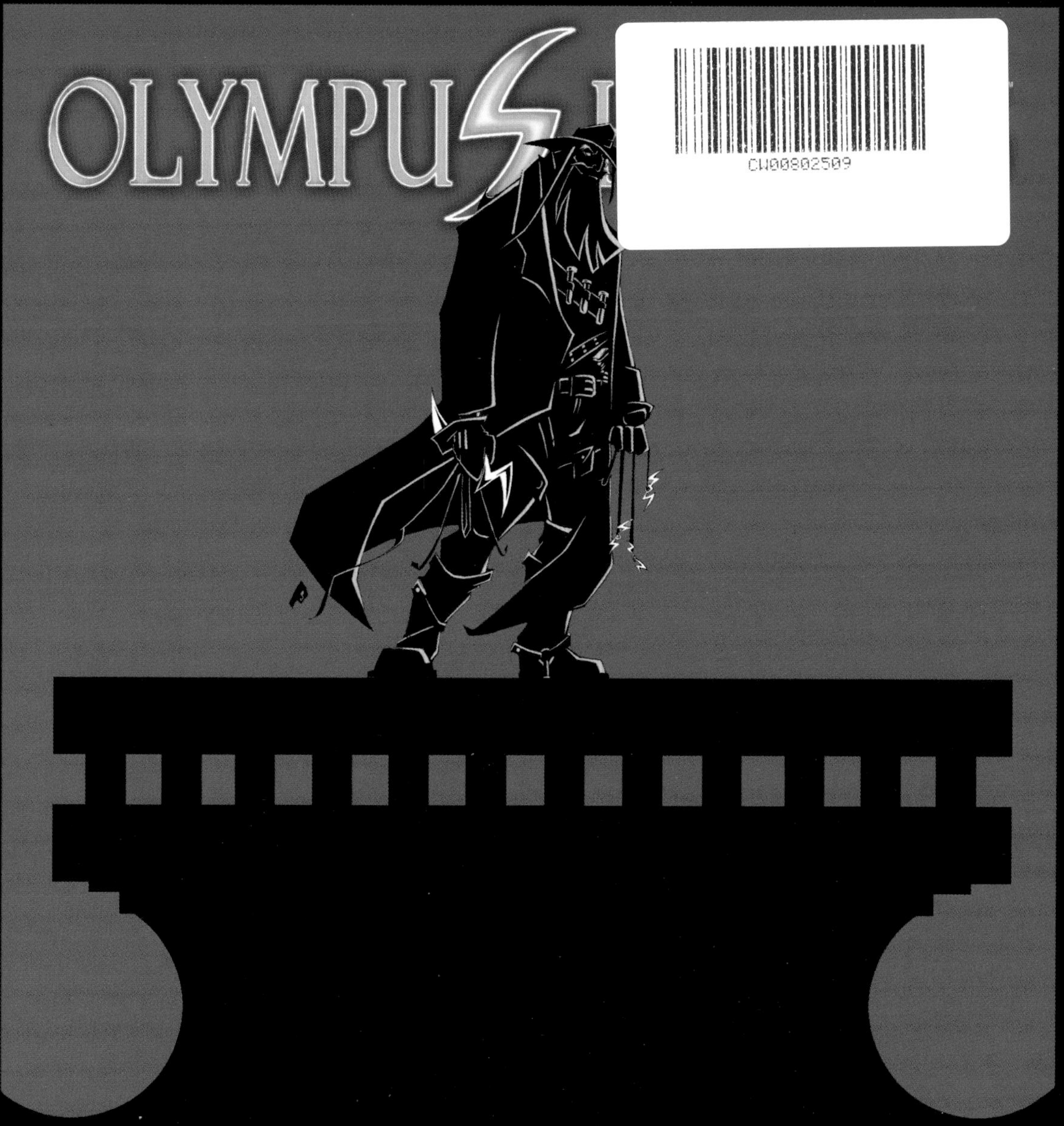
OLYMPUS

written and drawn by

Kevin Munroe

IDW

IDW Publishing
San Diego

OLYMPUS HEIGHTS

Kevin Munroe
story and art

Brian Beppu & Kevin Munroe
covers

Robbie Robbins & Cindy Chapman
letters

Cindy Chapman
design

Jeff Mariotte & Chris Ryall
original series editors

Chris Ryall
collection editor

www.IDWPUBLISHING.com

ISBN:1-932382-55-0

08 07 06 05   1 2 3 4 5

IDW Publishing is:
Ted Adams Publisher
Chris Ryall Editor-in-Chief
Robbie Robbins Design Director
Kris Oprisko Vice President
Alex Garner Art Director
Cindy Chapman Operations Manager
Tom B. Long Designer
Chance Boren Editorial Assistant
Yumiko Miyano Business Development
Rick Privman Business Development

INTRODUCTION

Thanks for picking up this book. If you're one of the few people who don't know me that will buy this book, you have no idea how flattered I am that ANYONE would buy this and allow themselves to be entertained by what I do.

Two children and a marriage of almost twelve years and I still was taught a very big lesson on what a "labor of love" is. I don't think I've ever worked so hard while loving and hating something at the same time so much in my entire life.

This book would not have happened without the love and support of my wife Lorelei who, for better or worse, suffered through a year of my half-listening "uh-huhs" while I was working and her near-tendonitis from erasing all of my inked pages.

Speaking of which, to Alexandra and Nathaniel, my kids and probably two of the funniest people I know—which says a lot, as I make a living surrounding myself with funny people—you're too young to realize it now, but one day you'll know how much it meant to me that you allowed me to miss so many dinners and just pencil pages while you played on the floor by the desk. You're better than coffee on a morning after only three hours sleep.

To Ted, Chris, Jeff, Robbie, Cindy, and everyone else at IDW Publishing. You are quite possibly the coolest people in the business and it was so reassuring to know that there is a reason why everyone speaks so highly of you. It is an honor to be in your club... even if I'm the red-headed second cousin who doesn't draw horror pictures.

To Brian Beppu, a good friend and one of the best painters I know. I'm so grateful that you agreed to paint the covers at no one's expense but your own. I'm sure you're most of the reason why anyone picked this book up in the first place after seeing your great work on the front. I'll never forget that.

To Dave Wilkins and Tony Washington—the better two-thirds of the *El Zombo Fantasma* team. Thanks for the great pin-up that really just made me wish you did the art for all of *Olympus* to begin with.

This story is filled with the stuff I daydream about—monsters, character ensembles, gadgets, and the concept that your ordinary life can be dramatically changed if you just look under the right rock. And that a family, however bizarre or out of the ordinary it is, is still a family. Whether it's the friend you meet for fruit smoothies every week to complain about work or the cacophonous ensemble that is the Friday night dinner table. Look around. Find yours and be thankful you have one.

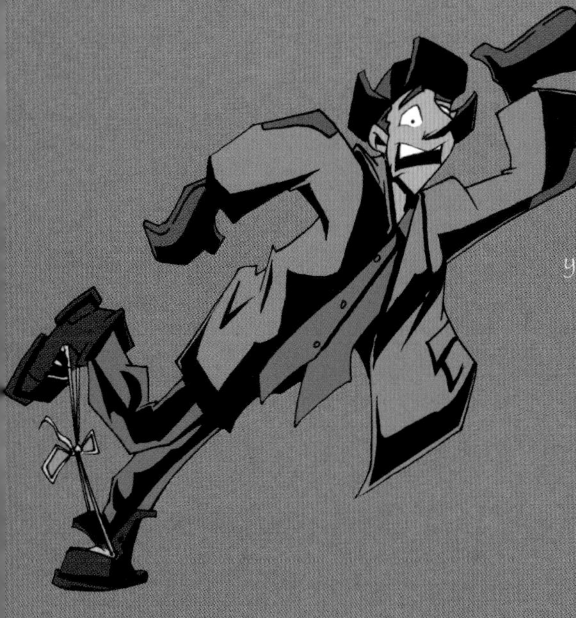

I know I am.

Enjoy,

Kevin Munroe
November 16, 2004

Chapter One

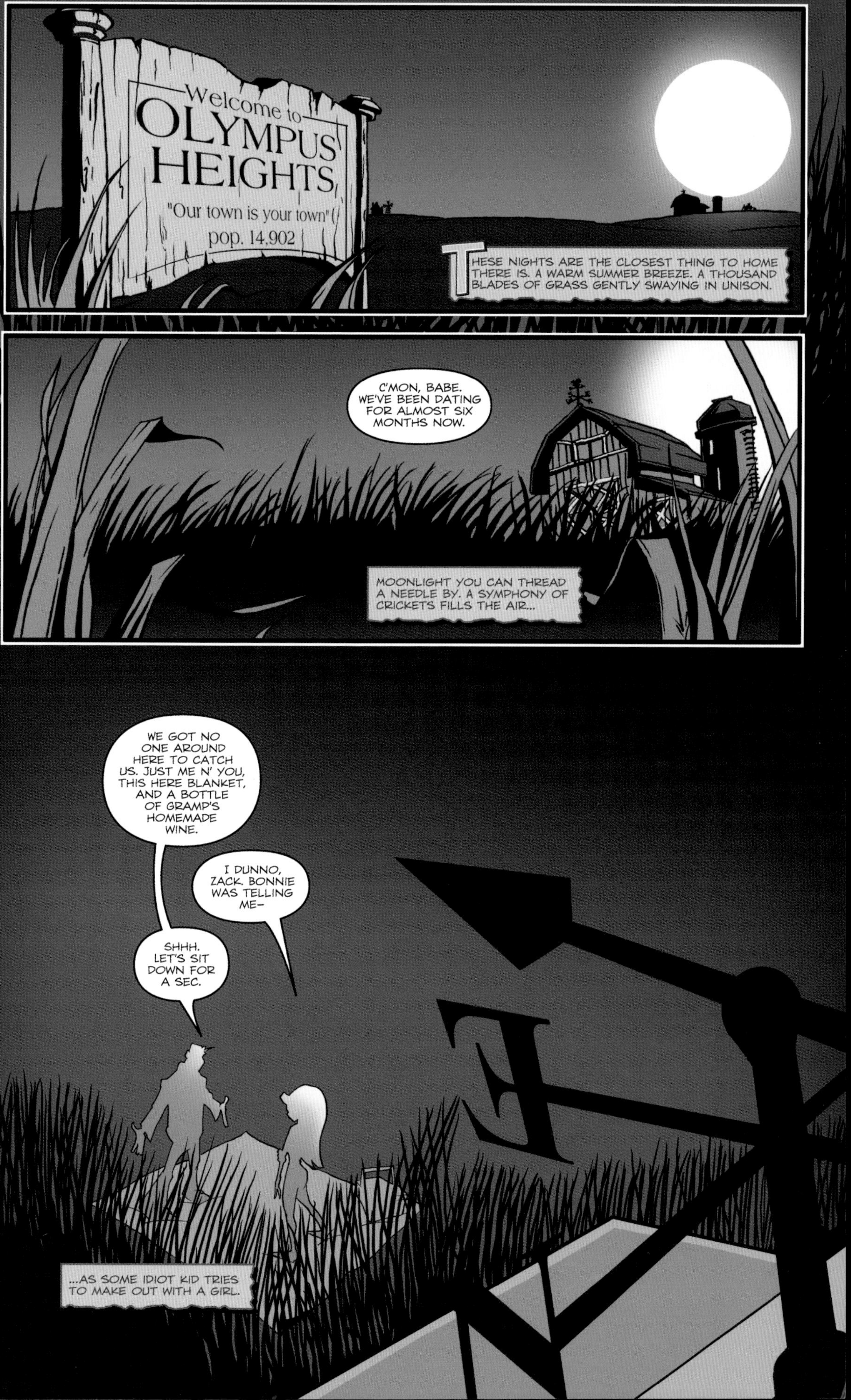
Welcome to OLYMPUS HEIGHTS
"Our town is your town"
pop. 14,902
THESE NIGHTS ARE THE CLOSEST THING TO HOME THERE IS. A WARM SUMMER BREEZE. A THOUSAND BLADES OF GRASS GENTLY SWAYING IN UNISON.
C'MON, BABE. WE'VE BEEN DATING FOR ALMOST SIX MONTHS NOW.
MOONLIGHT YOU CAN THREAD A NEEDLE BY. A SYMPHONY OF CRICKETS FILLS THE AIR...
WE GOT NO ONE AROUND HERE TO CATCH US. JUST ME N' YOU, THIS HERE BLANKET, AND A BOTTLE OF GRAMP'S HOMEMADE WINE.
I DUNNO, ZACK. BONNIE WAS TELLING ME–
SHHH. LET'S SIT DOWN FOR A SEC.
...AS SOME IDIOT KID TRIES TO MAKE OUT WITH A GIRL.

AND I HAVE TO WORK TONIGHT. BEEN MONTHS SINCE THE LAST ONE. HOPEFULLY IT'S JUST THE SENSORS TRIPPING AGAIN. HOPEFULLY.

BABY, IT'S TIME TO MOVE THINGS TO THE NEXT LEVEL.

BUT YOU SAID YOU JUST WANTED TO TALK.

I KNOW BABY. I WANTED TO TALK ABOUT *THIS.*

WHINNNNNY.

RUSTLE-RUSTLE

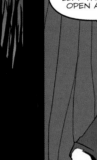

FREAKIN' SCOTTY. MUSTA LEFT THE GATE OPEN AGAIN.

SO BABE, LIKE I WAS SAYING—

WHINNNNNY.

TONIGHT, BABY, IT'S ALL ABOUT—

SMACK!

G'WAN BOY! GIT ON HOME!

—IT'S ALL ABOUT *YOU.*

GHRAAARRRR

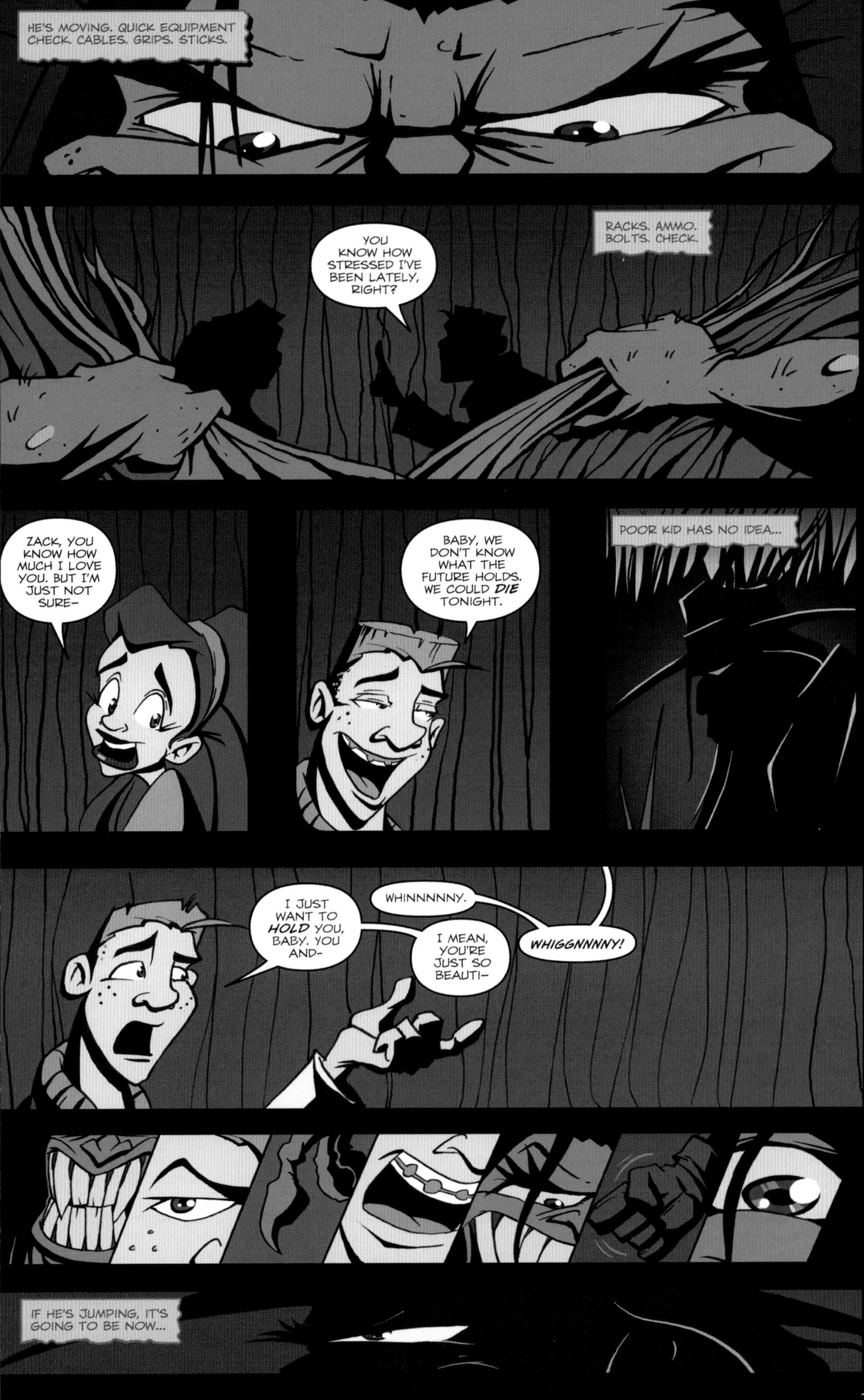
HE'S MOVING. QUICK EQUIPMENT CHECK. CABLES. GRIPS. STICKS.
RACKS. AMMO. BOLTS. CHECK.
YOU KNOW HOW STRESSED I'VE BEEN LATELY, RIGHT?
ZACK, YOU KNOW HOW MUCH I LOVE YOU. BUT I'M JUST NOT SURE-
BABY, WE DON'T KNOW WHAT THE FUTURE HOLDS. WE COULD *DIE* TONIGHT.
POOR KID HAS NO IDEA...
I JUST WANT TO *HOLD* YOU, BABY. YOU AND-
I MEAN, YOU'RE JUST SO BEAUTI-
WHINNNNNY.
WHIGGNNNNY!
IF HE'S JUMPING, IT'S GOING TO BE NOW...

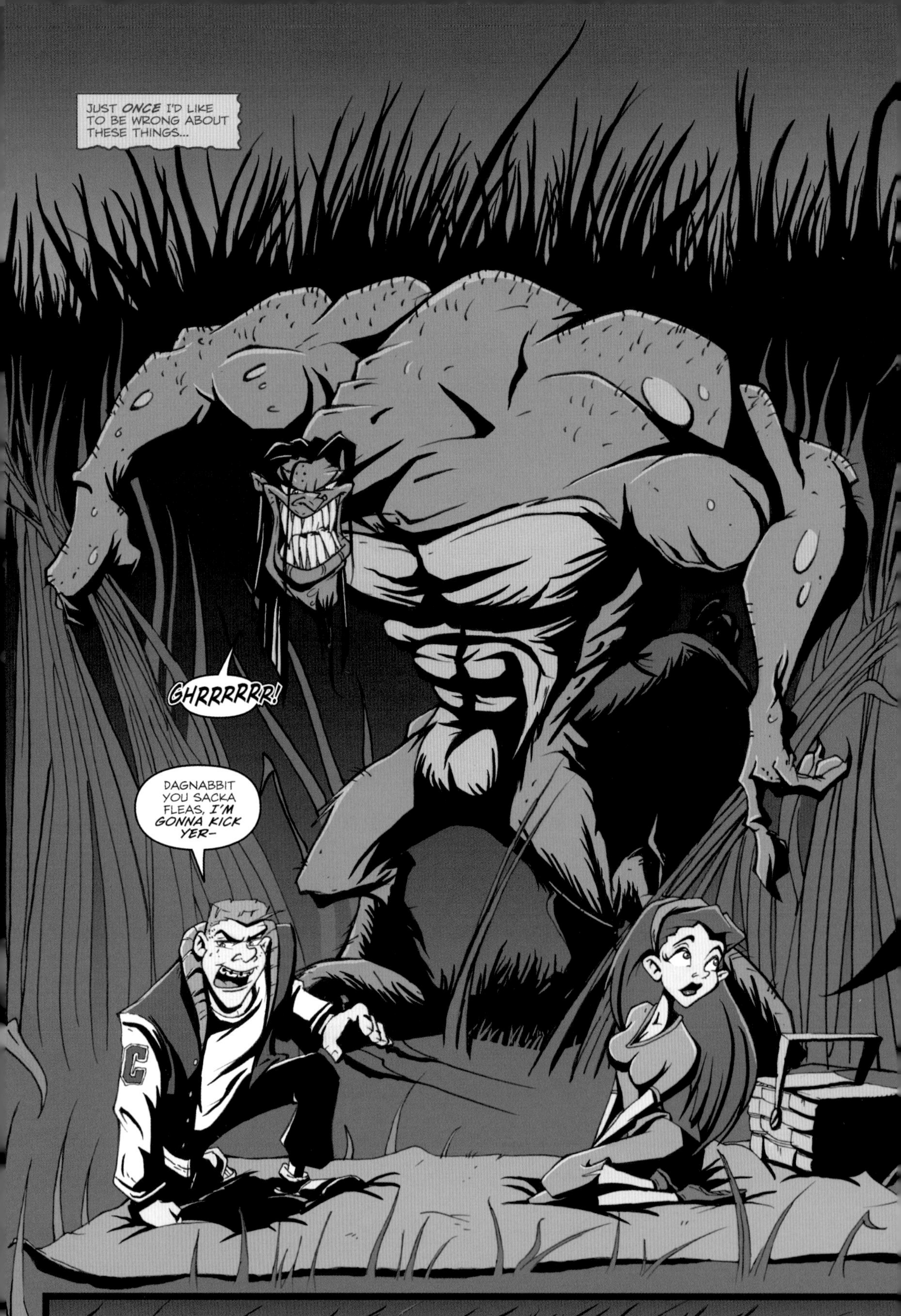

JUST *ONCE* I'D LIKE TO BE WRONG ABOUT THESE THINGS...
GHRRRRRR!
DAGNABBIT YOU SACKA FLEAS, *I'M GONNA KICK YER-*

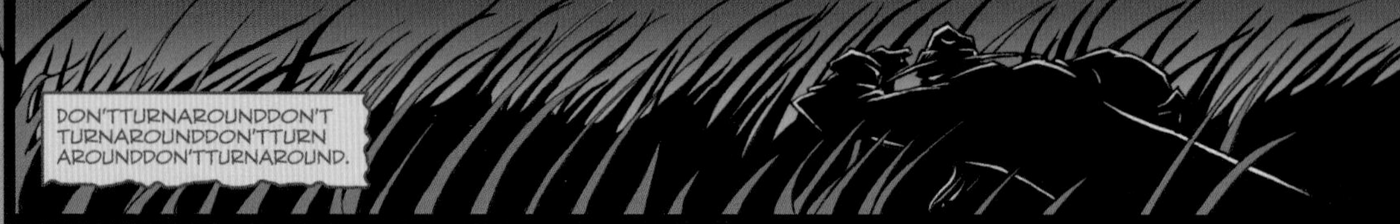

DON'TTURNAROUNDDON'T TURNAROUNDDON'TTURN AROUNDDON'TTURNAROUND.

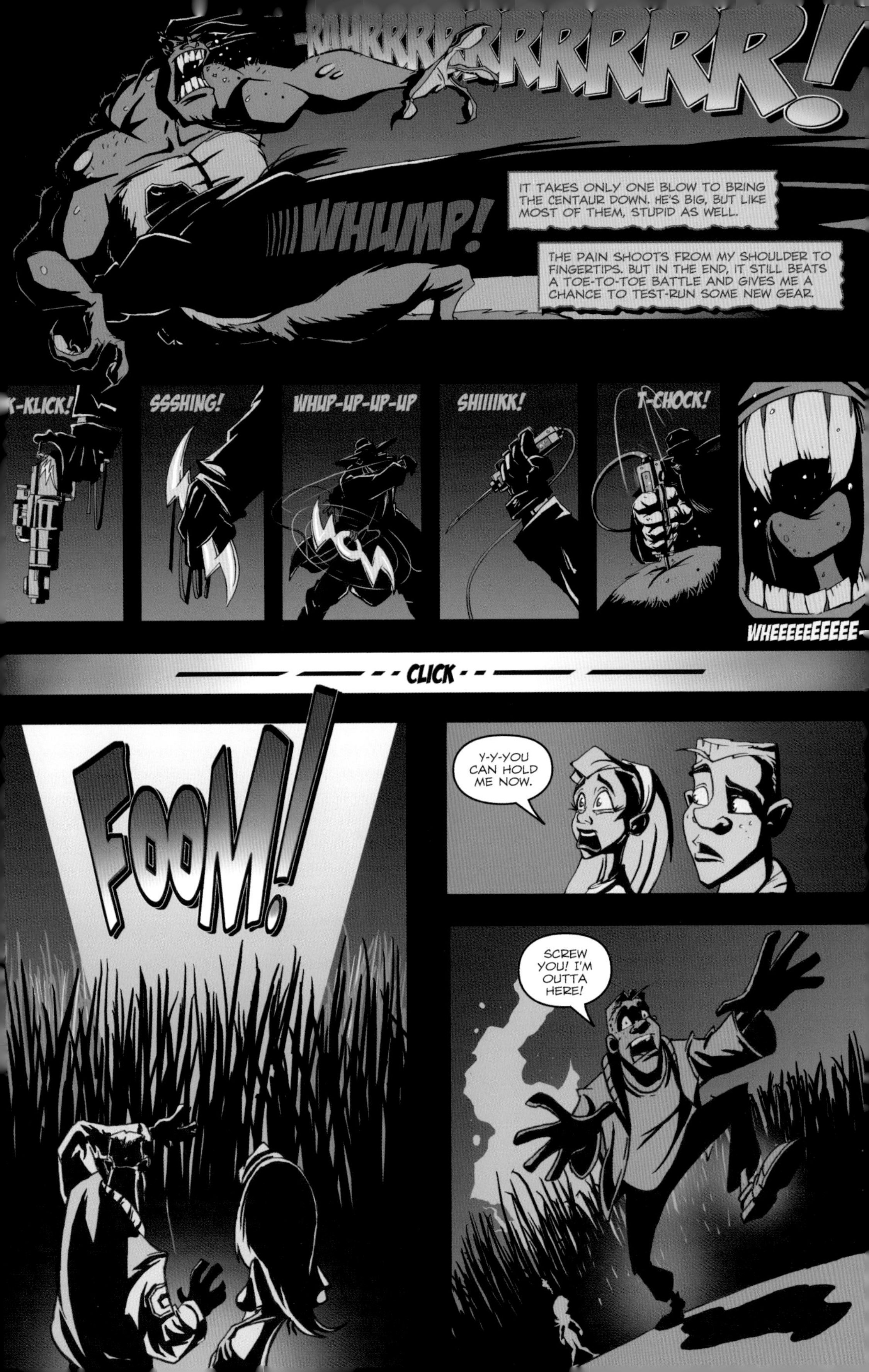
-RAHRRRRRRRRRRRR!
IT TAKES ONLY ONE BLOW TO BRING THE CENTAUR DOWN. HE'S BIG, BUT LIKE MOST OF THEM, STUPID AS WELL.
WHUMP!
THE PAIN SHOOTS FROM MY SHOULDER TO FINGERTIPS. BUT IN THE END, IT STILL BEATS A TOE-TO-TOE BATTLE AND GIVES ME A CHANCE TO TEST-RUN SOME NEW GEAR.
K-KLICK!
SSSHING!
WHUP-UP-UP-UP
SHIIIIKK!
T-CHOCK!
WHEEEEEEEEEE-
CLICK
FOOM!!
Y-Y-YOU CAN HOLD ME NOW.
SCREW YOU! I'M OUTTA HERE!

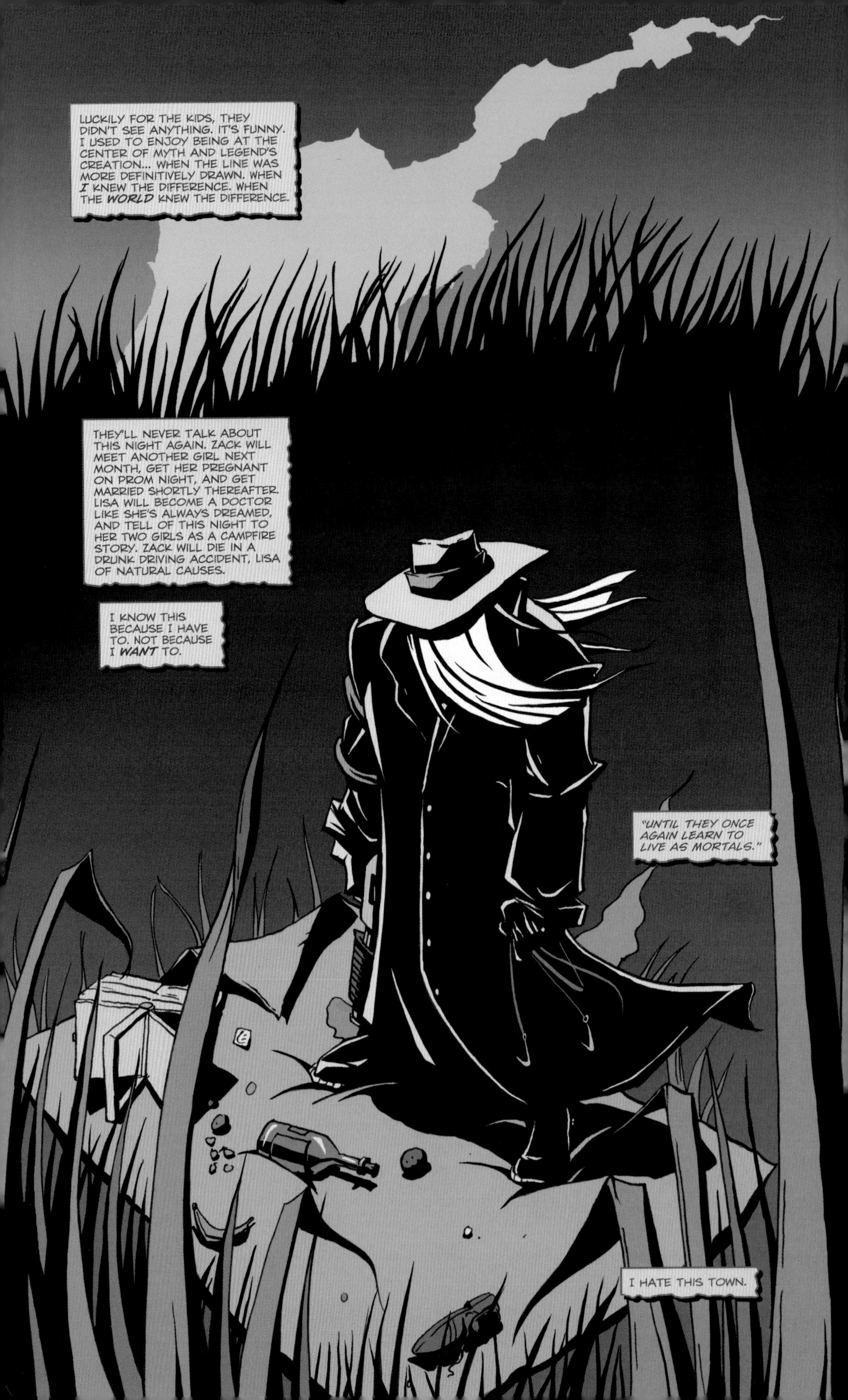
LUCKILY FOR THE KIDS, THEY DIDN'T SEE ANYTHING. IT'S FUNNY. I USED TO ENJOY BEING AT THE CENTER OF MYTH AND LEGEND'S CREATION... WHEN THE LINE WAS MORE DEFINITIVELY DRAWN. WHEN *I* KNEW THE DIFFERENCE. WHEN THE ***WORLD*** KNEW THE DIFFERENCE.
THEY'LL NEVER TALK ABOUT THIS NIGHT AGAIN. ZACK WILL MEET ANOTHER GIRL NEXT MONTH, GET HER PREGNANT ON PROM NIGHT, AND GET MARRIED SHORTLY THEREAFTER. LISA WILL BECOME A DOCTOR LIKE SHE'S ALWAYS DREAMED, AND TELL OF THIS NIGHT TO HER TWO GIRLS AS A CAMPFIRE STORY. ZACK WILL DIE IN A DRUNK DRIVING ACCIDENT, LISA OF NATURAL CAUSES.
I KNOW THIS BECAUSE I HAVE TO. NOT BECAUSE I ***WANT*** TO.
"UNTIL THEY ONCE AGAIN LEARN TO LIVE AS MORTALS."
I HATE THIS TOWN.

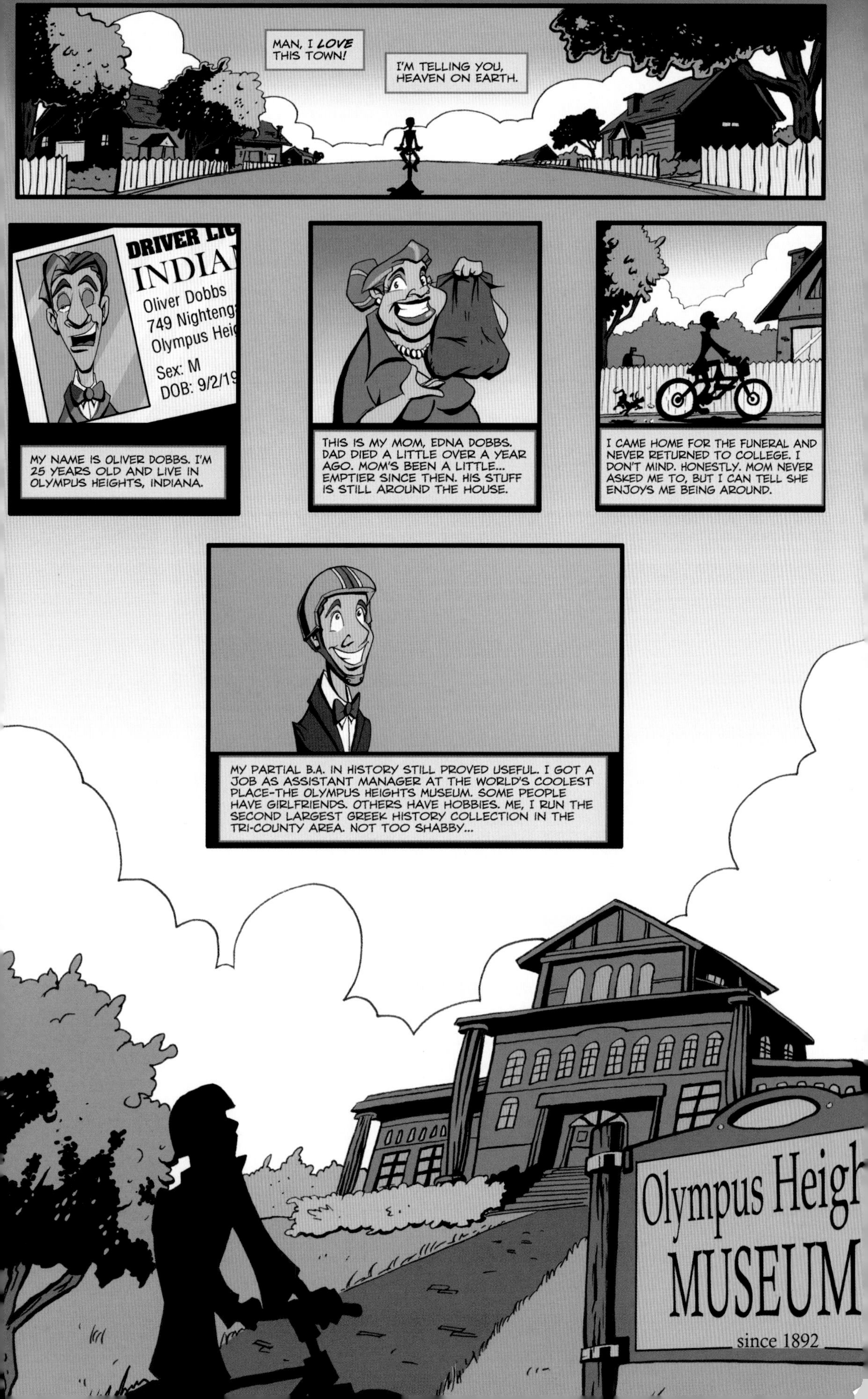
MAN, I LOVE THIS TOWN!
I'M TELLING YOU, HEAVEN ON EARTH.
DRIVER LIC
INDIA
Oliver Dobbs
749 Nighteng
Olympus Heig
Sex: M
DOB: 9/2/19
MY NAME IS OLIVER DOBBS. I'M 25 YEARS OLD AND LIVE IN OLYMPUS HEIGHTS, INDIANA.
THIS IS MY MOM, EDNA DOBBS. DAD DIED A LITTLE OVER A YEAR AGO. MOM'S BEEN A LITTLE... EMPTIER SINCE THEN. HIS STUFF IS STILL AROUND THE HOUSE.
I CAME HOME FOR THE FUNERAL AND NEVER RETURNED TO COLLEGE. I DON'T MIND. HONESTLY. MOM NEVER ASKED ME TO, BUT I CAN TELL SHE ENJOYS ME BEING AROUND.
MY PARTIAL B.A. IN HISTORY STILL PROVED USEFUL. I GOT A JOB AS ASSISTANT MANAGER AT THE WORLD'S COOLEST PLACE-THE OLYMPUS HEIGHTS MUSEUM. SOME PEOPLE HAVE GIRLFRIENDS. OTHERS HAVE HOBBIES. ME, I RUN THE SECOND LARGEST GREEK HISTORY COLLECTION IN THE TRI-COUNTY AREA. NOT TOO SHABBY...
Olympus Heigh
MUSEUM
since 1892

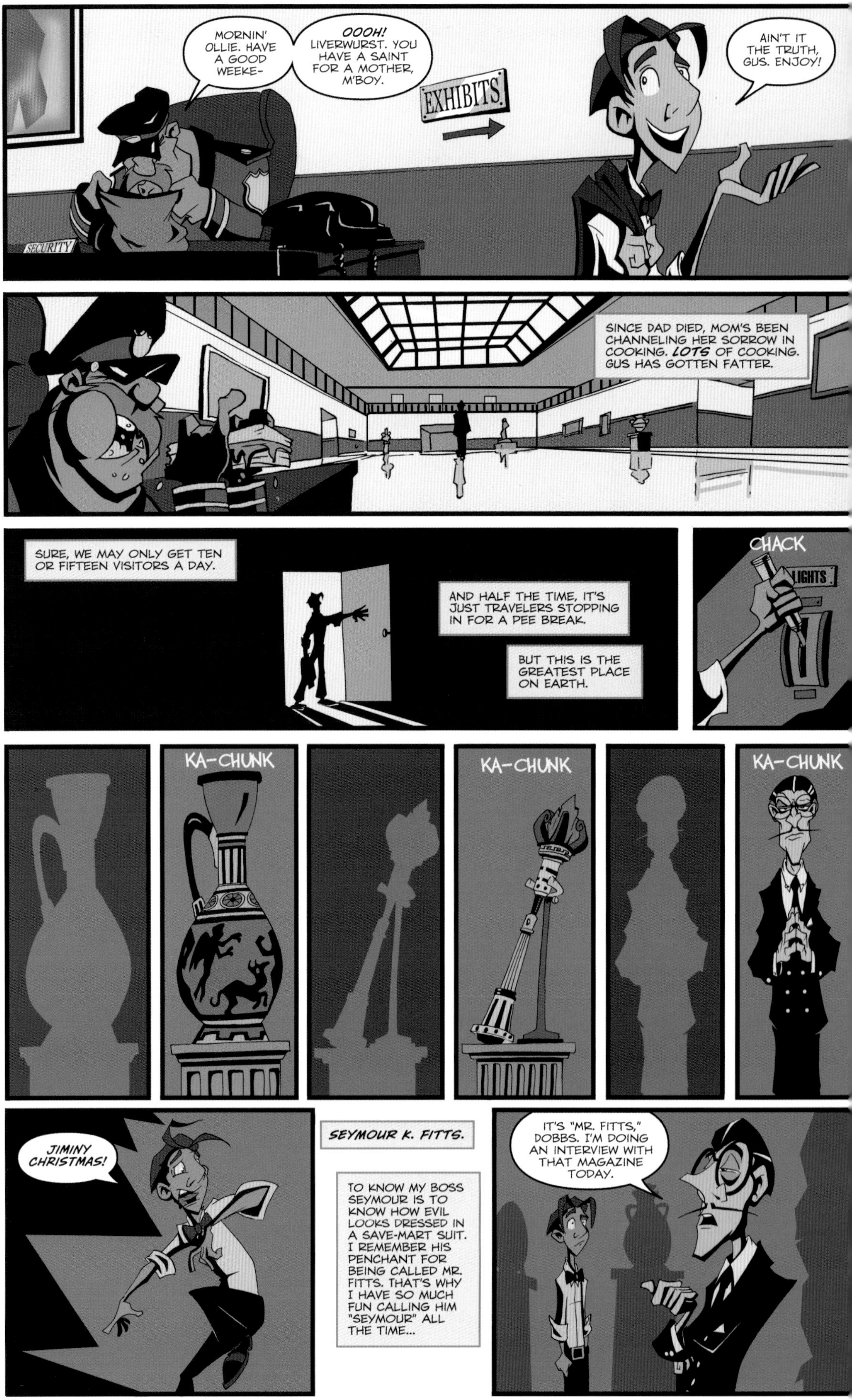

MORNIN' OLLIE. HAVE A GOOD WEEKE-
OOOH! LIVERWURST. YOU HAVE A SAINT FOR A MOTHER, M'BOY.
EXHIBITS
AIN'T IT THE TRUTH, GUS. ENJOY!
SECURITY
SINCE DAD DIED, MOM'S BEEN CHANNELING HER SORROW IN COOKING. LOTS OF COOKING. GUS HAS GOTTEN FATTER.
SURE, WE MAY ONLY GET TEN OR FIFTEEN VISITORS A DAY.
AND HALF THE TIME, IT'S JUST TRAVELERS STOPPING IN FOR A PEE BREAK.
BUT THIS IS THE GREATEST PLACE ON EARTH.
CHACK
LIGHTS
KA-CHUNK
KA-CHUNK
KA-CHUNK
JIMINY CHRISTMAS!
SEYMOUR K. FITTS.
TO KNOW MY BOSS SEYMOUR IS TO KNOW HOW EVIL LOOKS DRESSED IN A SAVE-MART SUIT. I REMEMBER HIS PENCHANT FOR BEING CALLED MR. FITTS. THAT'S WHY I HAVE SO MUCH FUN CALLING HIM "SEYMOUR" ALL THE TIME...
IT'S "MR. FITTS," DOBBS. I'M DOING AN INTERVIEW WITH THAT MAGAZINE TODAY.

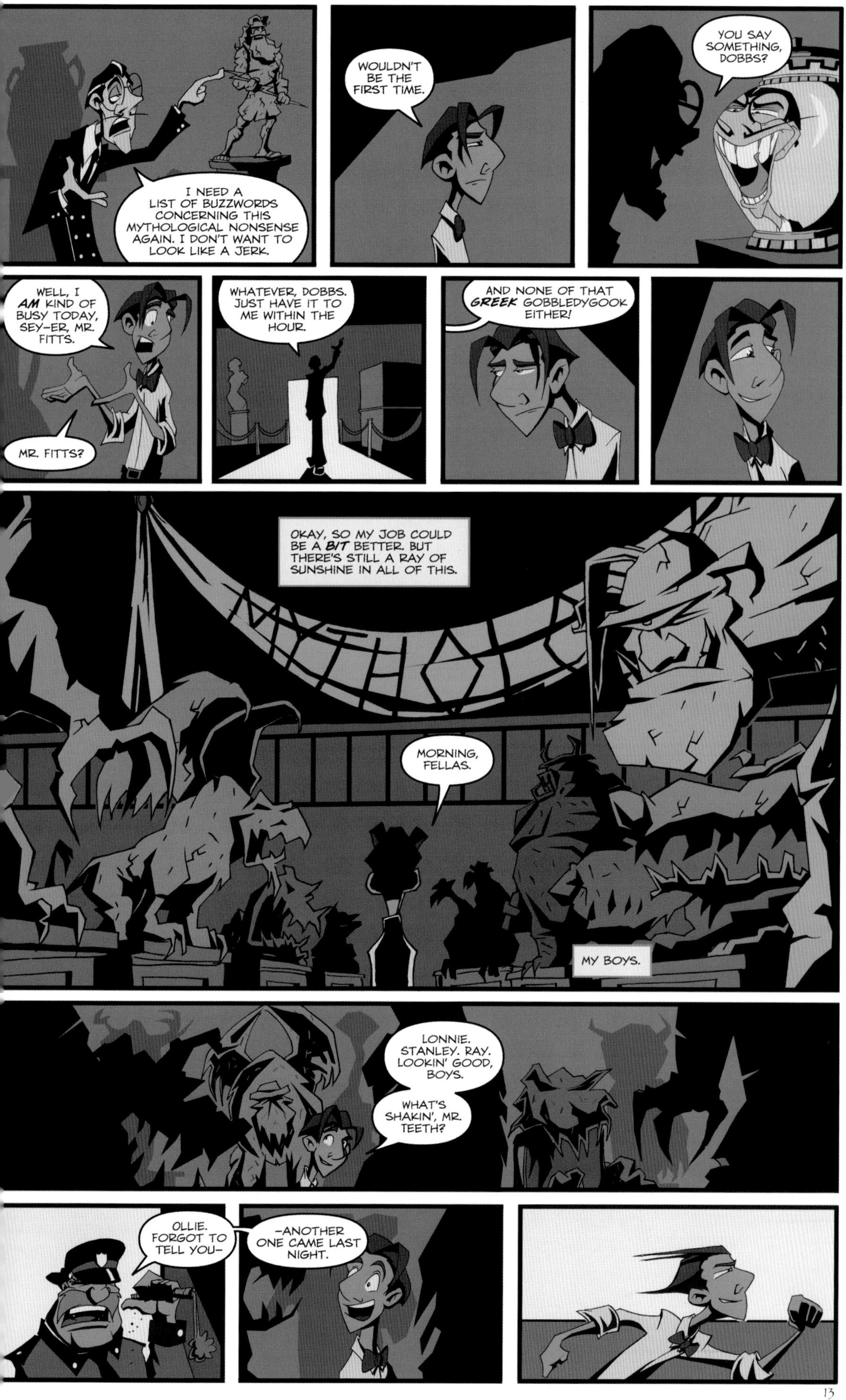
I NEED A LIST OF BUZZWORDS CONCERNING THIS MYTHOLOGICAL NONSENSE AGAIN. I DON'T WANT TO LOOK LIKE A JERK.
WOULDN'T BE THE FIRST TIME.
YOU SAY SOMETHING, DOBBS?
WELL, I AM KIND OF BUSY TODAY, SEY–ER, MR. FITTS.
MR. FITTS?
WHATEVER, DOBBS. JUST HAVE IT TO ME WITHIN THE HOUR.
AND NONE OF THAT GREEK GOBBLEDYGOOK EITHER!
OKAY, SO MY JOB COULD BE A BIT BETTER. BUT THERE'S STILL A RAY OF SUNSHINE IN ALL OF THIS.
MYTHO
MORNING, FELLAS.
MY BOYS.
LONNIE. STANLEY. RAY. LOOKIN' GOOD, BOYS.
WHAT'S SHAKIN', MR. TEETH?
OLLIE. FORGOT TO TELL YOU–
–ANOTHER ONE CAME LAST NIGHT.

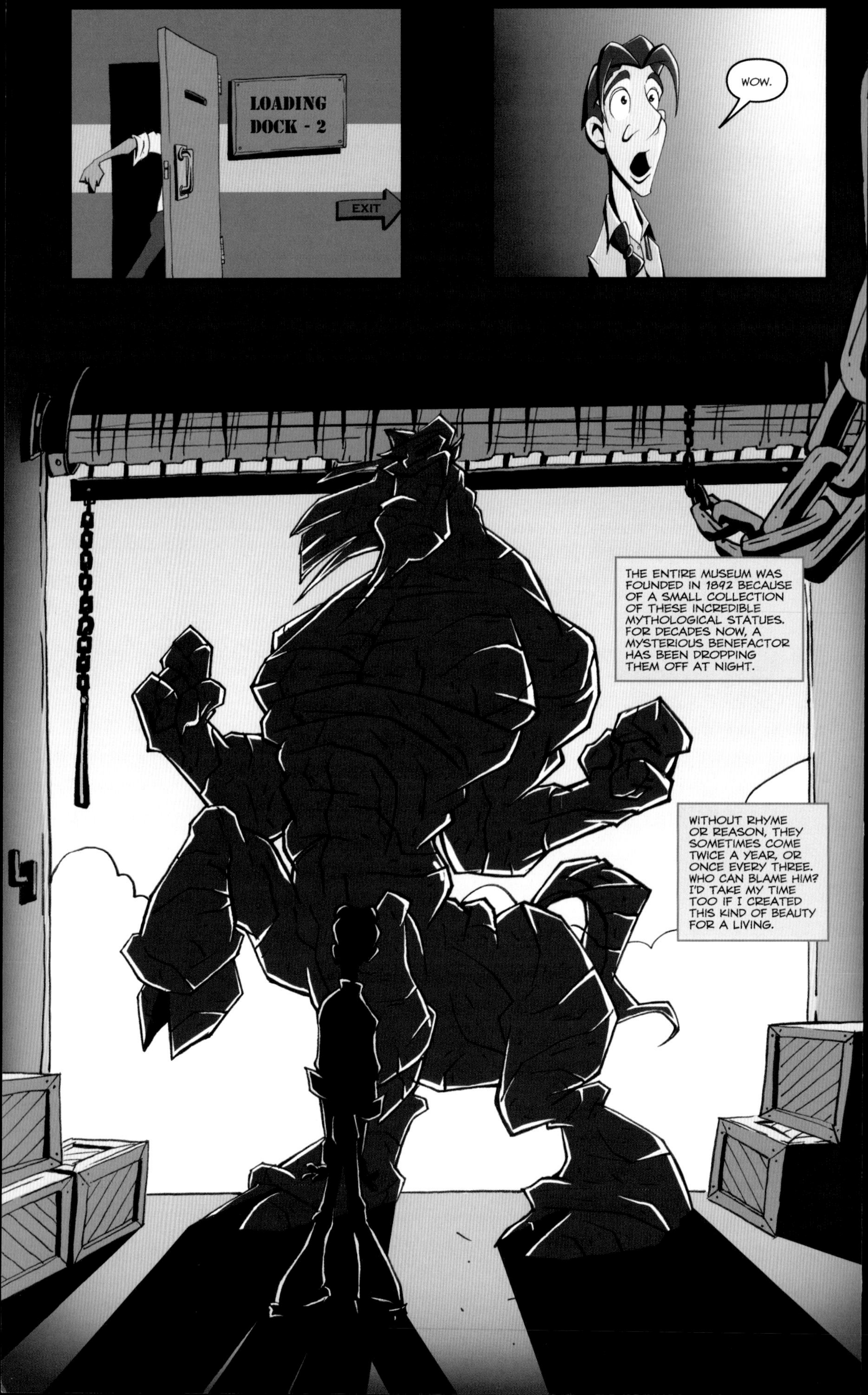
LOADING
DOCK - 2
EXIT
WOW.
THE ENTIRE MUSEUM WAS FOUNDED IN 1892 BECAUSE OF A SMALL COLLECTION OF THESE INCREDIBLE MYTHOLOGICAL STATUES. FOR DECADES NOW, A MYSTERIOUS BENEFACTOR HAS BEEN DROPPING THEM OFF AT NIGHT.
WITHOUT RHYME OR REASON, THEY SOMETIMES COME TWICE A YEAR, OR ONCE EVERY THREE. WHO CAN BLAME HIM? I'D TAKE MY TIME TOO IF I CREATED THIS KIND OF BEAUTY FOR A LIVING.

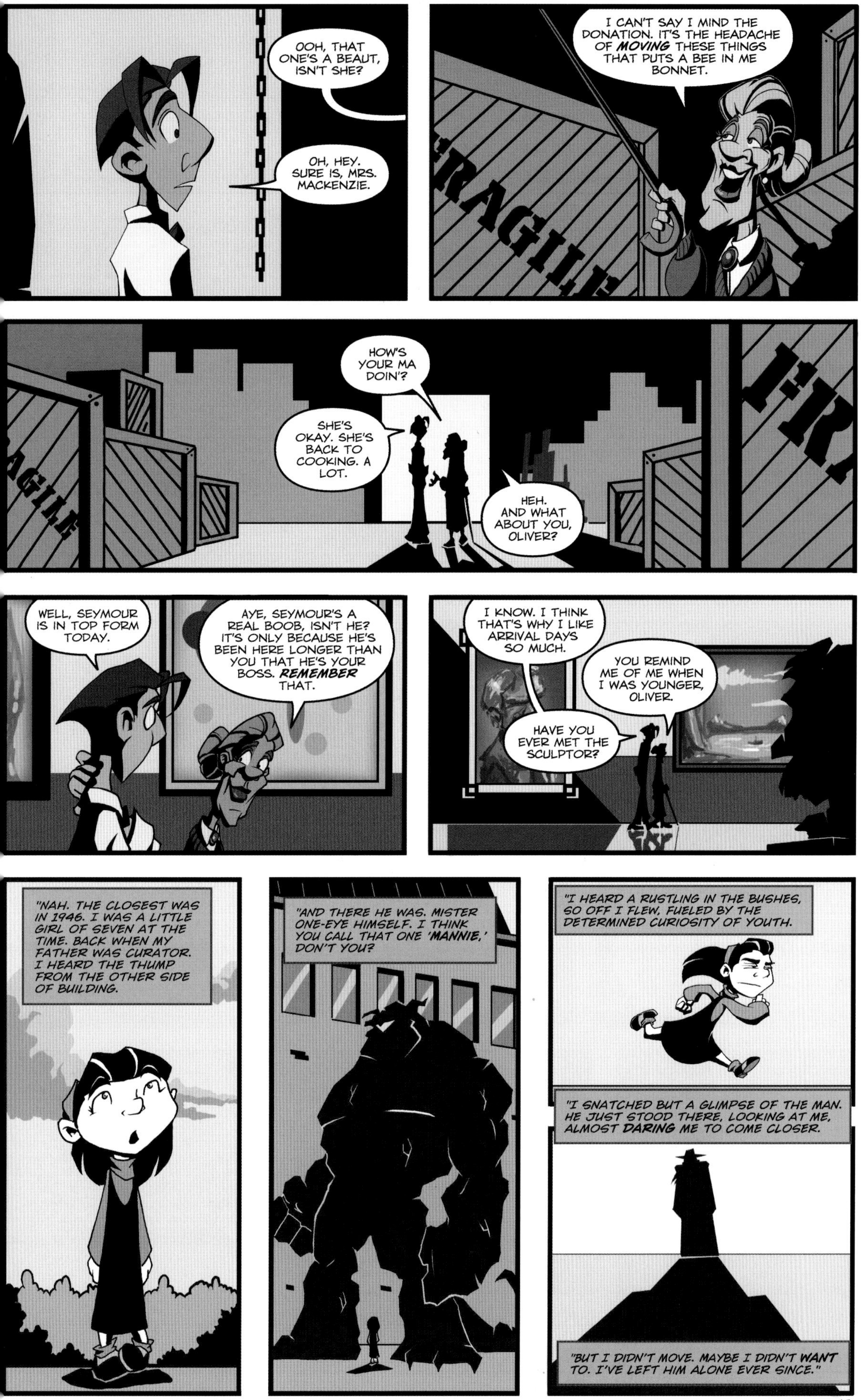
OOH, THAT ONE'S A BEAUT, ISN'T SHE?
OH, HEY. SURE IS, MRS. MACKENZIE.
I CAN'T SAY I MIND THE DONATION. IT'S THE HEADACHE OF MOVING THESE THINGS THAT PUTS A BEE IN ME BONNET.
FRAGILE
HOW'S YOUR MA DOIN'?
SHE'S OKAY. SHE'S BACK TO COOKING. A LOT.
HEH. AND WHAT ABOUT YOU, OLIVER?
WELL, SEYMOUR IS IN TOP FORM TODAY.
AYE, SEYMOUR'S A REAL BOOB, ISN'T HE? IT'S ONLY BECAUSE HE'S BEEN HERE LONGER THAN YOU THAT HE'S YOUR BOSS. REMEMBER THAT.
I KNOW. I THINK THAT'S WHY I LIKE ARRIVAL DAYS SO MUCH.
YOU REMIND ME OF ME WHEN I WAS YOUNGER, OLIVER.
HAVE YOU EVER MET THE SCULPTOR?
"NAH. THE CLOSEST WAS IN 1946. I WAS A LITTLE GIRL OF SEVEN AT THE TIME. BACK WHEN MY FATHER WAS CURATOR. I HEARD THE THUMP FROM THE OTHER SIDE OF BUILDING.
"AND THERE HE WAS. MISTER ONE-EYE HIMSELF. I THINK YOU CALL THAT ONE 'MANNIE,' DON'T YOU?
"I HEARD A RUSTLING IN THE BUSHES, SO OFF I FLEW, FUELED BY THE DETERMINED CURIOSITY OF YOUTH.
"I SNATCHED BUT A GLIMPSE OF THE MAN. HE JUST STOOD THERE, LOOKING AT ME, ALMOST DARING ME TO COME CLOSER.
"BUT I DIDN'T MOVE. MAYBE I DIDN'T WANT TO. I'VE LEFT HIM ALONE EVER SINCE."

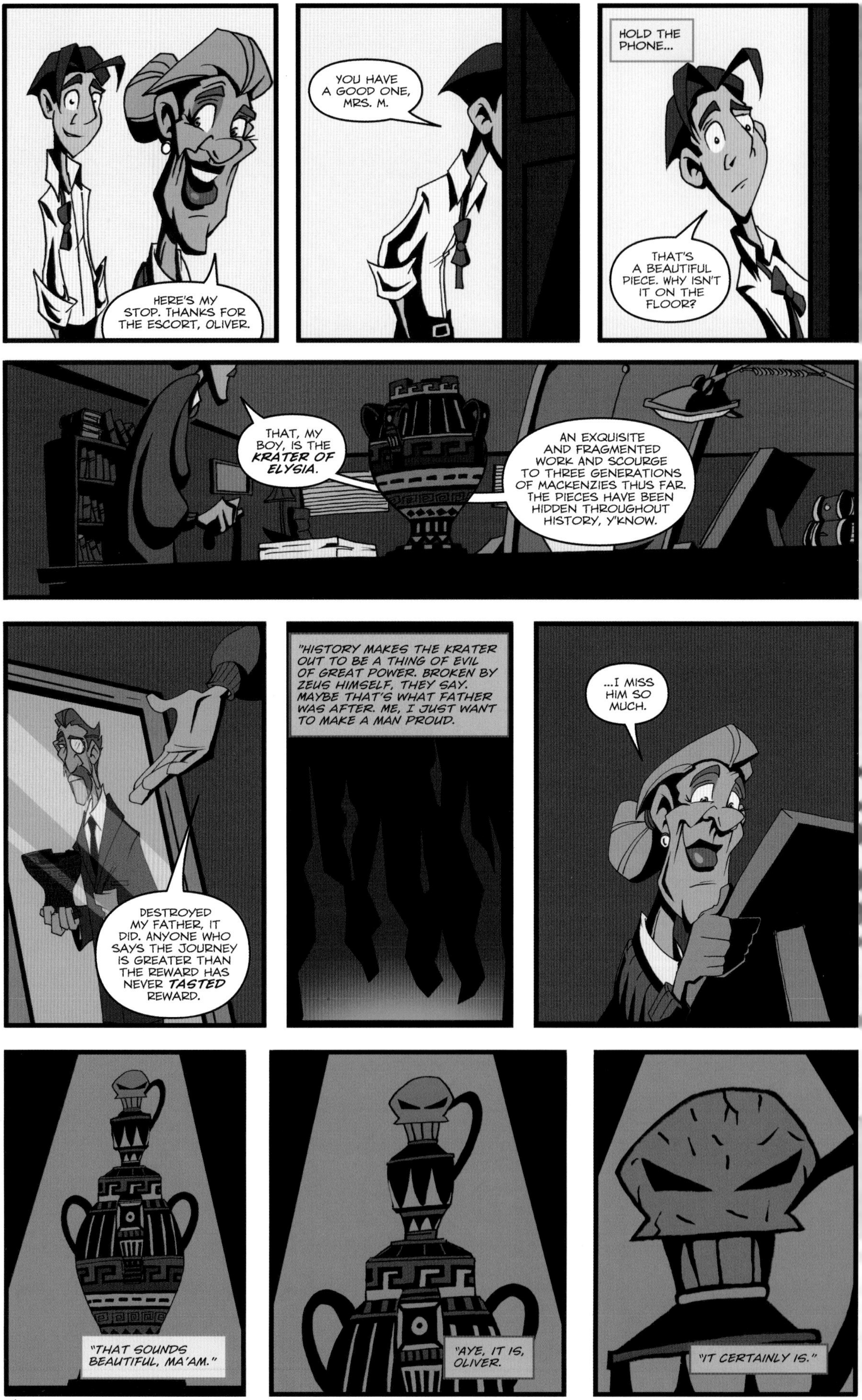
HERE'S MY STOP. THANKS FOR THE ESCORT, OLIVER.
YOU HAVE A GOOD ONE, MRS. M.
HOLD THE PHONE...
THAT'S A BEAUTIFUL PIECE. WHY ISN'T IT ON THE FLOOR?
THAT, MY BOY, IS THE KRATER OF ELYSIA.
AN EXQUISITE AND FRAGMENTED WORK AND SCOURGE TO THREE GENERATIONS OF MACKENZIES THUS FAR. THE PIECES HAVE BEEN HIDDEN THROUGHOUT HISTORY, Y'KNOW.
DESTROYED MY FATHER, IT DID. ANYONE WHO SAYS THE JOURNEY IS GREATER THAN THE REWARD HAS NEVER TASTED REWARD.
"HISTORY MAKES THE KRATER OUT TO BE A THING OF EVIL OF GREAT POWER. BROKEN BY ZEUS HIMSELF, THEY SAY. MAYBE THAT'S WHAT FATHER WAS AFTER. ME, I JUST WANT TO MAKE A MAN PROUD.
...I MISS HIM SO MUCH.
"THAT SOUNDS BEAUTIFUL, MA'AM."
"AYE, IT IS, OLIVER.
"IT CERTAINLY IS."

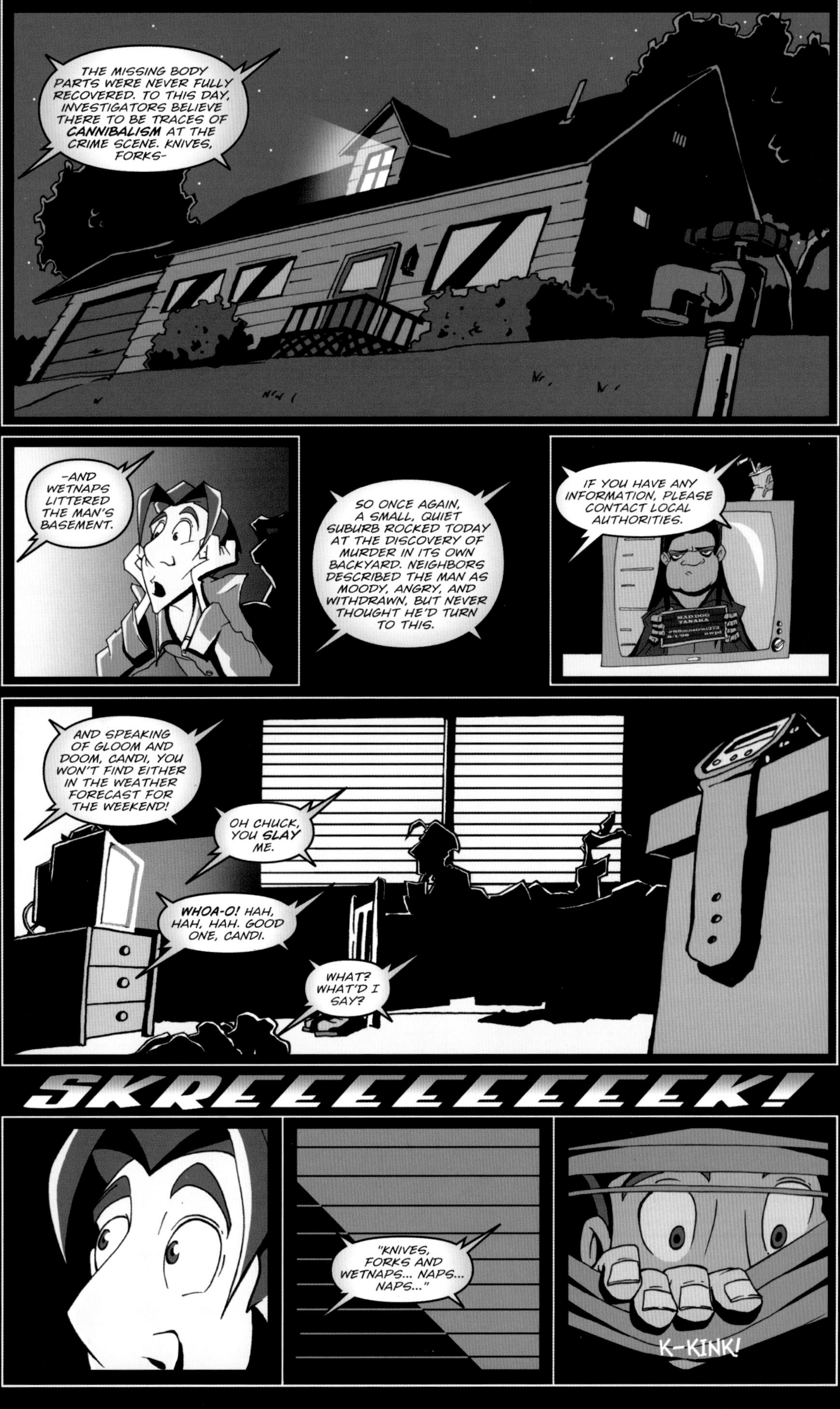

THE MISSING BODY PARTS WERE NEVER FULLY RECOVERED. TO THIS DAY, INVESTIGATORS BELIEVE THERE TO BE TRACES OF CANNIBALISM AT THE CRIME SCENE. KNIVES, FORKS-
-AND WETNAPS LITTERED THE MAN'S BASEMENT.
SO ONCE AGAIN, A SMALL, QUIET SUBURB ROCKED TODAY AT THE DISCOVERY OF MURDER IN ITS OWN BACKYARD. NEIGHBORS DESCRIBED THE MAN AS MOODY, ANGRY, AND WITHDRAWN, BUT NEVER THOUGHT HE'D TURN TO THIS.
IF YOU HAVE ANY INFORMATION, PLEASE CONTACT LOCAL AUTHORITIES.
MAD DOG TANAKA
AND SPEAKING OF GLOOM AND DOOM, CANDI, YOU WON'T FIND EITHER IN THE WEATHER FORECAST FOR THE WEEKEND!
OH CHUCK, YOU SLAY ME.
WHOA-O! HAH, HAH, HAH. GOOD ONE, CANDI.
WHAT? WHAT'D I SAY?
SKREEEEEEEEEK!
"KNIVES, FORKS AND WETNAPS... NAPS... NAPS..."
K-KINK!

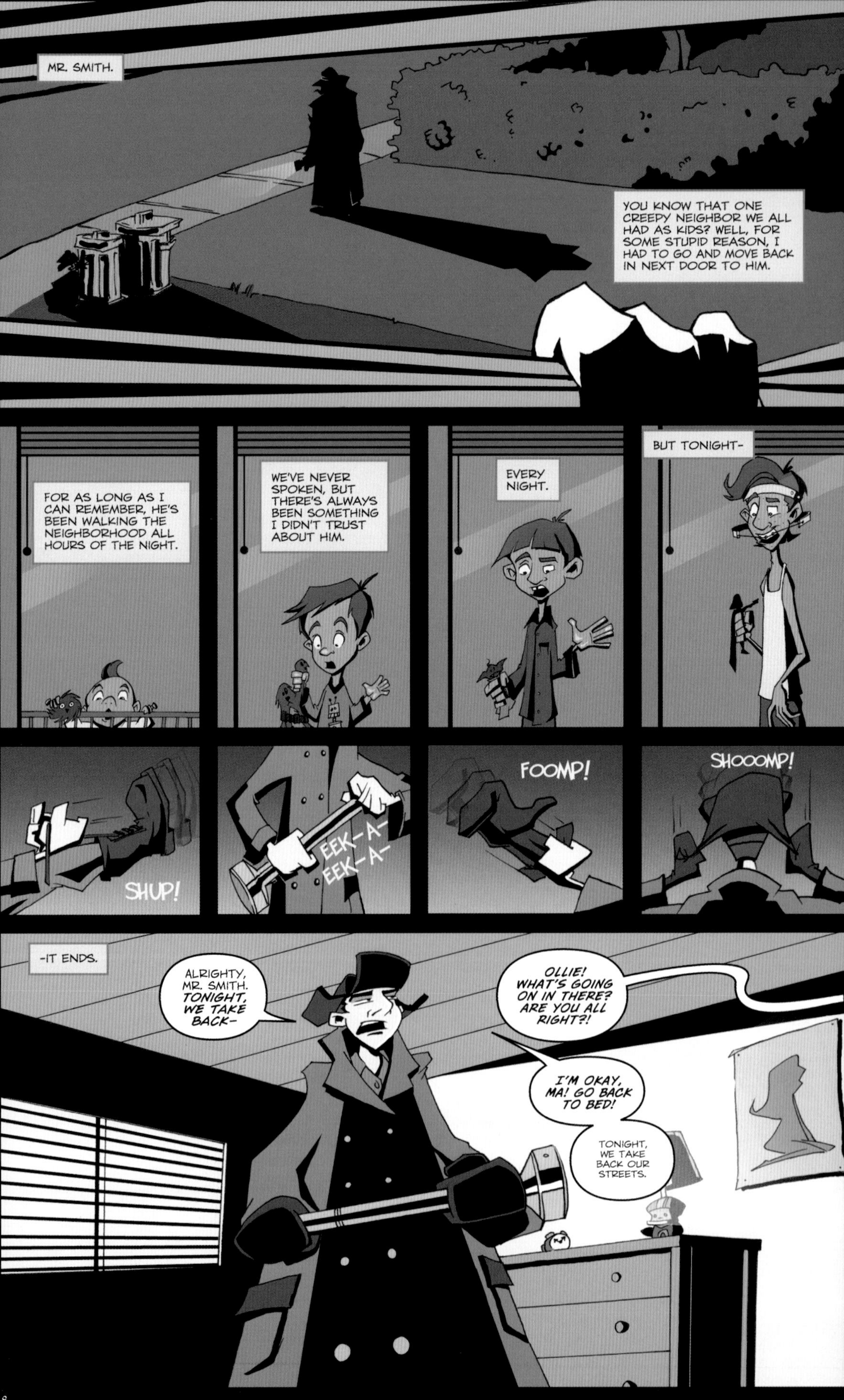
MR. SMITH.
YOU KNOW THAT ONE CREEPY NEIGHBOR WE ALL HAD AS KIDS? WELL, FOR SOME STUPID REASON, I HAD TO GO AND MOVE BACK IN NEXT DOOR TO HIM.
FOR AS LONG AS I CAN REMEMBER, HE'S BEEN WALKING THE NEIGHBORHOOD ALL HOURS OF THE NIGHT.
WE'VE NEVER SPOKEN, BUT THERE'S ALWAYS BEEN SOMETHING I DIDN'T TRUST ABOUT HIM.
EVERY NIGHT.
BUT TONIGHT-
SHUP!
EEK-A-EEK-A-
FOOMP!
SHOOOMP!
-IT ENDS.
ALRIGHTY, MR. SMITH. TONIGHT, WE TAKE BACK-
OLLIE! WHAT'S GOING ON IN THERE? ARE YOU ALL RIGHT?!
I'M OKAY, MA! GO BACK TO BED!
TONIGHT, WE TAKE BACK OUR STREETS.

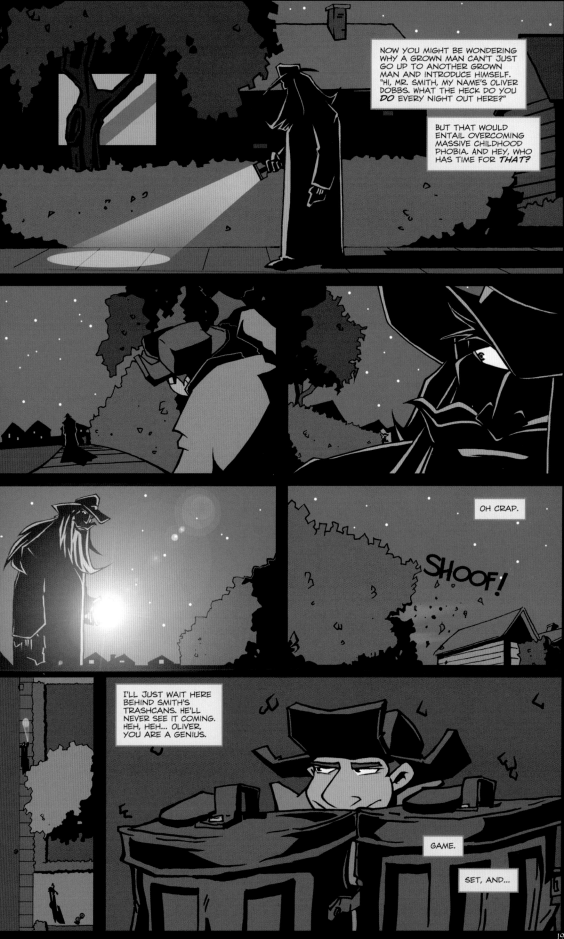

NOW YOU MIGHT BE WONDERING WHY A GROWN MAN CAN'T JUST GO UP TO ANOTHER GROWN MAN AND INTRODUCE HIMSELF. "HI, MR. SMITH, MY NAME'S OLIVER DOBBS. WHAT THE HECK DO YOU *DO* EVERY NIGHT OUT HERE?"

BUT THAT WOULD ENTAIL OVERCOMING MASSIVE CHILDHOOD PHOBIA. AND HEY, WHO HAS TIME FOR *THAT?*

OH CRAP.

SHOOF!

I'LL JUST WAIT HERE BEHIND SMITH'S TRASHCANS. HE'LL NEVER SEE IT COMING. HEH, HEH... OLIVER, YOU ARE A GENIUS.

GAME.

SET, AND...

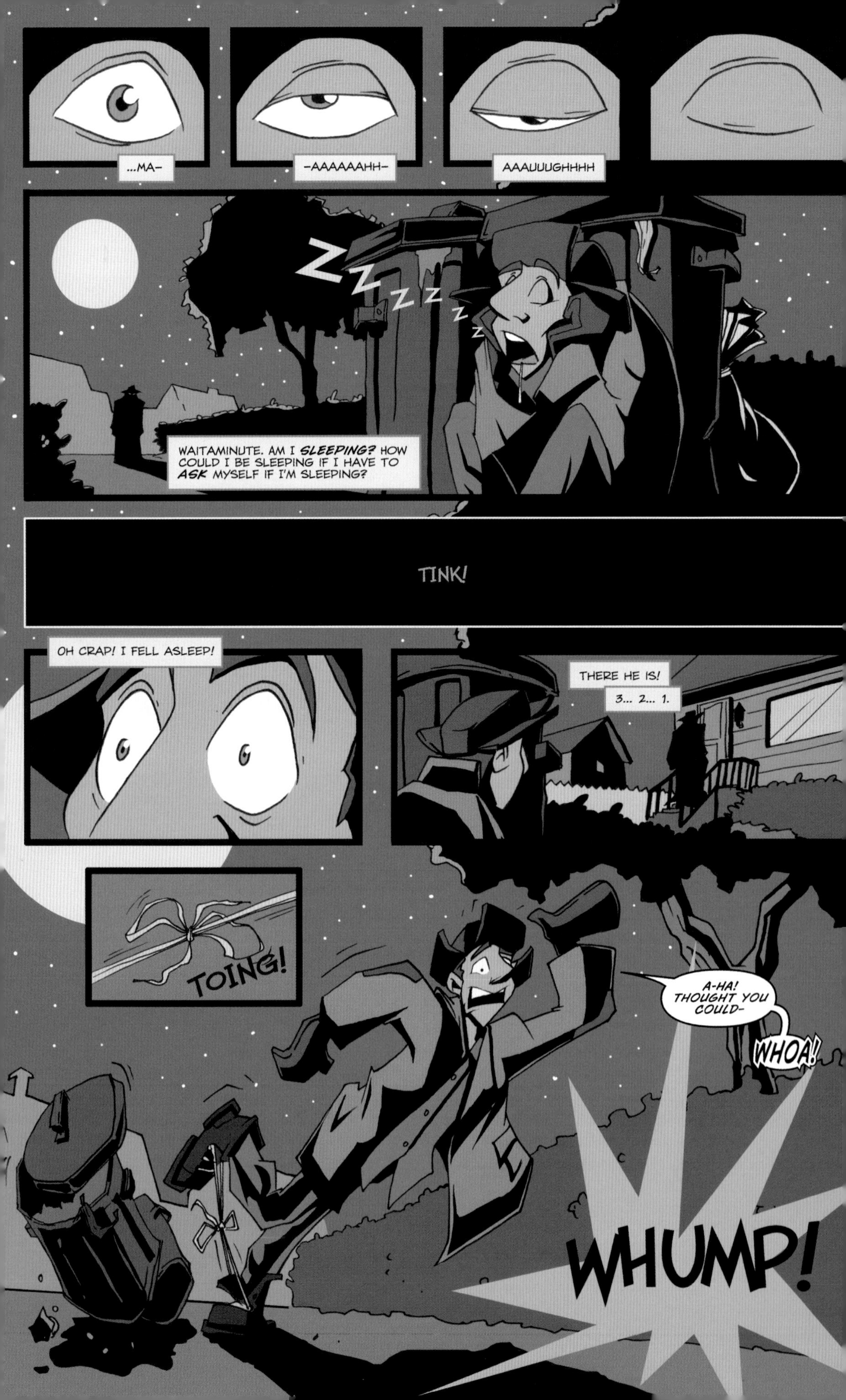
...MA-
-AAAAAAHH-
AAAUUUGHHHH
ZZZZZZ
WAITAMINUTE. AM I SLEEPING? HOW COULD I BE SLEEPING IF I HAVE TO ASK MYSELF IF I'M SLEEPING?
TINK!
OH CRAP! I FELL ASLEEP!
THERE HE IS!
3... 2... 1.
TOING!
A-HA! THOUGHT YOU COULD-
WHOA!
WHUMP!

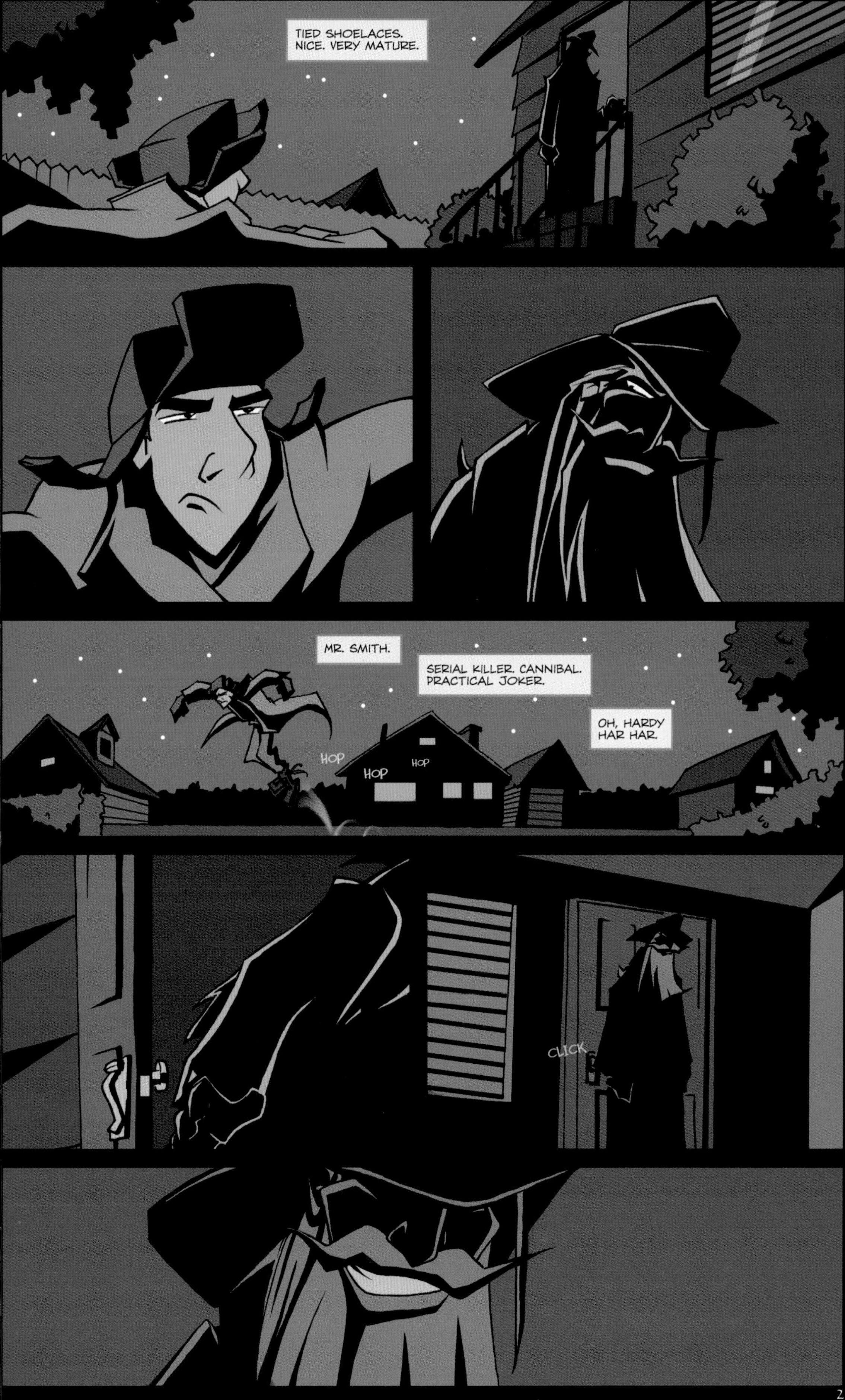
TIED SHOELACES. NICE. VERY MATURE.
MR. SMITH.
SERIAL KILLER. CANNIBAL. PRACTICAL JOKER.
OH, HARDY HAR HAR.
HOP
HOP
HOP
CLICK

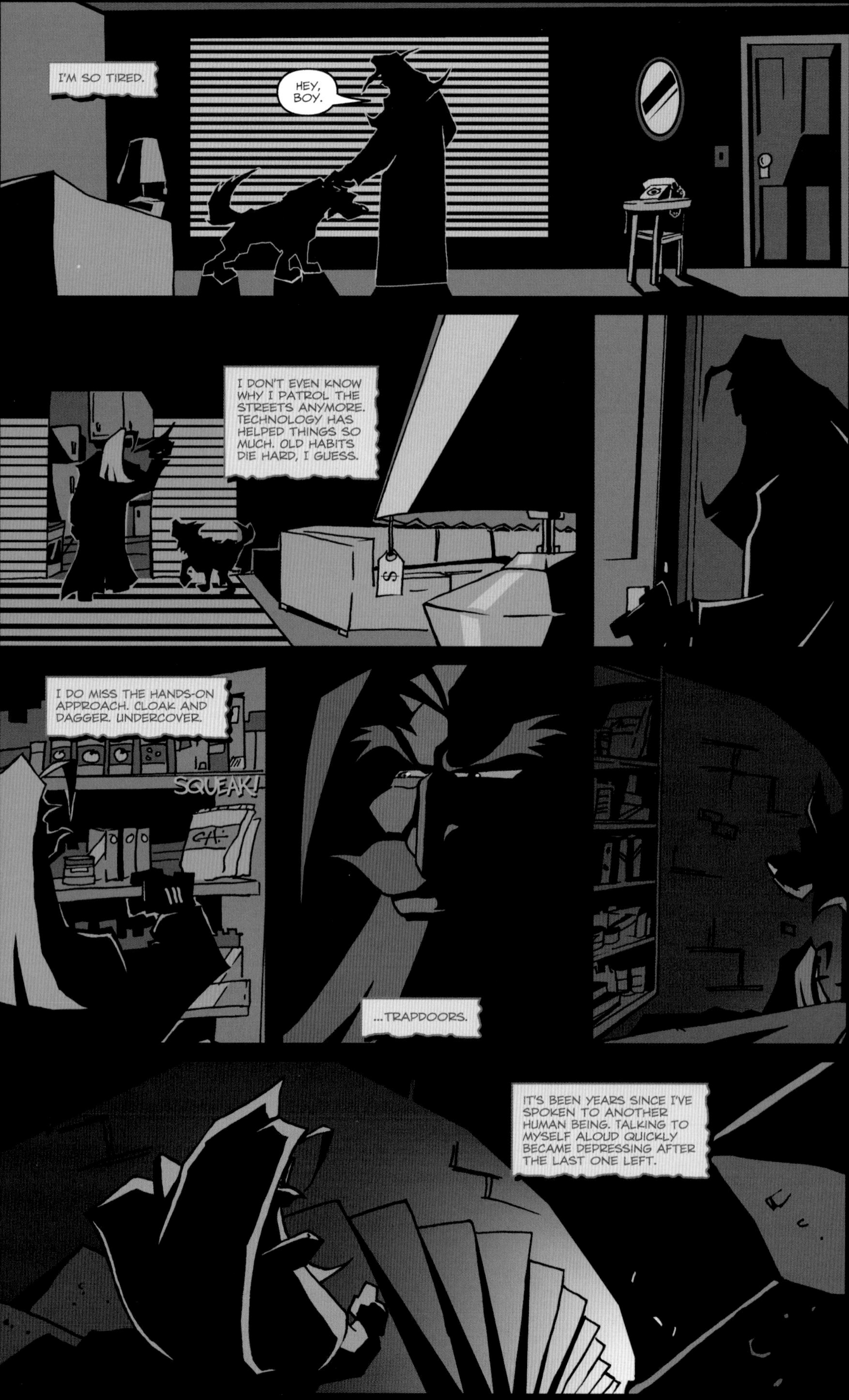
I'M SO TIRED.
HEY, BOY.
I DON'T EVEN KNOW WHY I PATROL THE STREETS ANYMORE. TECHNOLOGY HAS HELPED THINGS SO MUCH. OLD HABITS DIE HARD, I GUESS.
I DO MISS THE HANDS-ON APPROACH. CLOAK AND DAGGER. UNDERCOVER.
SQUEAK!
...TRAPDOORS.
IT'S BEEN YEARS SINCE I'VE SPOKEN TO ANOTHER HUMAN BEING. TALKING TO MYSELF ALOUD QUICKLY BECAME DEPRESSING AFTER THE LAST ONE LEFT.

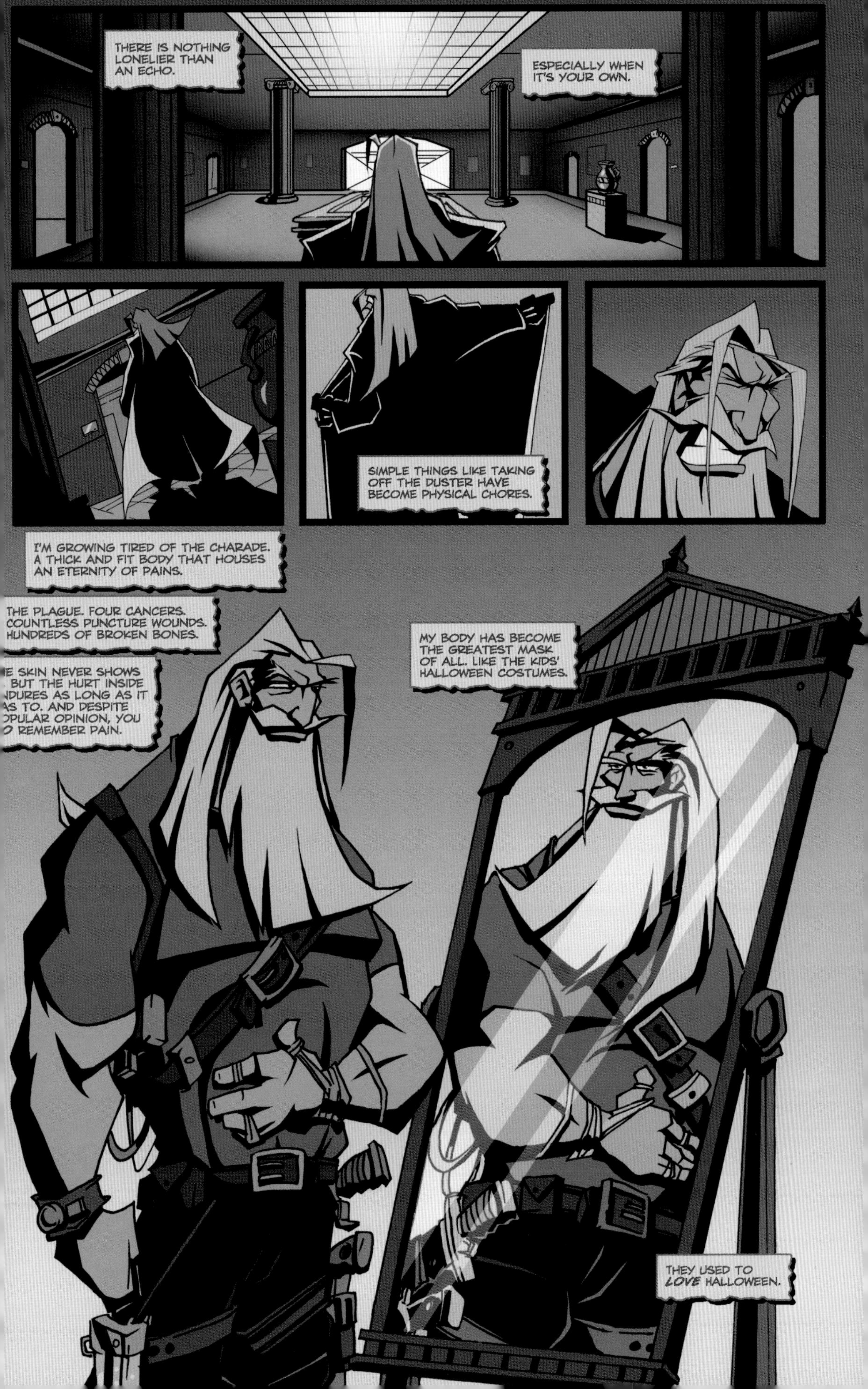
THERE IS NOTHING LONELIER THAN AN ECHO.
ESPECIALLY WHEN IT'S YOUR OWN.
SIMPLE THINGS LIKE TAKING OFF THE DUSTER HAVE BECOME PHYSICAL CHORES.
I'M GROWING TIRED OF THE CHARADE. A THICK AND FIT BODY THAT HOUSES AN ETERNITY OF PAINS.
THE PLAGUE. FOUR CANCERS. COUNTLESS PUNCTURE WOUNDS. HUNDREDS OF BROKEN BONES.
E SKIN NEVER SHOWS BUT THE HURT INSIDE NDURES AS LONG AS IT AS TO. AND DESPITE OPULAR OPINION, YOU O REMEMBER PAIN.
MY BODY HAS BECOME THE GREATEST MASK OF ALL. LIKE THE KIDS' HALLOWEEN COSTUMES.
THEY USED TO *LOVE* HALLOWEEN.

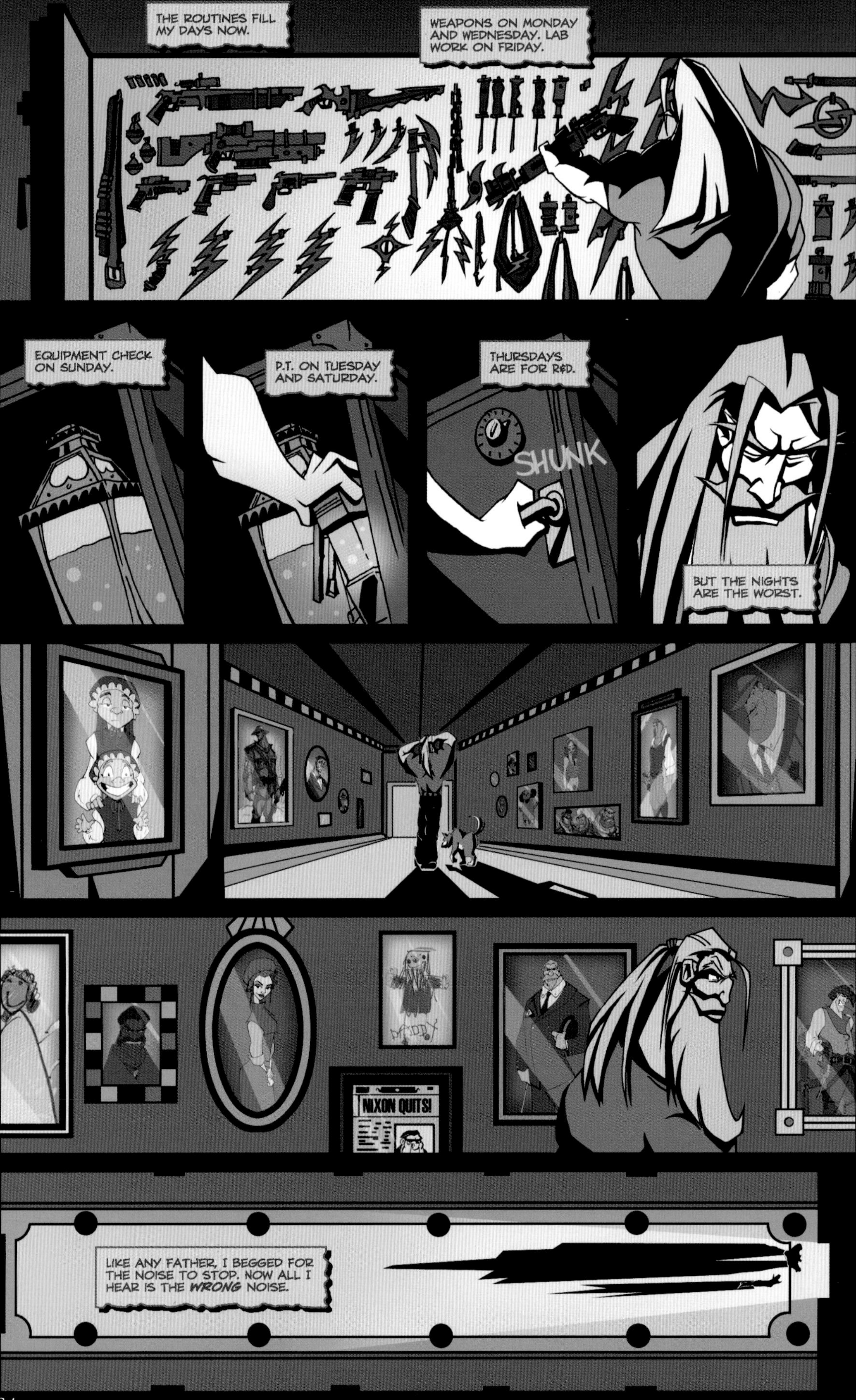
THE ROUTINES FILL MY DAYS NOW.
WEAPONS ON MONDAY AND WEDNESDAY. LAB WORK ON FRIDAY.
EQUIPMENT CHECK ON SUNDAY.
P.T. ON TUESDAY AND SATURDAY.
THURSDAYS ARE FOR R&D.
SHUNK
BUT THE NIGHTS ARE THE WORST.
NIXON QUITS!
LIKE ANY FATHER, I BEGGED FOR THE NOISE TO STOP. NOW ALL I HEAR IS THE *WRONG* NOISE.

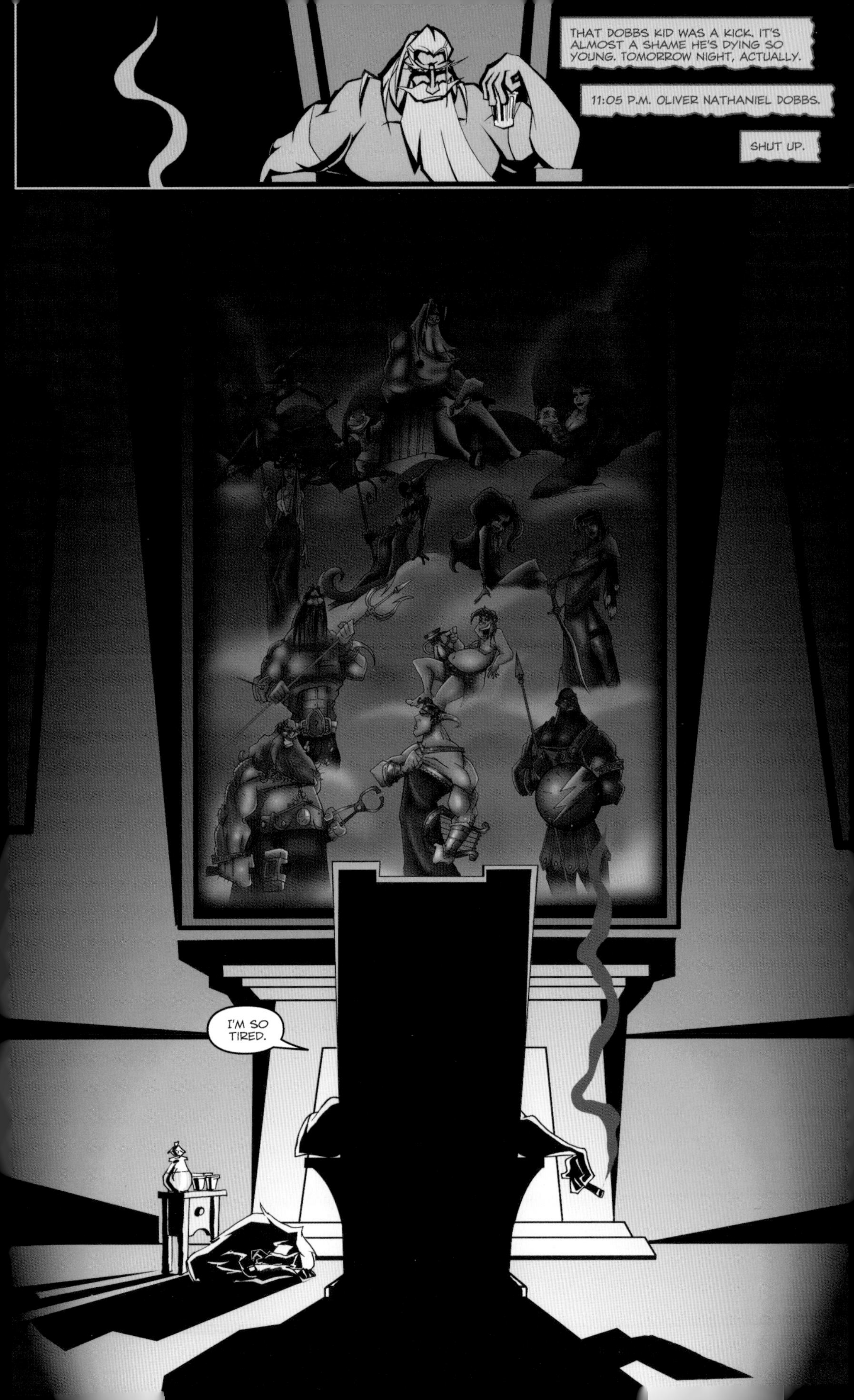
THAT DOBBS KID WAS A KICK. IT'S ALMOST A SHAME HE'S DYING SO YOUNG. TOMORROW NIGHT, ACTUALLY.
11:05 P.M. OLIVER NATHANIEL DOBBS.
SHUT UP.
I'M SO TIRED.

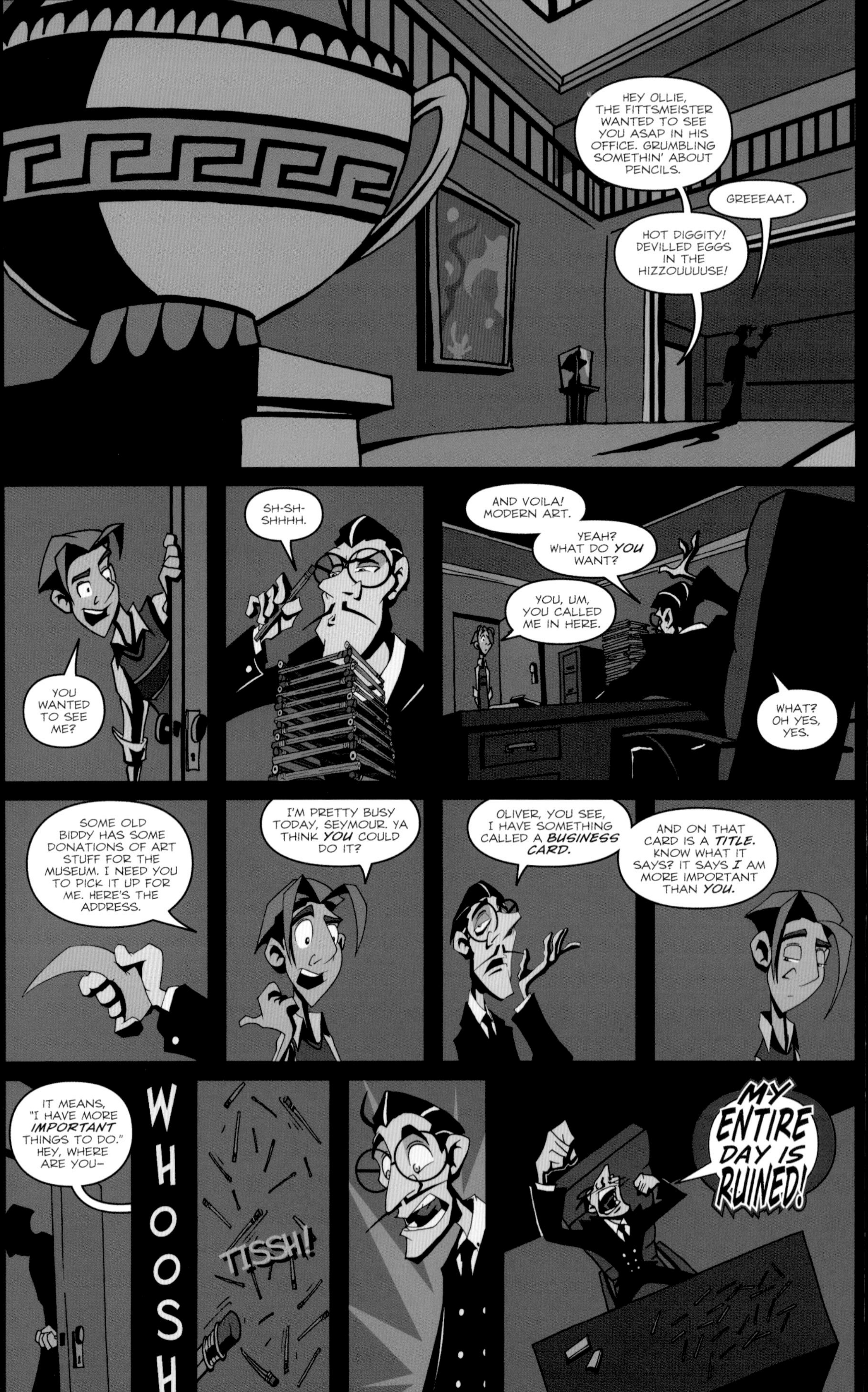

HEY OLLIE, THE FITTSMEISTER WANTED TO SEE YOU ASAP IN HIS OFFICE. GRUMBLING SOMETHIN' ABOUT PENCILS.
GREEEAAT.
HOT DIGGITY! DEVILLED EGGS IN THE HIZZOUUUUSE!
YOU WANTED TO SEE ME?
SH-SH-SHHHH.
AND VOILA! MODERN ART.
YEAH? WHAT DO YOU WANT?
YOU, UM, YOU CALLED ME IN HERE.
WHAT? OH YES, YES.
SOME OLD BIDDY HAS SOME DONATIONS OF ART STUFF FOR THE MUSEUM. I NEED YOU TO PICK IT UP FOR ME. HERE'S THE ADDRESS.
I'M PRETTY BUSY TODAY, SEYMOUR. YA THINK YOU COULD DO IT?
OLIVER, YOU SEE, I HAVE SOMETHING CALLED A BUSINESS CARD.
AND ON THAT CARD IS A TITLE. KNOW WHAT IT SAYS? IT SAYS I AM MORE IMPORTANT THAN YOU.
IT MEANS, "I HAVE MORE IMPORTANT THINGS TO DO." HEY, WHERE ARE YOU–
WHOOSH
TISSH!
MY ENTIRE DAY IS RUINED!

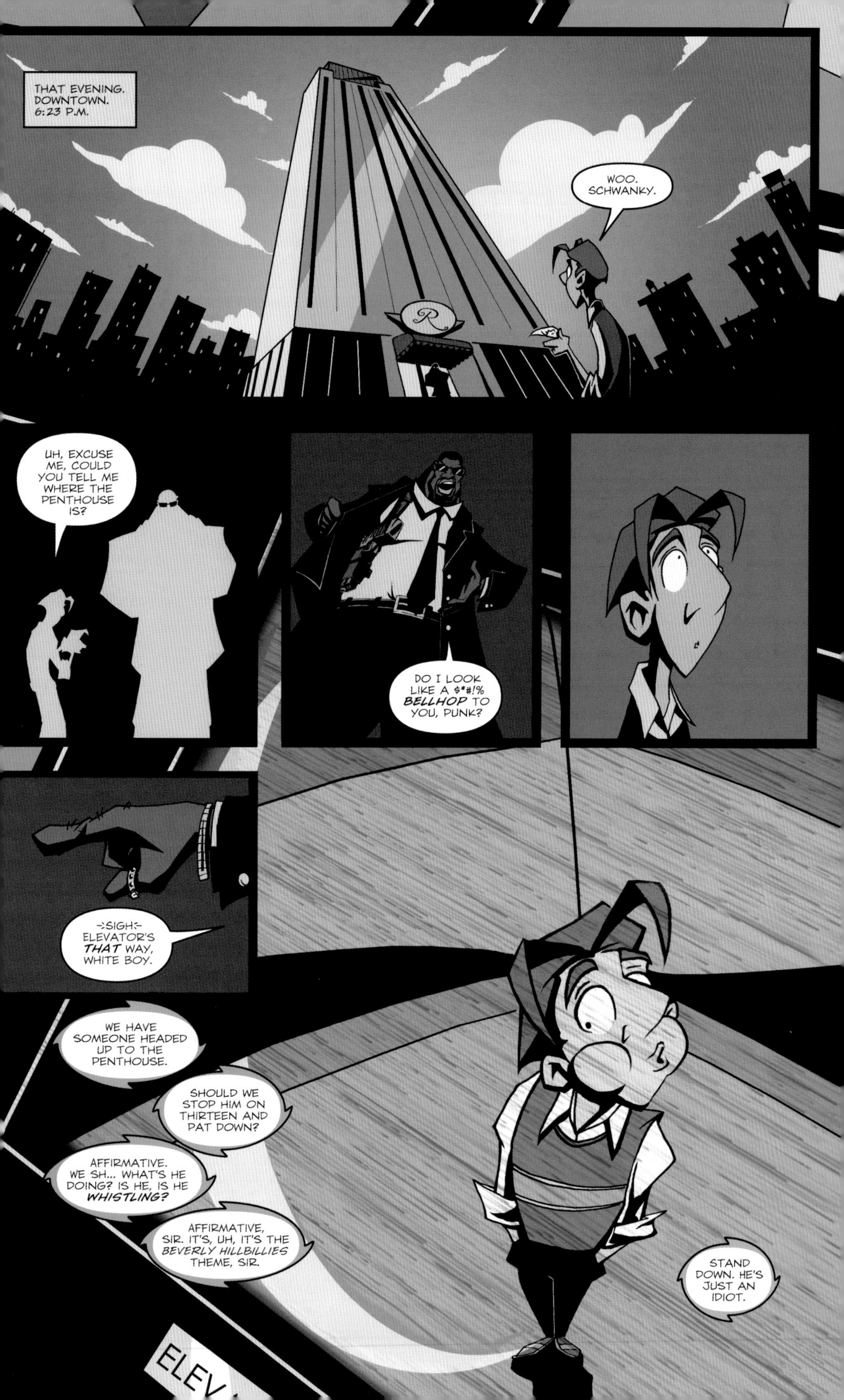
THAT EVENING. DOWNTOWN. 6:23 P.M.
WOO. SCHWANKY.
UH, EXCUSE ME, COULD YOU TELL ME WHERE THE PENTHOUSE IS?
DO I LOOK LIKE A $*#!% BELLHOP TO YOU, PUNK?
-SIGH- ELEVATOR'S THAT WAY, WHITE BOY.
WE HAVE SOMEONE HEADED UP TO THE PENTHOUSE.
SHOULD WE STOP HIM ON THIRTEEN AND PAT DOWN?
AFFIRMATIVE. WE SH... WHAT'S HE DOING? IS HE, IS HE WHISTLING?
AFFIRMATIVE, SIR. IT'S, UH, IT'S THE BEVERLY HILLBILLIES THEME, SIR.
STAND DOWN. HE'S JUST AN IDIOT.
ELEV

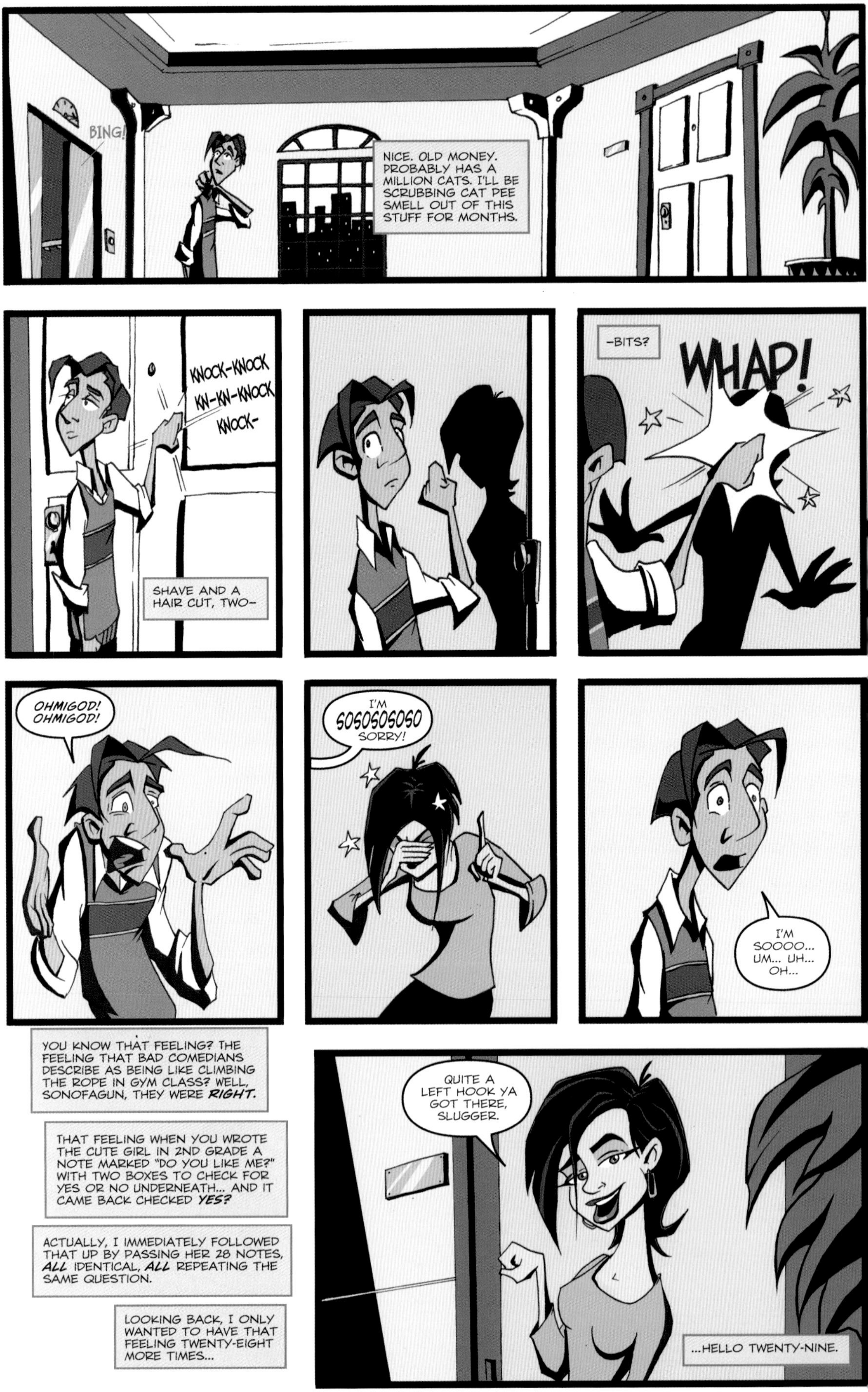

BING!
NICE. OLD MONEY. PROBABLY HAS A MILLION CATS. I'LL BE SCRUBBING CAT PEE SMELL OUT OF THIS STUFF FOR MONTHS.
KNOCK-KNOCK
KN-KN-KNOCK
KNOCK-
SHAVE AND A HAIR CUT, TWO-
-BITS?
WHAP!
OHMIGOD! OHMIGOD!
I'M SOSOSOSOSO SORRY!
I'M SOOOO... UM... UH... OH...
YOU KNOW THAT FEELING? THE FEELING THAT BAD COMEDIANS DESCRIBE AS BEING LIKE CLIMBING THE ROPE IN GYM CLASS? WELL, SONOFAGUN, THEY WERE RIGHT.
THAT FEELING WHEN YOU WROTE THE CUTE GIRL IN 2ND GRADE A NOTE MARKED "DO YOU LIKE ME?" WITH TWO BOXES TO CHECK FOR YES OR NO UNDERNEATH... AND IT CAME BACK CHECKED YES?
ACTUALLY, I IMMEDIATELY FOLLOWED THAT UP BY PASSING HER 28 NOTES, ALL IDENTICAL, ALL REPEATING THE SAME QUESTION.
LOOKING BACK, I ONLY WANTED TO HAVE THAT FEELING TWENTY-EIGHT MORE TIMES...
QUITE A LEFT HOOK YA GOT THERE, SLUGGER.
...HELLO TWENTY-NINE.

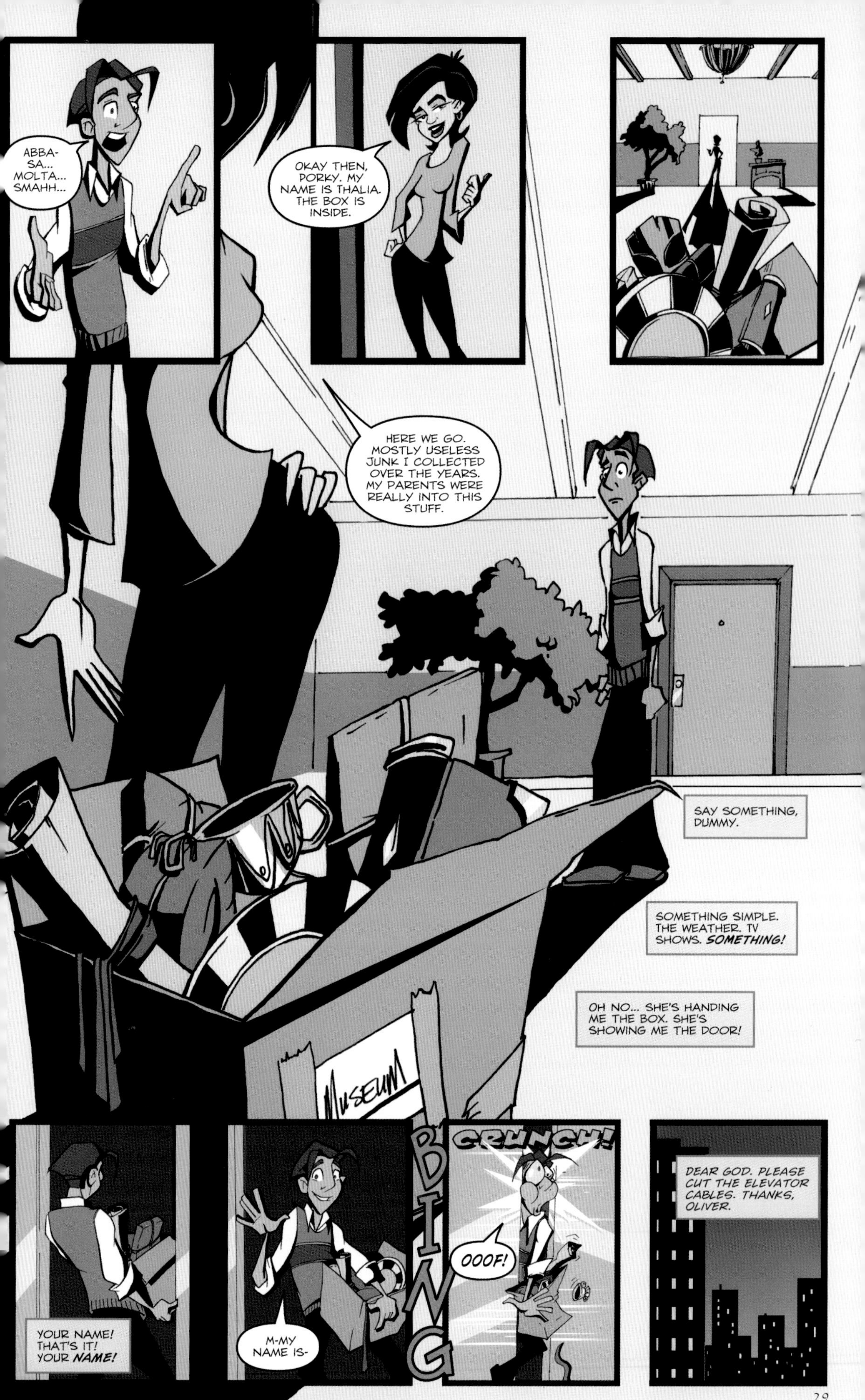
ABBA-SA... MOLTA... SMAHH...
OKAY THEN, PORKY. MY NAME IS THALIA. THE BOX IS INSIDE.
HERE WE GO. MOSTLY USELESS JUNK I COLLECTED OVER THE YEARS. MY PARENTS WERE REALLY INTO THIS STUFF.
SAY SOMETHING, DUMMY.
SOMETHING SIMPLE. THE WEATHER. TV SHOWS. SOMETHING!
OH NO... SHE'S HANDING ME THE BOX. SHE'S SHOWING ME THE DOOR!
MUSEUM
YOUR NAME! THAT'S IT! YOUR NAME!
M-MY NAME IS-
BING
CRUNCH!
OOOF!
DEAR GOD. PLEASE CUT THE ELEVATOR CABLES. THANKS, OLIVER.

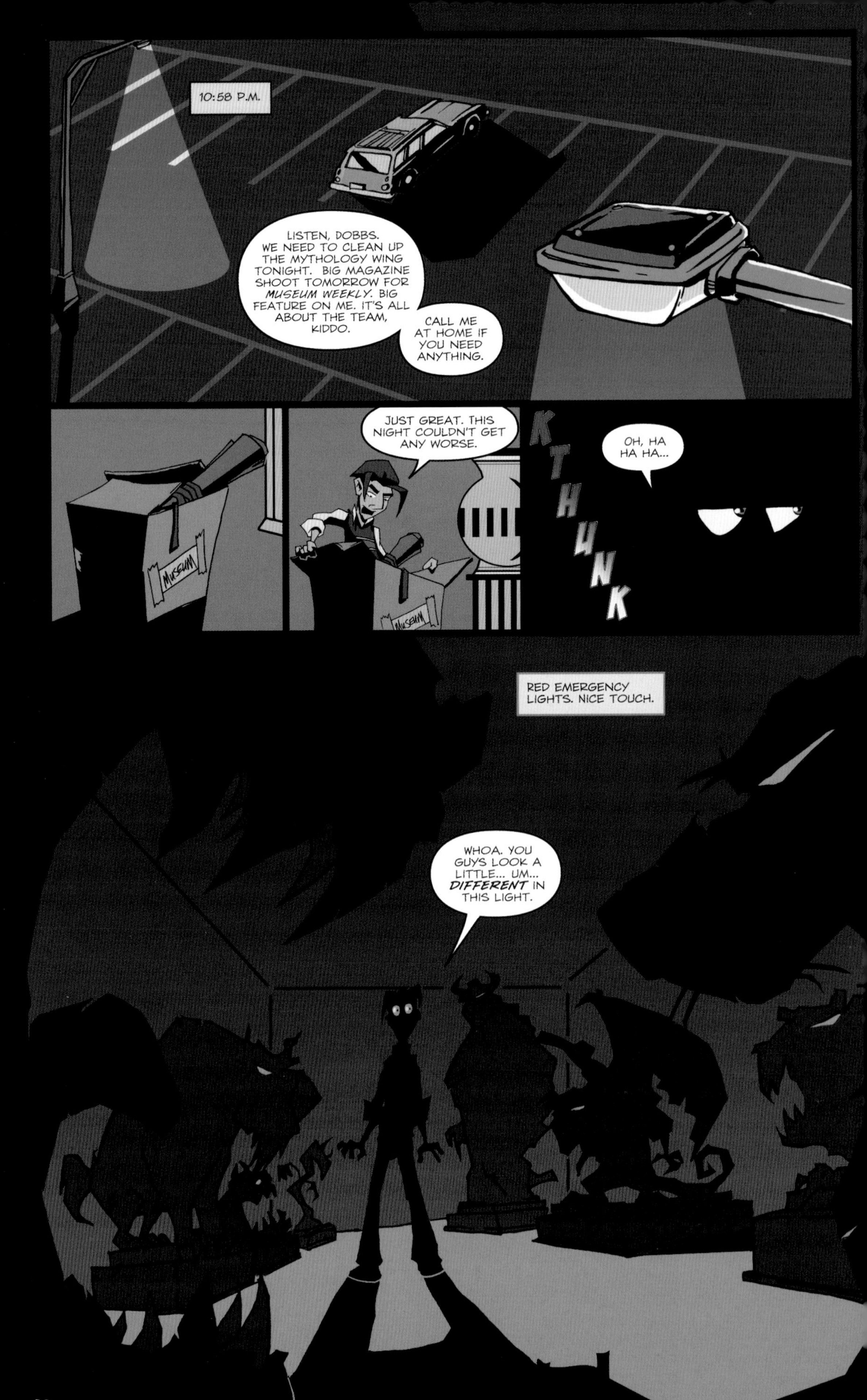
10:58 P.M.
LISTEN, DOBBS. WE NEED TO CLEAN UP THE MYTHOLOGY WING TONIGHT. BIG MAGAZINE SHOOT TOMORROW FOR MUSEUM WEEKLY. BIG FEATURE ON ME. IT'S ALL ABOUT THE TEAM, KIDDO.
CALL ME AT HOME IF YOU NEED ANYTHING.
MUSEUM
JUST GREAT. THIS NIGHT COULDN'T GET ANY WORSE.
MUSEUM
KTHUNK
OH, HA HA HA...
RED EMERGENCY LIGHTS. NICE TOUCH.
WHOA. YOU GUYS LOOK A LITTLE... UM... DIFFERENT IN THIS LIGHT.

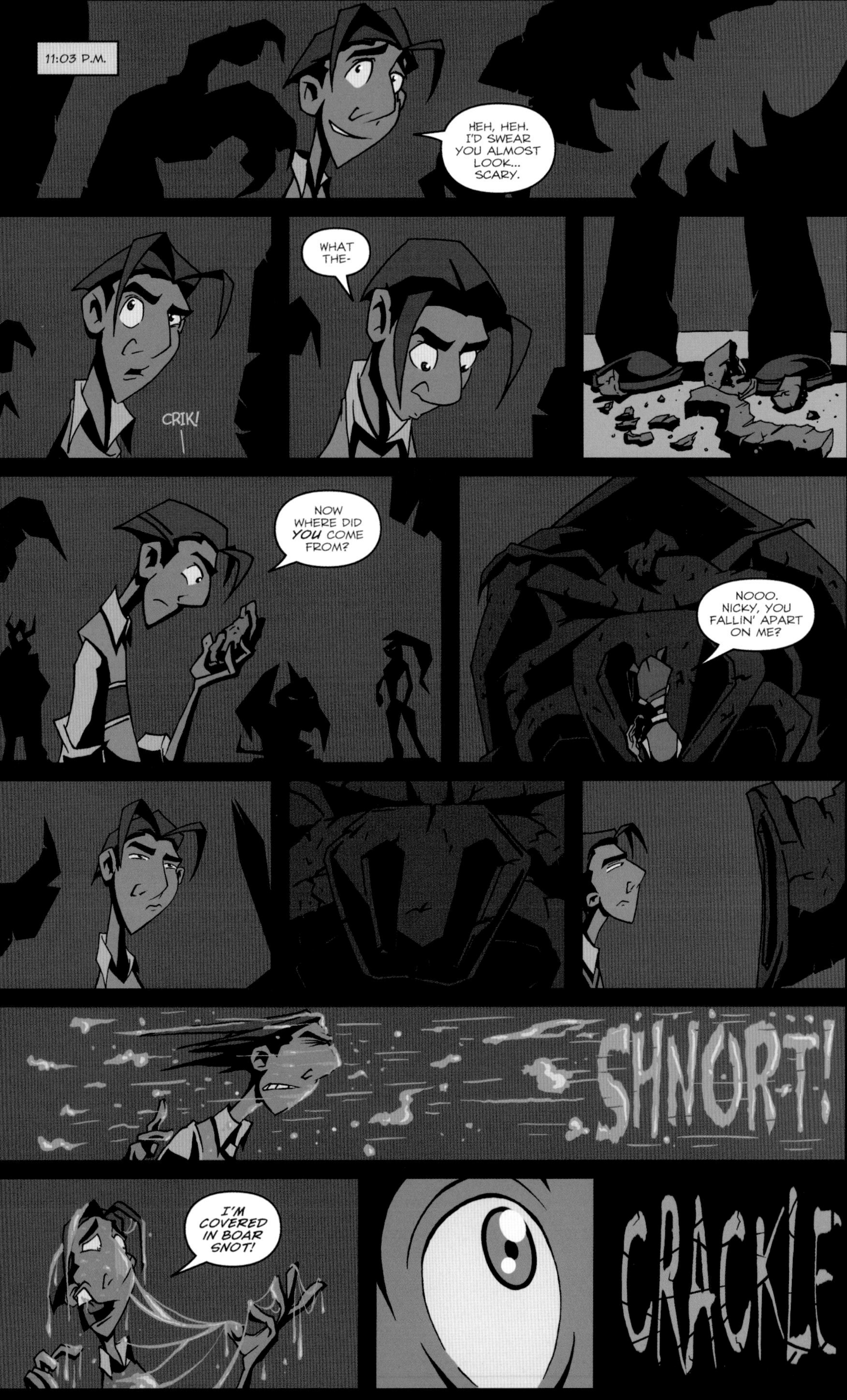
11:03 P.M.
HEH, HEH. I'D SWEAR YOU ALMOST LOOK... SCARY.
CRIK!
WHAT THE-
NOW WHERE DID YOU COME FROM?
NOOO. NICKY, YOU FALLIN' APART ON ME?
SHNORT!
I'M COVERED IN BOAR SNOT!
CRACKLE

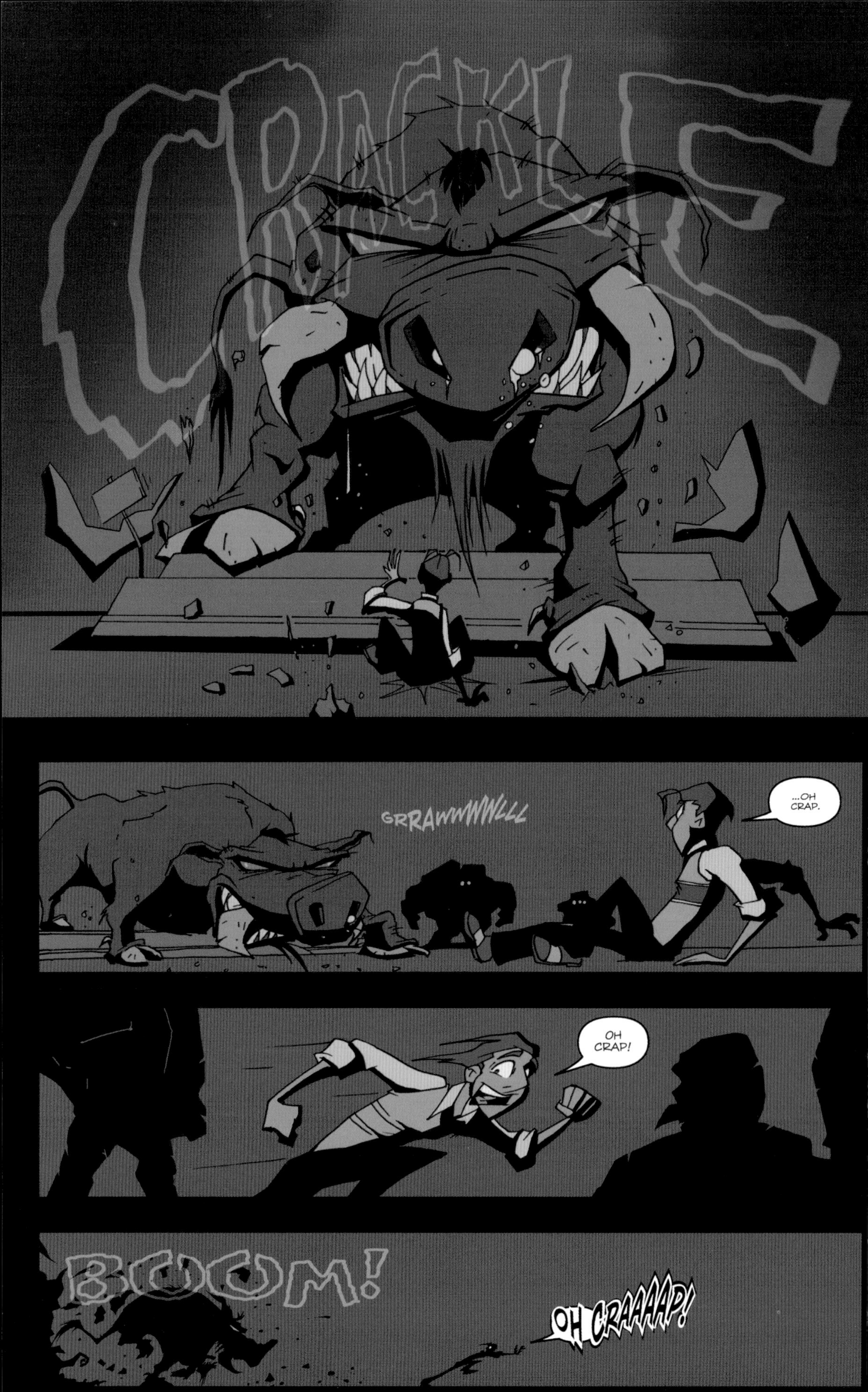
CRACKLE
GRRAWWWWLLL
...OH CRAP.
OH CRAP!
BOOM!
OH CRAAAAP!

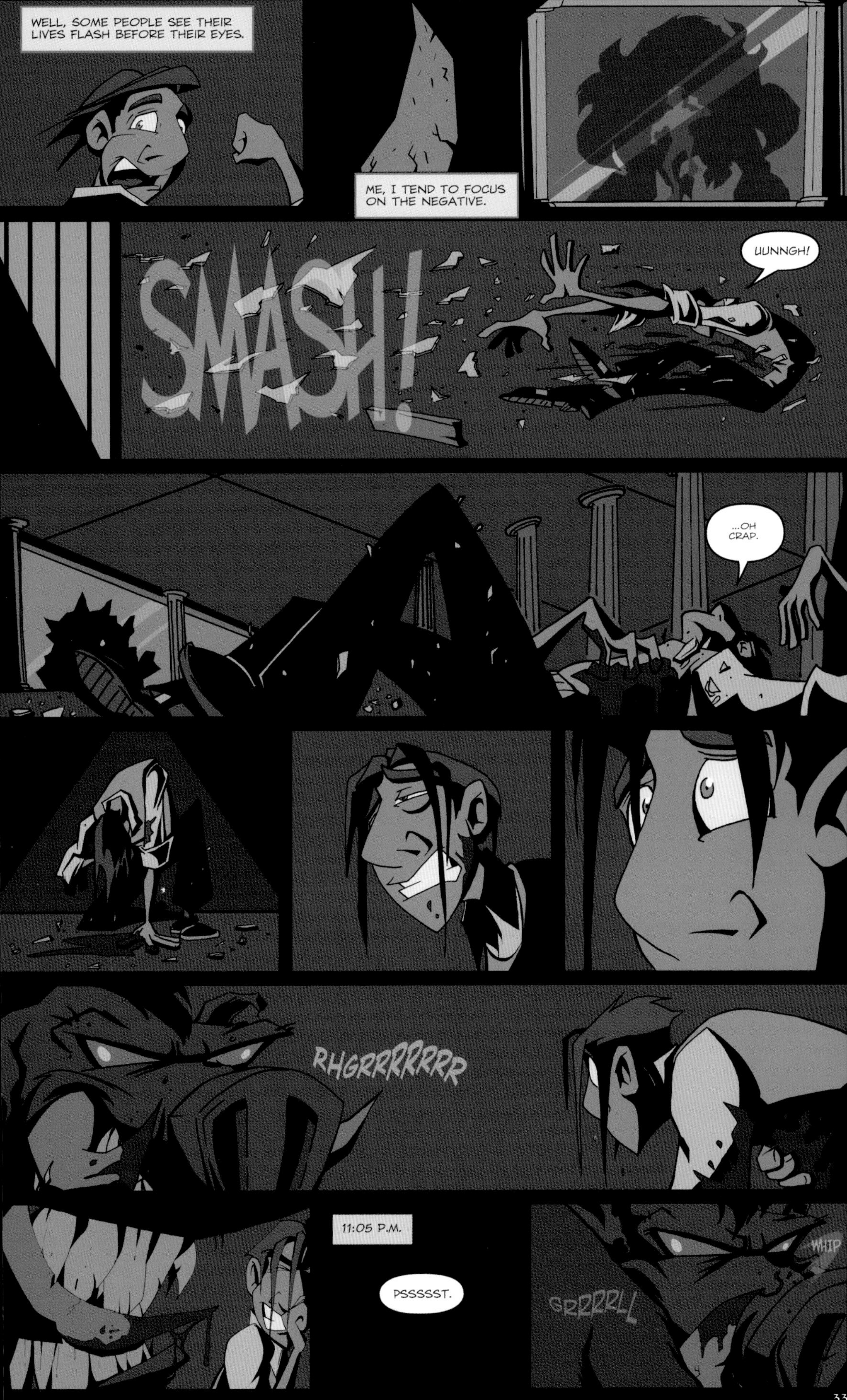
WELL, SOME PEOPLE SEE THEIR LIVES FLASH BEFORE THEIR EYES.
ME, I TEND TO FOCUS ON THE NEGATIVE.
SMASH!
UUNNGH!
...OH CRAP.
RHGRRRRRRR
11:05 P.M.
PSSSSST.
WHIP
GRRRRLL

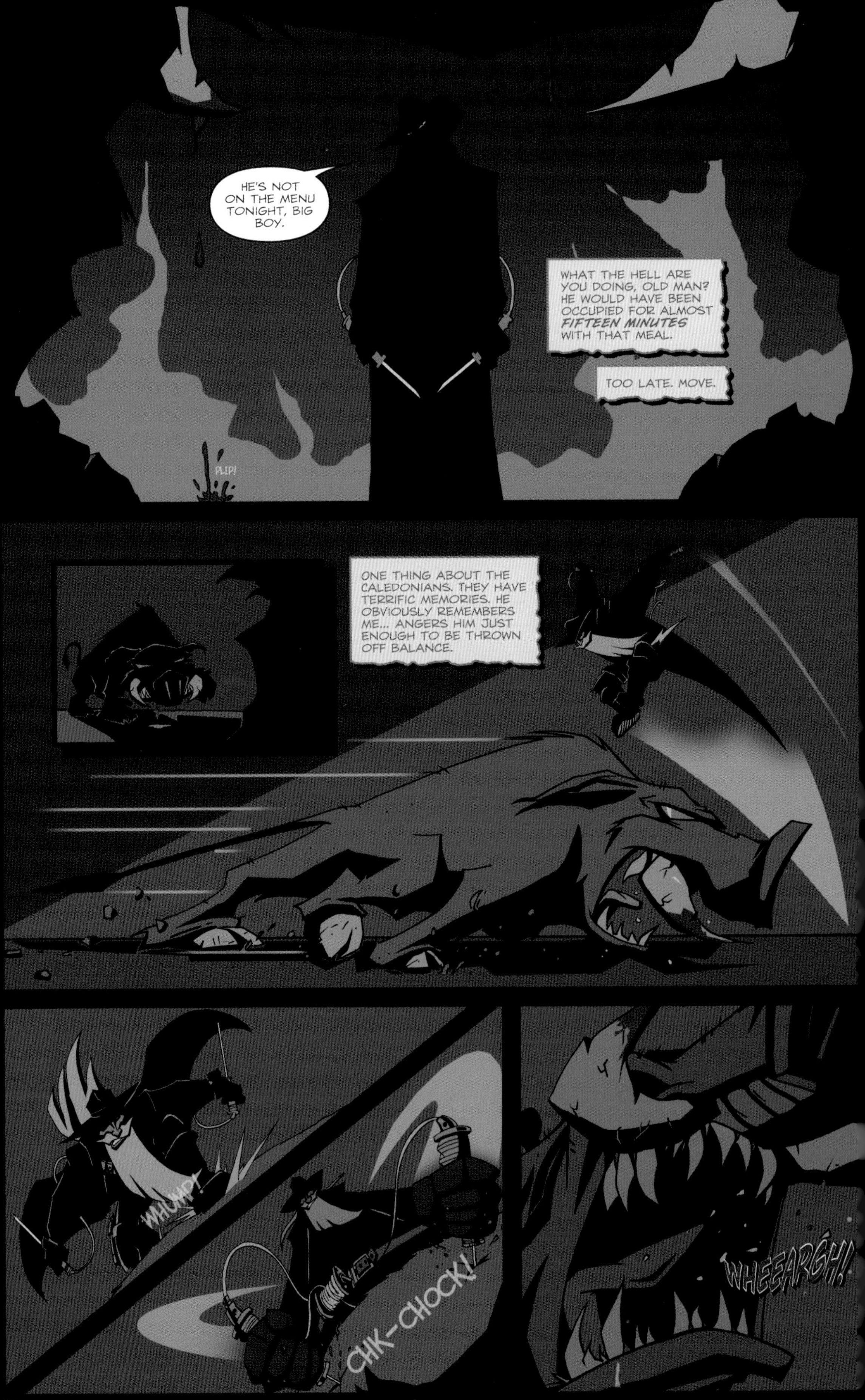
HE'S NOT ON THE MENU TONIGHT, BIG BOY.
WHAT THE HELL ARE YOU DOING, OLD MAN? HE WOULD HAVE BEEN OCCUPIED FOR ALMOST FIFTEEN MINUTES WITH THAT MEAL.
TOO LATE. MOVE.
PLIP!
ONE THING ABOUT THE CALEDONIANS. THEY HAVE TERRIFIC MEMORIES. HE OBVIOUSLY REMEMBERS ME... ANGERS HIM JUST ENOUGH TO BE THROWN OFF BALANCE.
WHUMP!
CHK-CHOCK!
WHEEARGH!

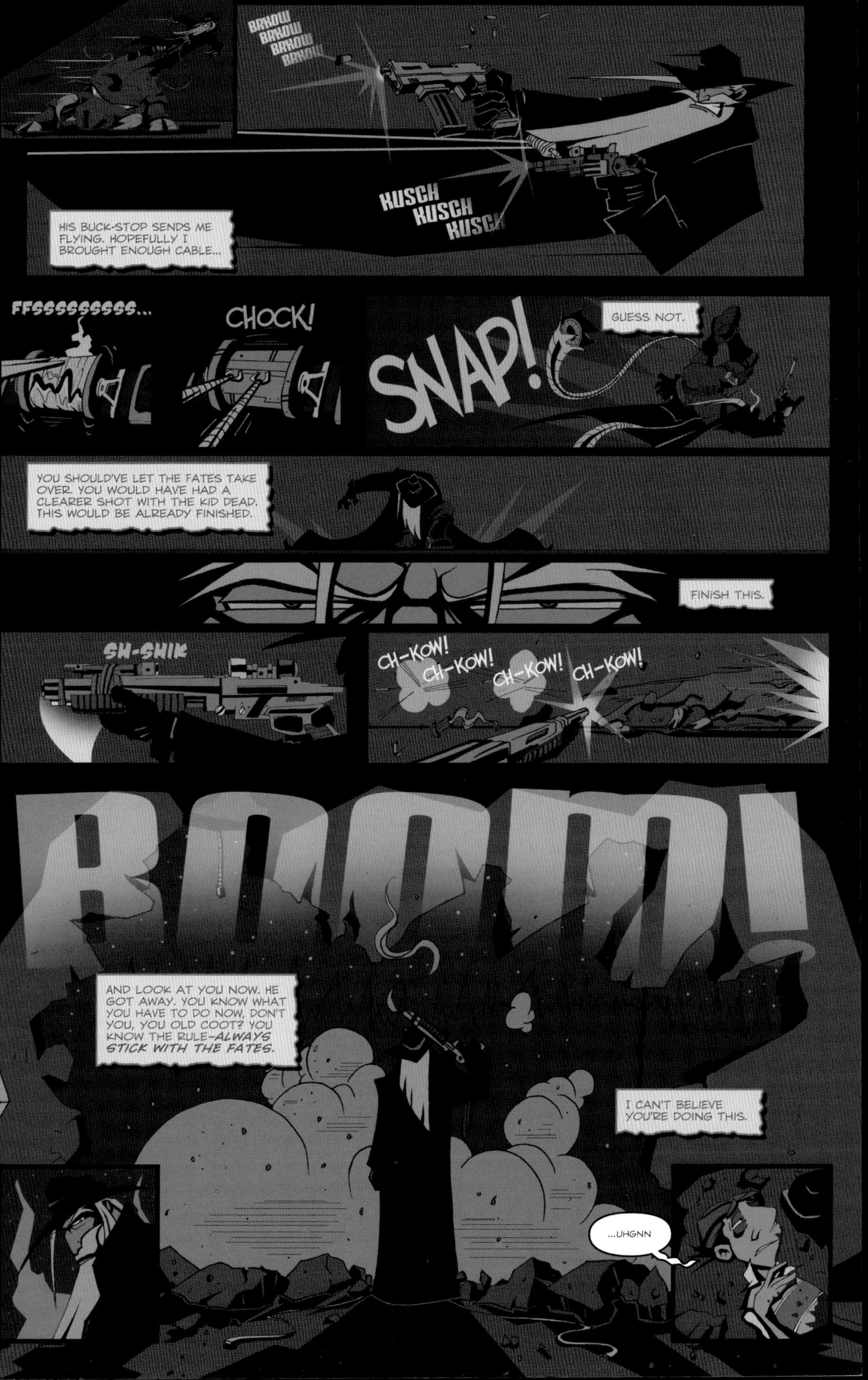
BRKOW BRKOW BRKOW BRKOW
KUSCH KUSCH KUSCH
HIS BUCK-STOP SENDS ME FLYING. HOPEFULLY I BROUGHT ENOUGH CABLE...
FFSSSSSSSSS...
CHOCK!
SNAP!
GUESS NOT.
YOU SHOULD'VE LET THE FATES TAKE OVER. YOU WOULD HAVE HAD A CLEARER SHOT WITH THE KID DEAD. THIS WOULD BE ALREADY FINISHED.
FINISH THIS.
SH-SHIK
CH-KOW! CH-KOW! CH-KOW! CH-KOW!
BOOOM!
AND LOOK AT YOU NOW. HE GOT AWAY. YOU KNOW WHAT YOU HAVE TO DO NOW, DON'T YOU, YOU OLD COOT? YOU KNOW THE RULE--ALWAYS STICK WITH THE FATES.
I CAN'T BELIEVE YOU'RE DOING THIS.
...UHGNN

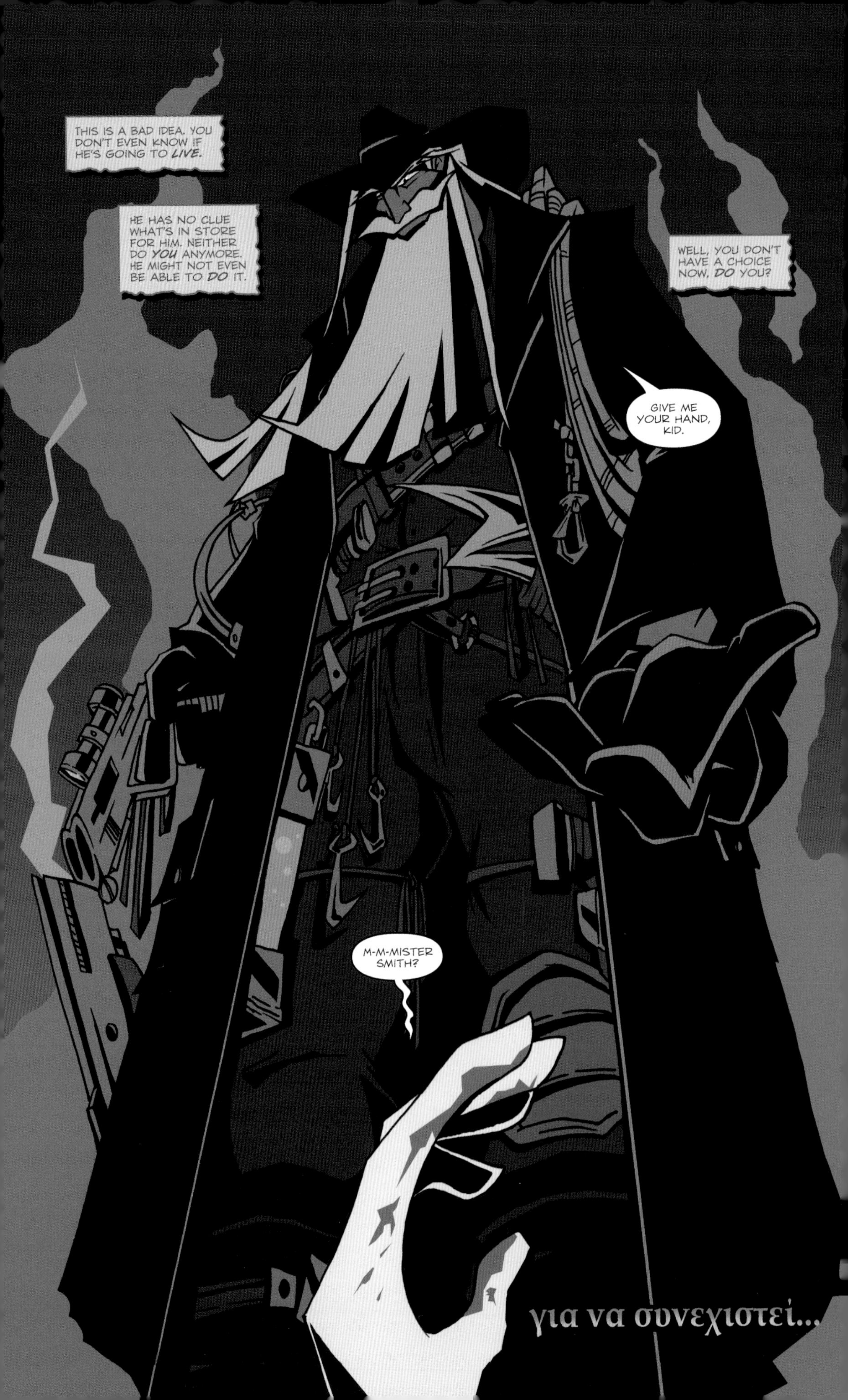

THIS IS A BAD IDEA. YOU DON'T EVEN KNOW IF HE'S GOING TO *LIVE.*
HE HAS NO CLUE WHAT'S IN STORE FOR HIM. NEITHER DO *YOU* ANYMORE. HE MIGHT NOT EVEN BE ABLE TO *DO* IT.
WELL, YOU DON'T HAVE A CHOICE NOW, *DO* YOU?
GIVE ME YOUR HAND, KID.
M-M-MISTER SMITH?
για να συνεχιστεί...

THE DEATH OF MISTER SMITH

"M-m-mister Smith?"

The words barely left Oliver's lips before his head fell back onto the granite floor with an unconscious thump. It was enough to give the bearded man standing over him pause. As the man holstered his smoking weapon, his face was grim. For he knew that should he continue down this path, there would be a good chance he would no longer be known by that name.

"Mister Smith."

What a dumb name, he thought. *Suppose that's what I get for letting the kids pick it themselves.* He couldn't help but grin at the idea of all the pet fish and cats they'd outlived, buried, or lost, burdened by such unfortunate monikers as "Turkey Lips," "Mr. Chum Chum," "Peanut Butter," "Poop," and "Stupid Dummy Face."

Maybe "Mister Smith" wasn't all that bad after all...

Smith scooped Oliver up and threw him over his shoulder, the mysterious green glowing liquid bouncing its sheen off Oliver's face. Smith involuntarily groaned. His muscles tensed up much quicker now after exertion than they did years ago. This was one brute of a battle... and he felt it from head to toe. But why? Why did the statue process not work this time? What could be changing?

As he walked through the rubble and out the hole in the museum wall, Smith remembered back to the first time he faced the Boar. Villages in the area were being terrorized by a creature that came out of the woods at night and stormed into their wooden shacks. It was only when a villager barely escaped an attack that Smith realized the key. Once the Boar tasted the blood of a victim, it developed an immediate taste for that blood alone. The Boar managed to kill that man the next night, but Smith quickly used himself as bait. That's where the faded scar on his upper shoulder came from.

When the Boar rounded back the next night, Smith was prepared along with his brother and two of his sons. After a heart-pounding chase through the woods (it was, after all, a little more thrilling back then), the Boar was caught in the triangulation of their harpoons. Smith turned back, walked right up to the oversized snout and jammed two sticks into its maw. It immediately turned to stone. On all fours. For the next five hundred and thirty-six years. Until tonight.

Maybe Smith could bring the kid back to his own house. Slip him into his own bed and then quietly escape out the window and deny the whole thing. Maybe just leave him at the museum, and everyone would assume it was a burglary of some sort. No one would ever believe Oliver's story about a statue coming to life and attacking him. He doesn't need to be a part of this world. Truth be told, it was probably the words of Smith's ex-wife buzzing in the back of his head. He knew very well what had happened to the other three he allowed in. But this one was different. There was something about Oliver. But what was it?

And with that, a drop of blood ran down Oliver's limp hand, balled at the end of his index finger, and splattered onto Smith's boot.

Smith needed Oliver. Plain and simple.

Carefully looking both ways, Smith dashed across the street to a large black truck tucked away in an unassuming alley. Despite the museum's ringing alarm, no one had arrived at the scene yet. Thank the Gods for small towns and a drunken sheriff.

The vehicle looked like an old fire truck from 1932... only with nitrous gas canisters and an ammo dispenser where a stereo would normally go. Oliver slumped over in his seat. The cab smelled like sweat and leather. Smith stood there, with the passenger side open knowing that should he start the truck, there was no turning back. Smith paused, giving himself a final out...

...and then Oliver shivered. Smith couldn't help but think of every child he had ever created. Alone. Helpless. He took off his worn trenchcoat, removed the sharp lightning bolt-shaped blades from the inside and draped it over Oliver. Then Smith slowly closed the door. Ka-chick.

And thus marked the death of "Mister Smith"...

Opposite page: Kevin Munroe's first rendering of Zeus

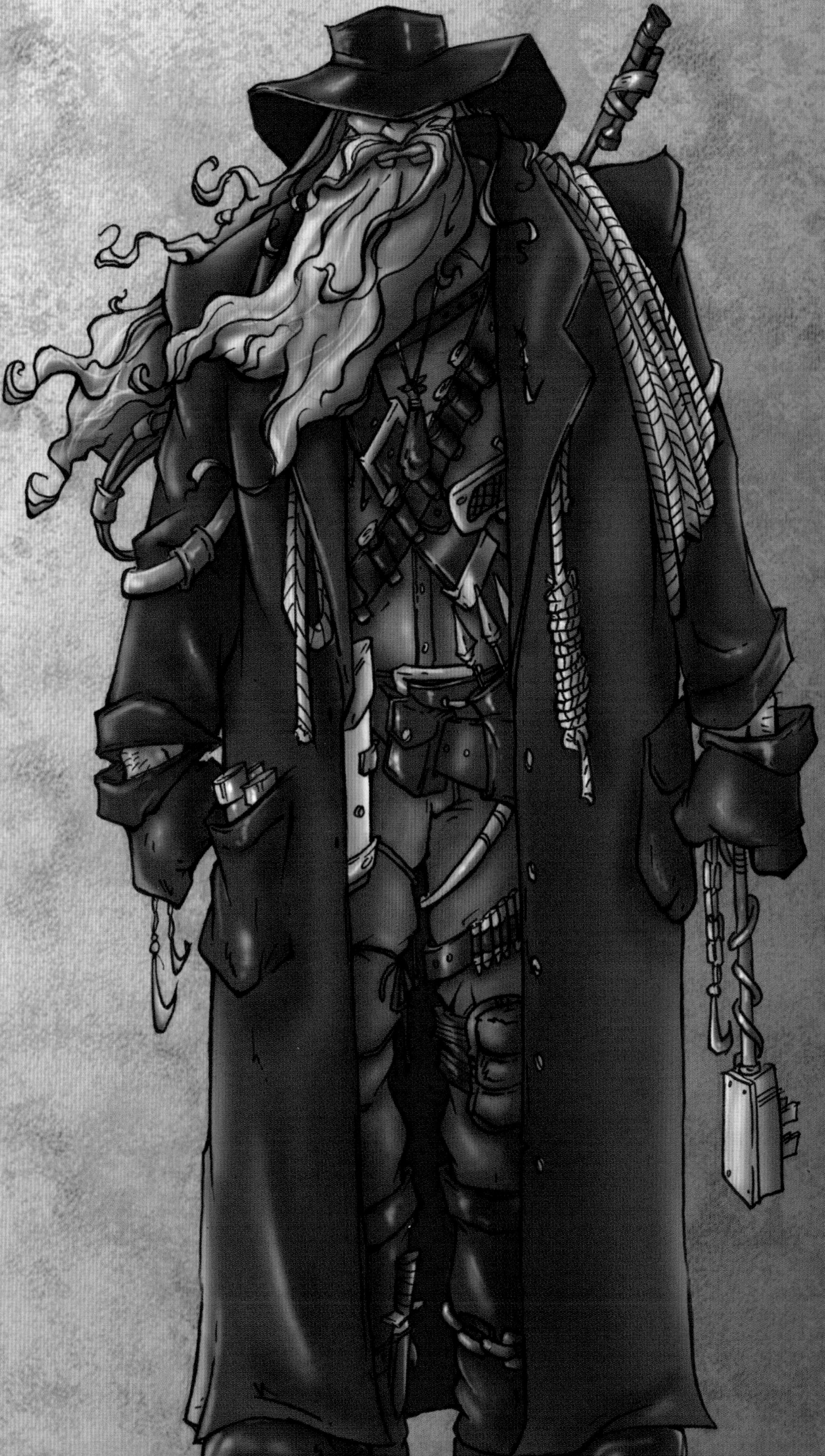

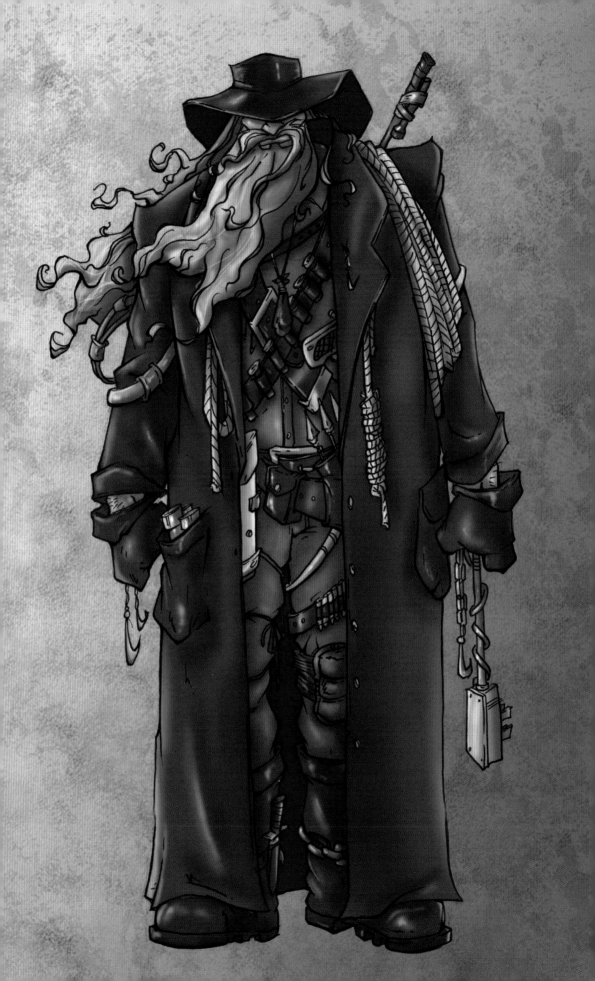

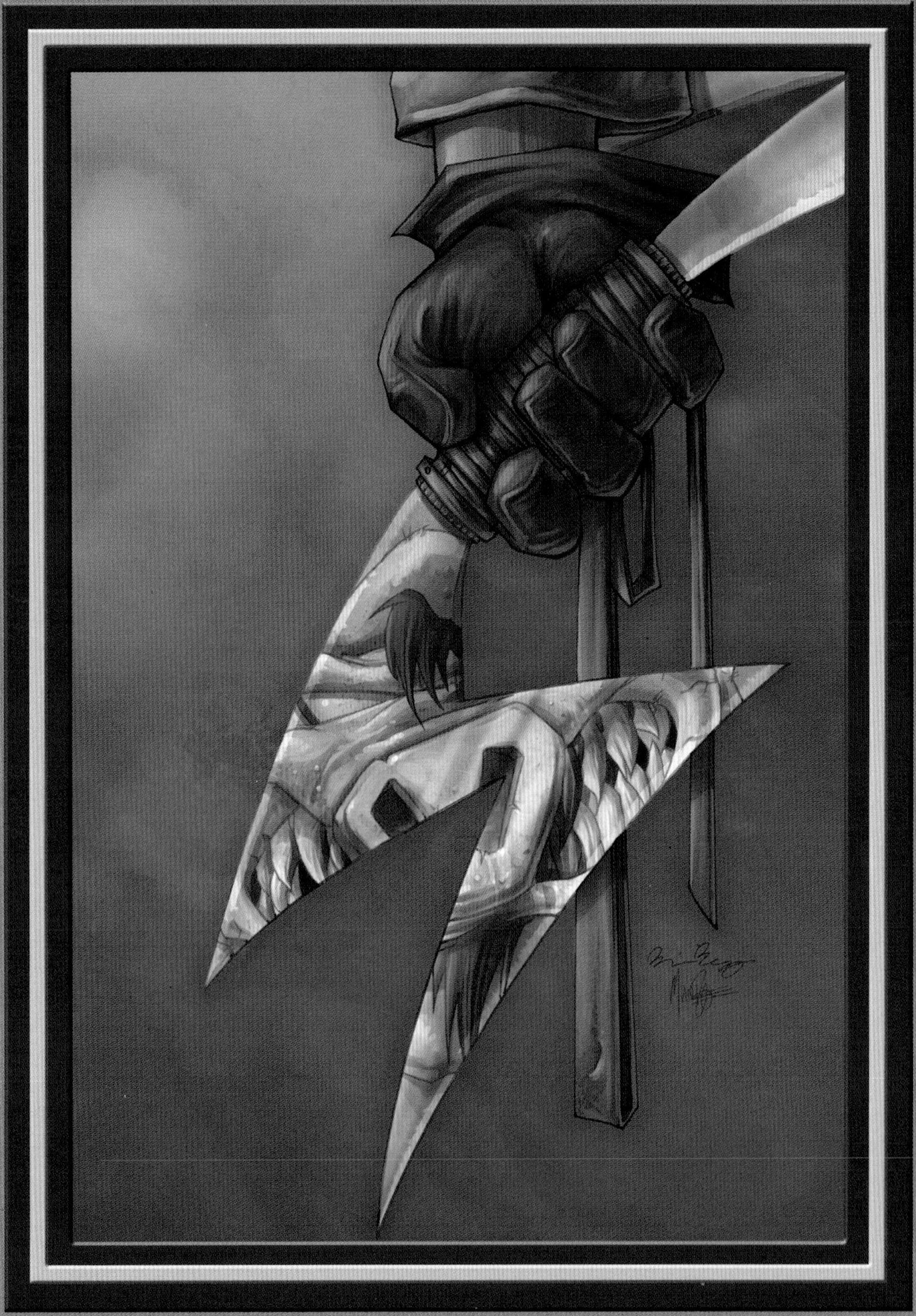

Chapter Two

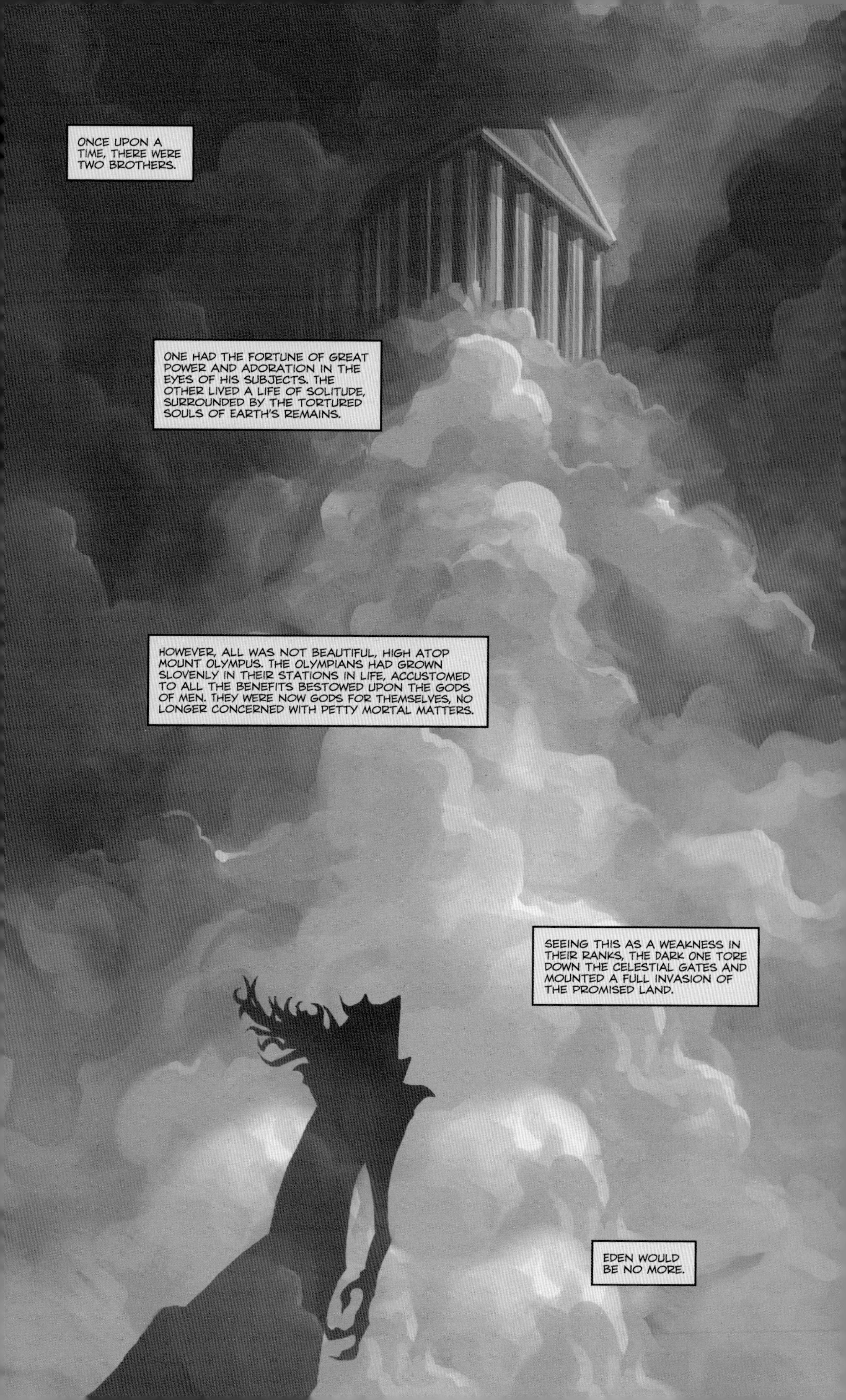
ONCE UPON A TIME, THERE WERE TWO BROTHERS.
ONE HAD THE FORTUNE OF GREAT POWER AND ADORATION IN THE EYES OF HIS SUBJECTS. THE OTHER LIVED A LIFE OF SOLITUDE, SURROUNDED BY THE TORTURED SOULS OF EARTH'S REMAINS.
HOWEVER, ALL WAS NOT BEAUTIFUL, HIGH ATOP MOUNT OLYMPUS. THE OLYMPIANS HAD GROWN SLOVENLY IN THEIR STATIONS IN LIFE, ACCUSTOMED TO ALL THE BENEFITS BESTOWED UPON THE GODS OF MEN. THEY WERE NOW GODS FOR THEMSELVES, NO LONGER CONCERNED WITH PETTY MORTAL MATTERS.
SEEING THIS AS A WEAKNESS IN THEIR RANKS, THE DARK ONE TORE DOWN THE CELESTIAL GATES AND MOUNTED A FULL INVASION OF THE PROMISED LAND.
EDEN WOULD BE NO MORE.

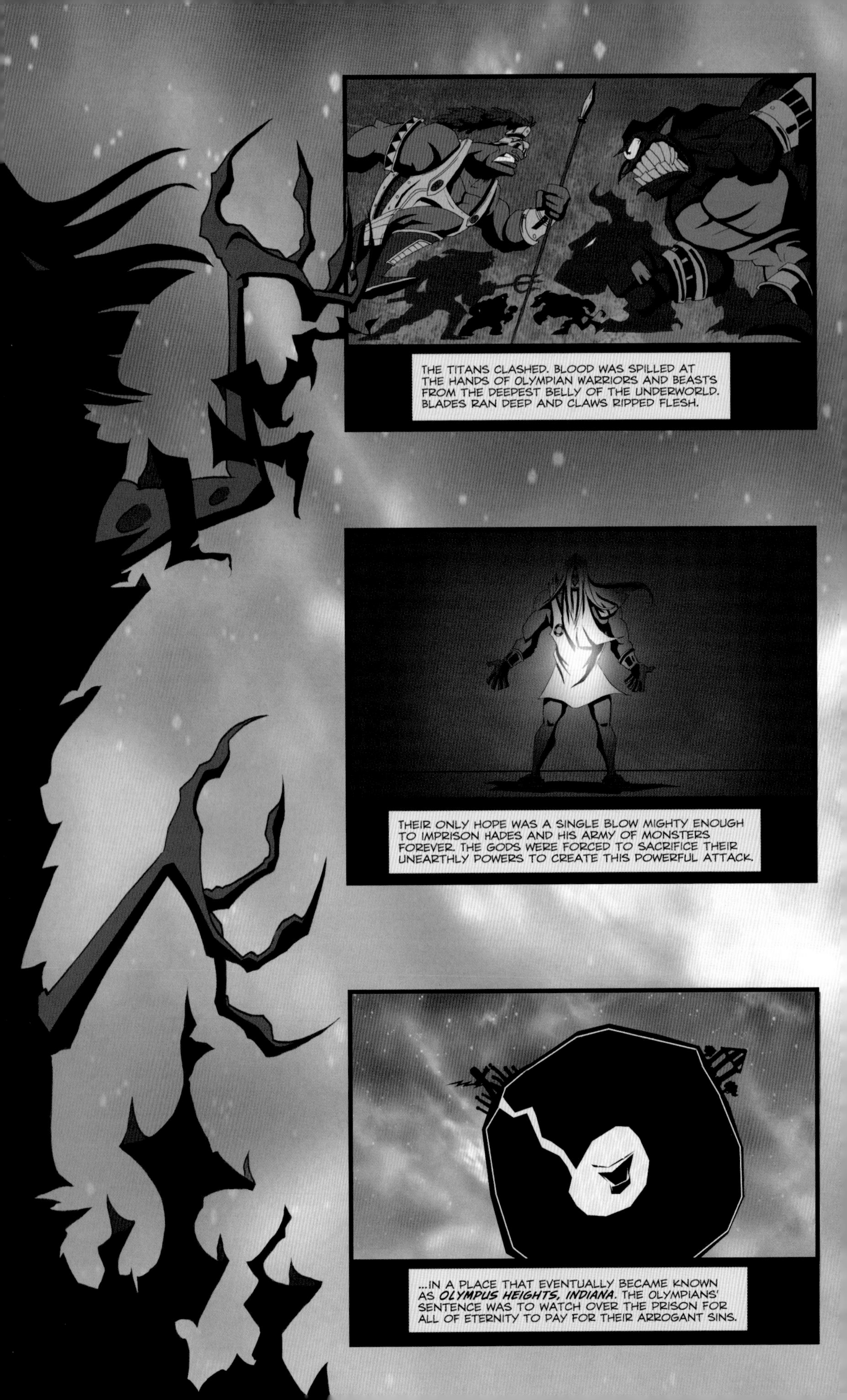
THE TITANS CLASHED. BLOOD WAS SPILLED AT THE HANDS OF OLYMPIAN WARRIORS AND BEASTS FROM THE DEEPEST BELLY OF THE UNDERWORLD. BLADES RAN DEEP AND CLAWS RIPPED FLESH.
THEIR ONLY HOPE WAS A SINGLE BLOW MIGHTY ENOUGH TO IMPRISON HADES AND HIS ARMY OF MONSTERS FOREVER. THE GODS WERE FORCED TO SACRIFICE THEIR UNEARTHLY POWERS TO CREATE THIS POWERFUL ATTACK.
...IN A PLACE THAT EVENTUALLY BECAME KNOWN AS OLYMPUS HEIGHTS, INDIANA. THE OLYMPIANS' SENTENCE WAS TO WATCH OVER THE PRISON FOR ALL OF ETERNITY TO PAY FOR THEIR ARROGANT SINS.

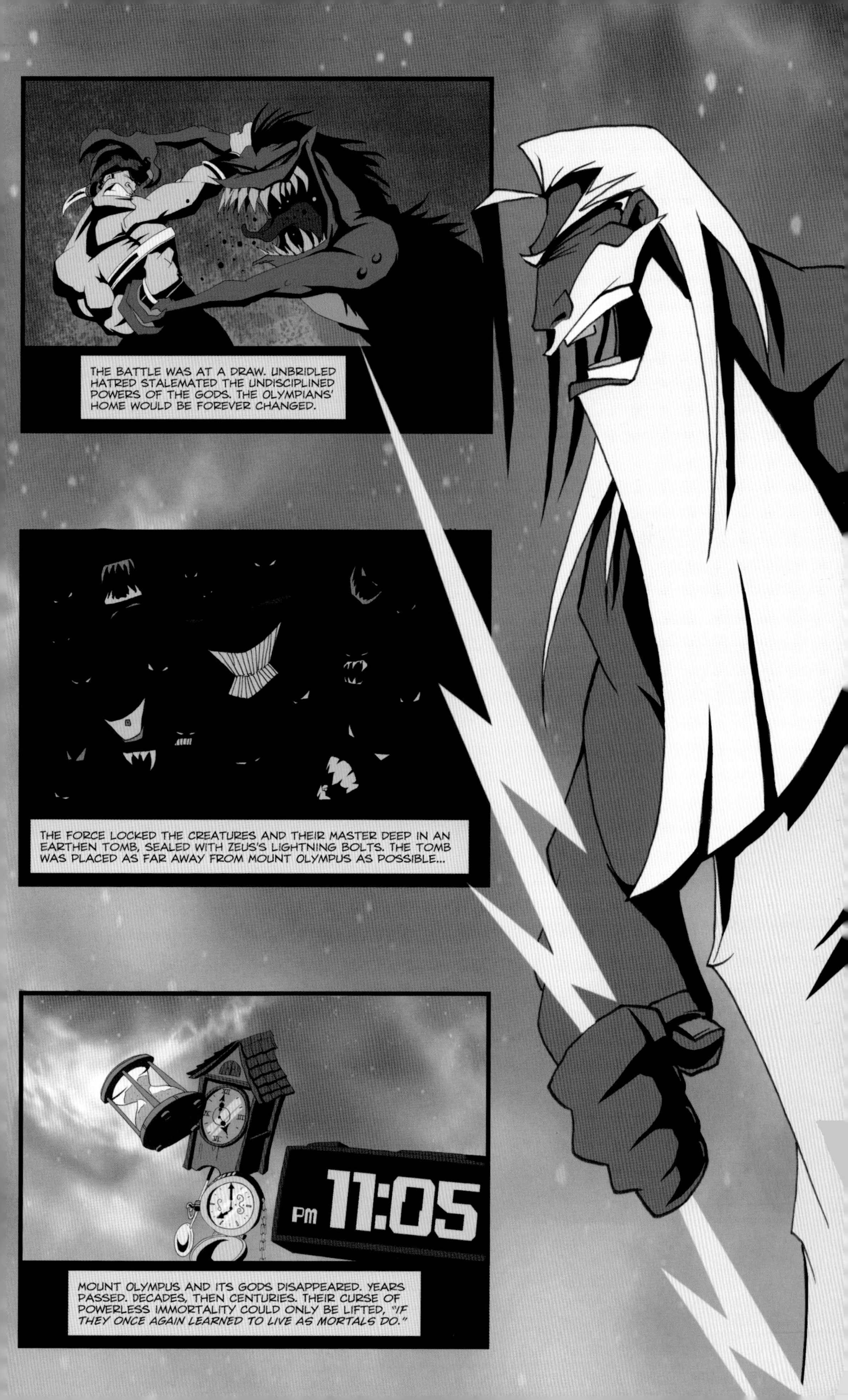
THE BATTLE WAS AT A DRAW. UNBRIDLED HATRED STALEMATED THE UNDISCIPLINED POWERS OF THE GODS. THE OLYMPIANS' HOME WOULD BE FOREVER CHANGED.
THE FORCE LOCKED THE CREATURES AND THEIR MASTER DEEP IN AN EARTHEN TOMB, SEALED WITH ZEUS'S LIGHTNING BOLTS. THE TOMB WAS PLACED AS FAR AWAY FROM MOUNT OLYMPUS AS POSSIBLE...
PM 11:05
MOUNT OLYMPUS AND ITS GODS DISAPPEARED. YEARS PASSED. DECADES, THEN CENTURIES. THEIR CURSE OF POWERLESS IMMORTALITY COULD ONLY BE LIFTED, "IF THEY ONCE AGAIN LEARNED TO LIVE AS MORTALS DO."

THE OLYMPIANS STOOD SHOULDER TO SHOULDER IN THEIR WATCH.

AN ENTIRE FAMILY, STRONG AND PROUD.

HOWEVER, AS FAMILIES DO, THEY SOON GREW APART.

DREAMS REPLACED DUTY.

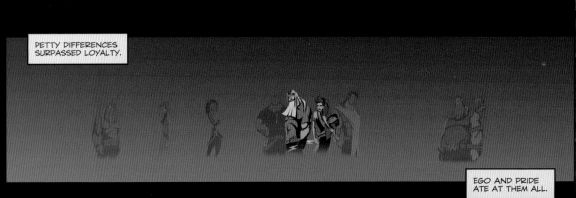

PETTY DIFFERENCES SURPASSED LOYALTY.

EGO AND PRIDE ATE AT THEM ALL.

UNTIL...

...THERE WAS ONE.

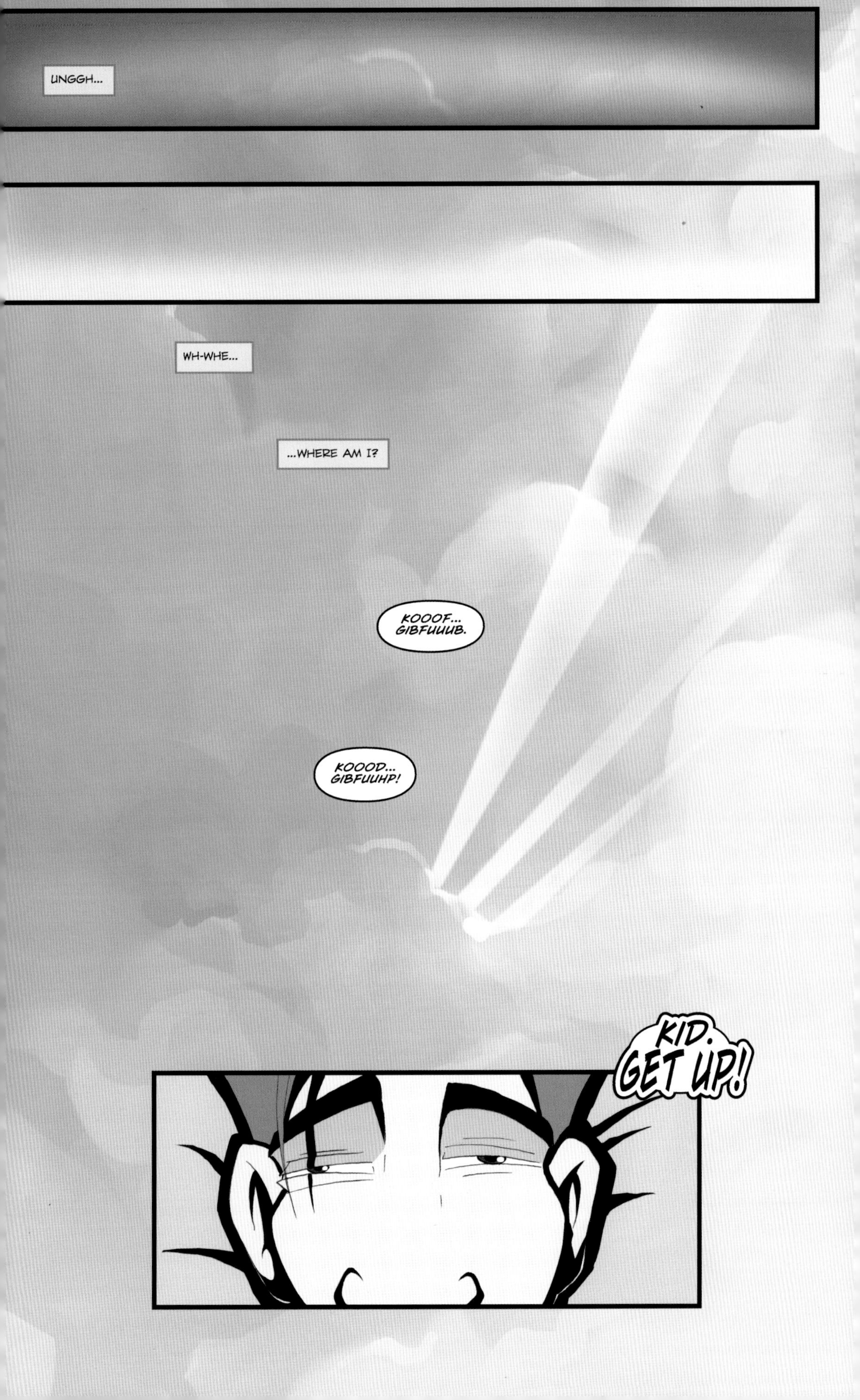
UNGGH...
WH-WHE...
...WHERE AM I?
KOOOF... GIBFUUUB.
KOOOD... GIBFUUHP!
KID. GET UP!

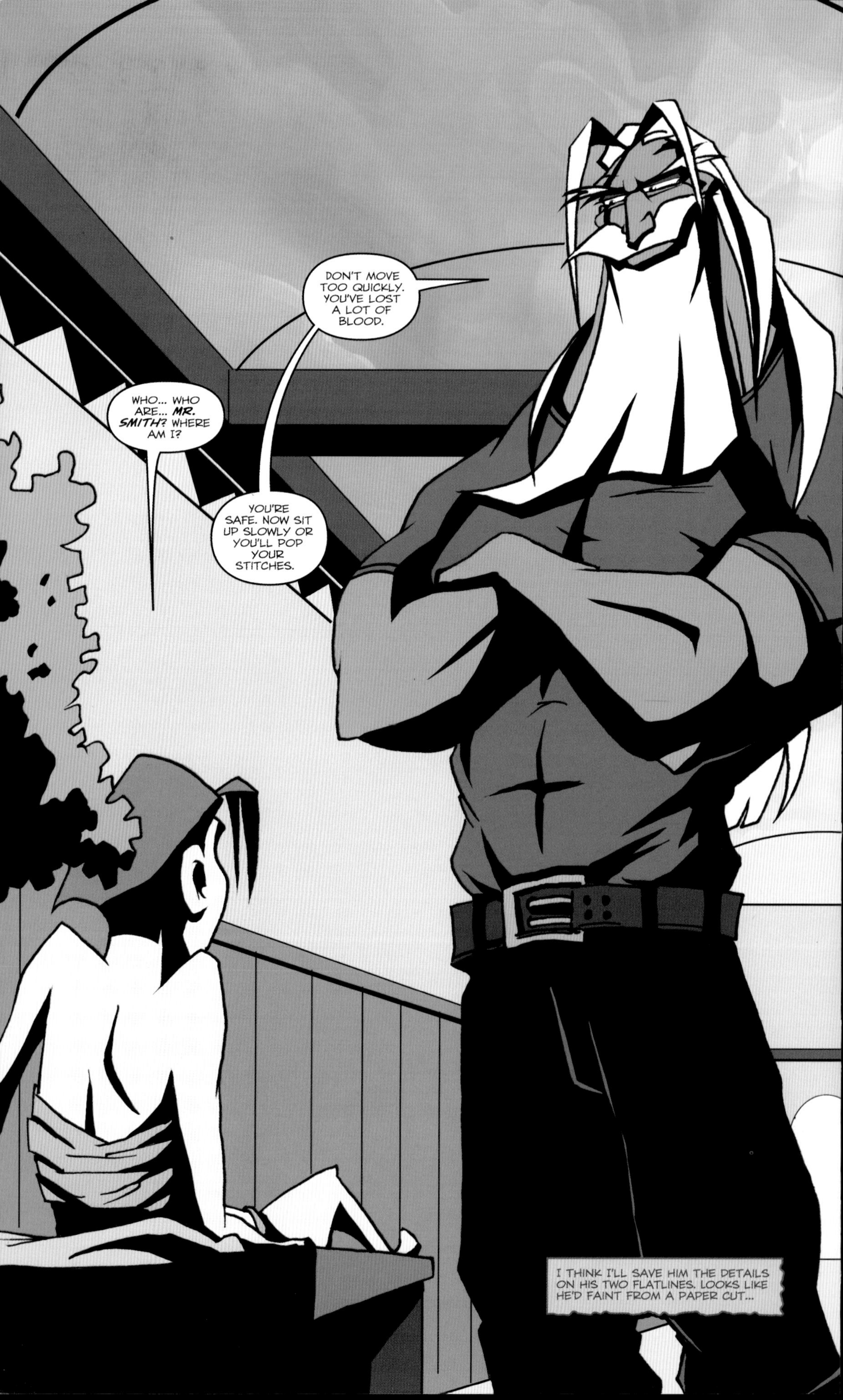
DON'T MOVE TOO QUICKLY. YOU'VE LOST A LOT OF BLOOD.
WHO... WHO ARE... MR. SMITH? WHERE AM I?
YOU'RE SAFE. NOW SIT UP SLOWLY OR YOU'LL POP YOUR STITCHES.
I THINK I'LL SAVE HIM THE DETAILS ON HIS TWO FLATLINES. LOOKS LIKE HE'D FAINT FROM A PAPER CUT...

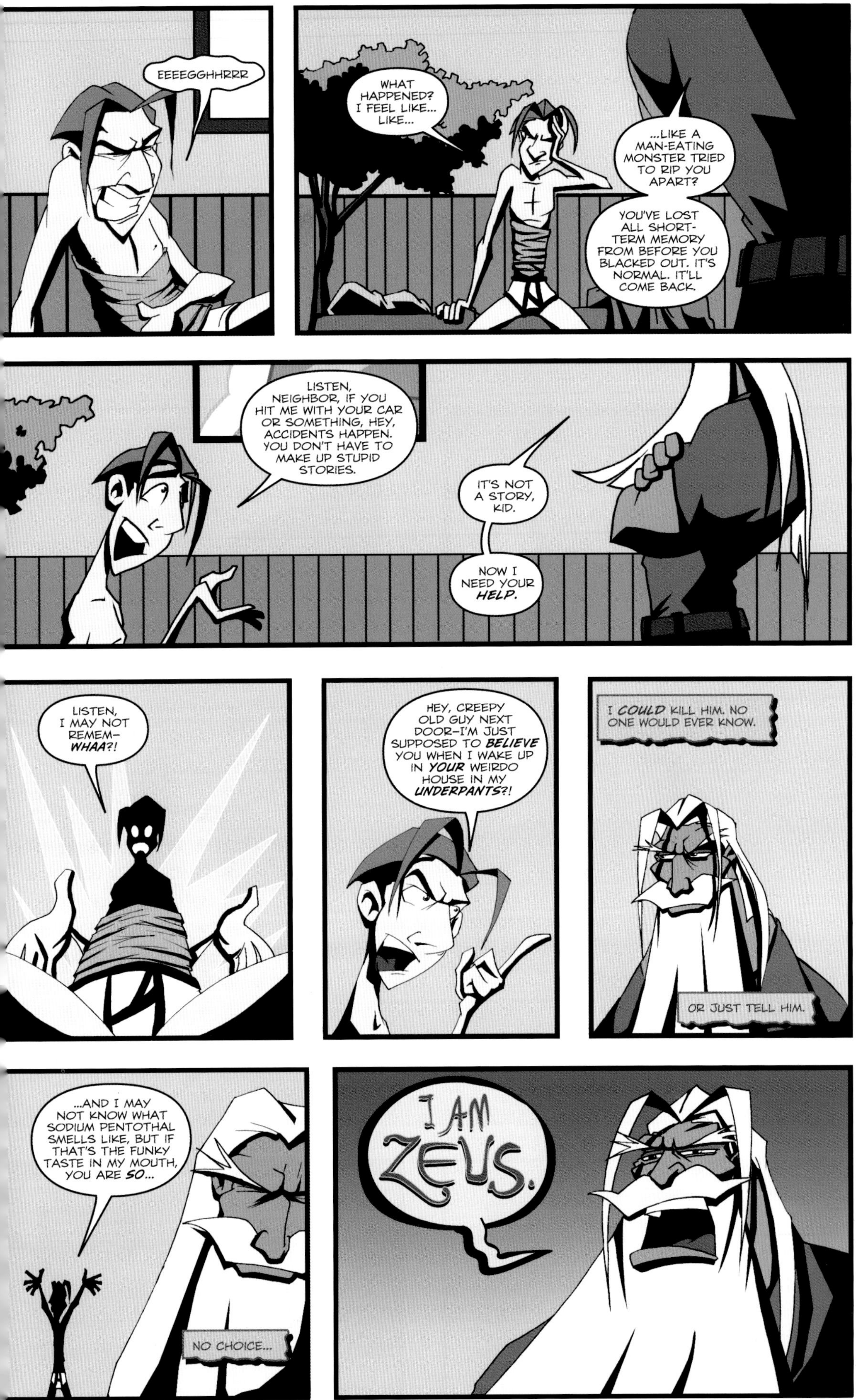

EEEEGGHHRRR
WHAT HAPPENED? I FEEL LIKE... LIKE...
...LIKE A MAN-EATING MONSTER TRIED TO RIP YOU APART?
YOU'VE LOST ALL SHORT-TERM MEMORY FROM BEFORE YOU BLACKED OUT. IT'S NORMAL. IT'LL COME BACK.
LISTEN, NEIGHBOR, IF YOU HIT ME WITH YOUR CAR OR SOMETHING, HEY, ACCIDENTS HAPPEN. YOU DON'T HAVE TO MAKE UP STUPID STORIES.
IT'S NOT A STORY, KID.
NOW I NEED YOUR HELP.
LISTEN, I MAY NOT REMEM-WHAA?!
HEY, CREEPY OLD GUY NEXT DOOR–I'M JUST SUPPOSED TO BELIEVE YOU WHEN I WAKE UP IN YOUR WEIRDO HOUSE IN MY UNDERPANTS?!
I COULD KILL HIM. NO ONE WOULD EVER KNOW.
OR JUST TELL HIM.
...AND I MAY NOT KNOW WHAT SODIUM PENTOTHAL SMELLS LIKE, BUT IF THAT'S THE FUNKY TASTE IN MY MOUTH, YOU ARE SO...
NO CHOICE...
I AM ZEUS.

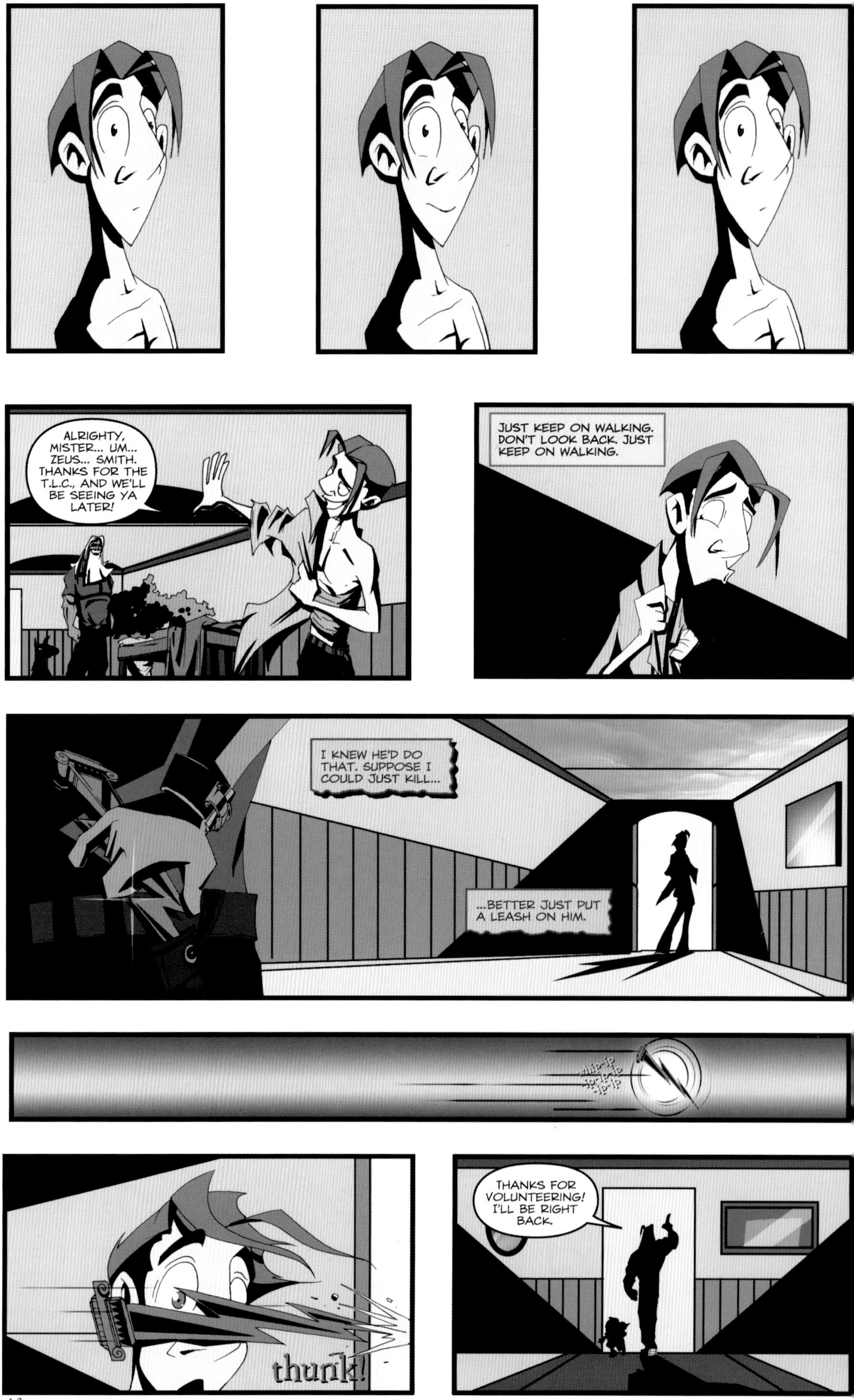
ALRIGHTY, MISTER... UM... ZEUS... SMITH. THANKS FOR THE T.L.C., AND WE'LL BE SEEING YA LATER!
JUST KEEP ON WALKING. DON'T LOOK BACK. JUST KEEP ON WALKING.
I KNEW HE'D DO THAT. SUPPOSE I COULD JUST KILL...
...BETTER JUST PUT A LEASH ON HIM.
whip-ip-ip-ip-ip-ip-ip
thunk!
THANKS FOR VOLUNTEERING! I'LL BE RIGHT BACK.

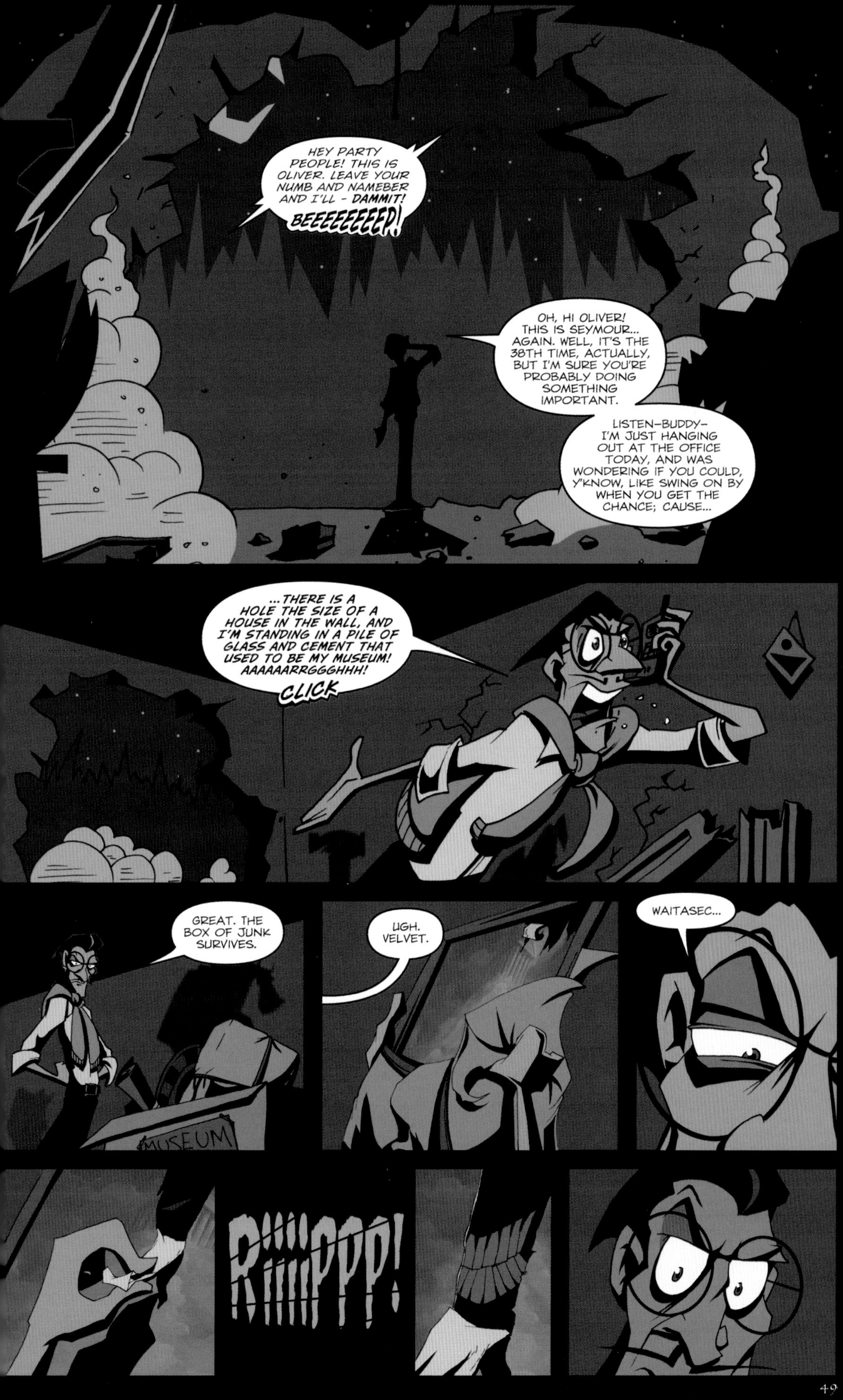
HEY PARTY PEOPLE! THIS IS OLIVER. LEAVE YOUR NUMB AND NAMEBER AND I'LL - DAMMIT!
BEEEEEEEEEP!
OH, HI OLIVER! THIS IS SEYMOUR... AGAIN. WELL, IT'S THE 38TH TIME, ACTUALLY, BUT I'M SURE YOU'RE PROBABLY DOING SOMETHING IMPORTANT.
LISTEN-BUDDY- I'M JUST HANGING OUT AT THE OFFICE TODAY, AND WAS WONDERING IF YOU COULD, Y'KNOW, LIKE SWING ON BY WHEN YOU GET THE CHANCE; CAUSE...
...THERE IS A HOLE THE SIZE OF A HOUSE IN THE WALL, AND I'M STANDING IN A PILE OF GLASS AND CEMENT THAT USED TO BE MY MUSEUM! AAAAAARRGGGHHH!
CLICK
GREAT. THE BOX OF JUNK SURVIVES.
MUSEUM
UGH. VELVET.
WAITASEC...
RIIIIPPPP!

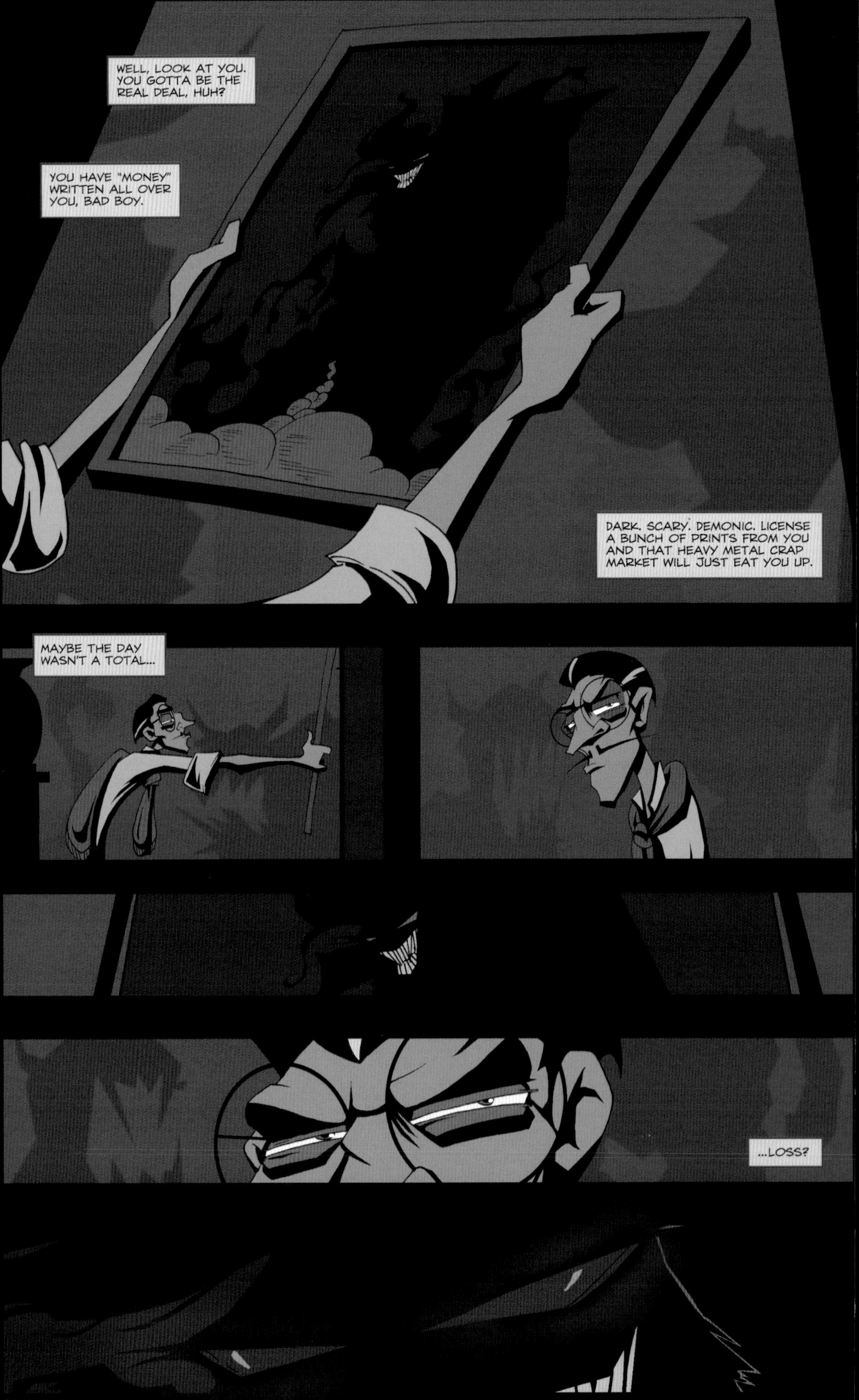
WELL, LOOK AT YOU. YOU GOTTA BE THE REAL DEAL, HUH?
YOU HAVE "MONEY" WRITTEN ALL OVER YOU, BAD BOY.
DARK. SCARY. DEMONIC. LICENSE A BUNCH OF PRINTS FROM YOU AND THAT HEAVY METAL CRAP MARKET WILL JUST EAT YOU UP.
MAYBE THE DAY WASN'T A TOTAL...
...LOSS?

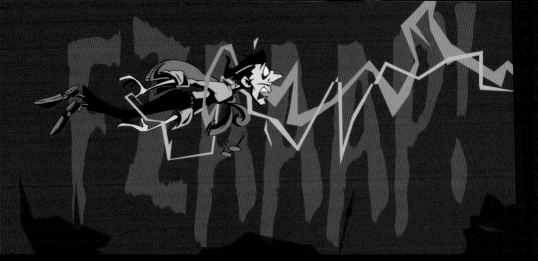

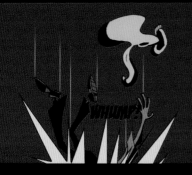

STAND... STAND UP... NOW, YOU SACK OF FLESH!

THIS IS NIIIICE. A LITTLE SCRAWNY FOR MY TASTES, BUT I'LL TAKE IT.

MMMM. SMELL THAT NIGHT AIR

THANK YOU, LADIES AND GENTLEMEN, IT'S GOOD TO BE BACK...

...NOW LET'S TAKE THIS BABY OUT FOR A TEST DRIVE.

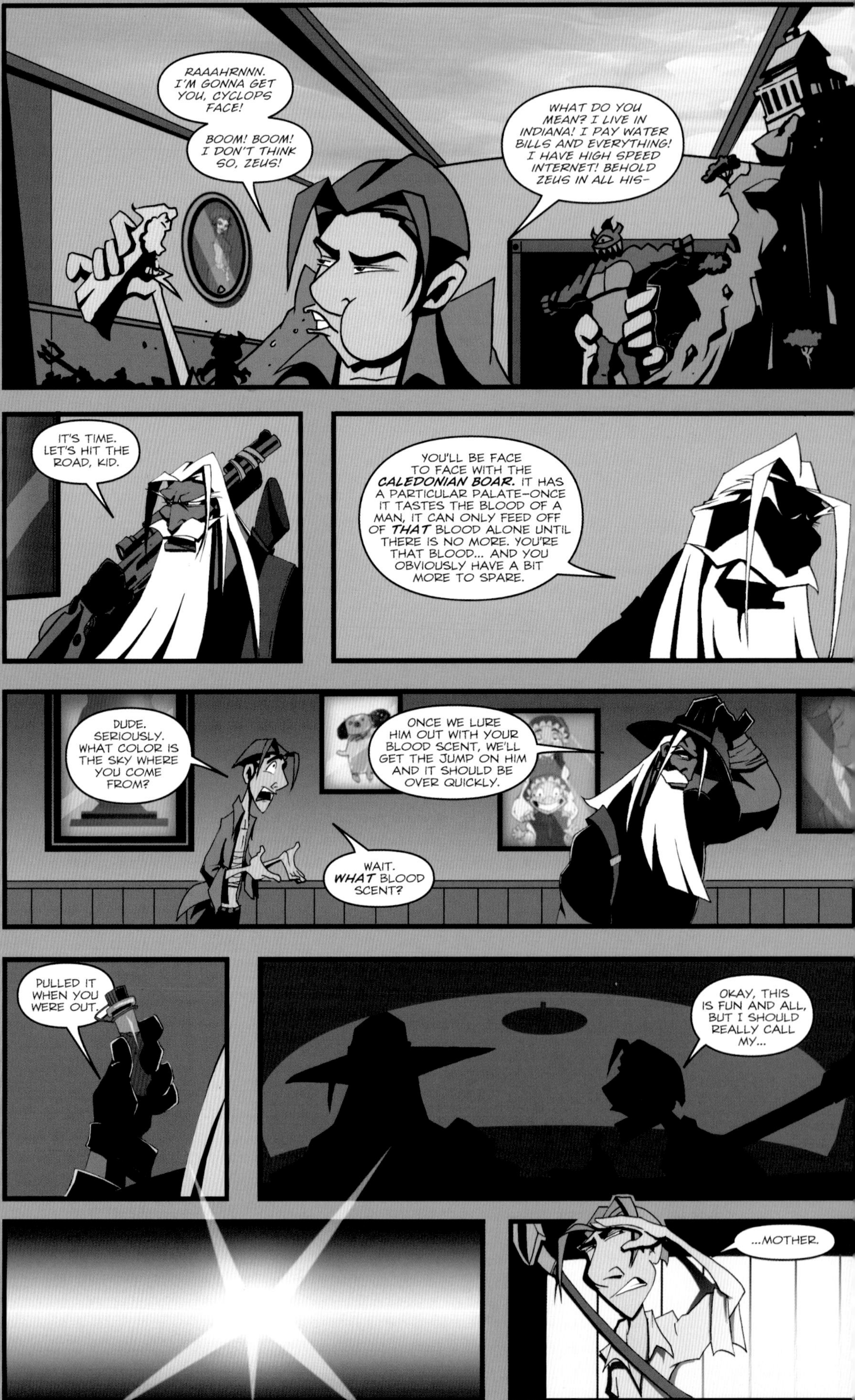
RAAAHRNNN. I'M GONNA GET YOU, CYCLOPS FACE!
BOOM! BOOM! I DON'T THINK SO, ZEUS!
WHAT DO YOU MEAN? I LIVE IN INDIANA! I PAY WATER BILLS AND EVERYTHING! I HAVE HIGH SPEED INTERNET! BEHOLD ZEUS IN ALL HIS-
IT'S TIME. LET'S HIT THE ROAD, KID.
YOU'LL BE FACE TO FACE WITH THE CALEDONIAN BOAR. IT HAS A PARTICULAR PALATE-ONCE IT TASTES THE BLOOD OF A MAN, IT CAN ONLY FEED OFF OF THAT BLOOD ALONE UNTIL THERE IS NO MORE. YOU'RE THAT BLOOD... AND YOU OBVIOUSLY HAVE A BIT MORE TO SPARE.
DUDE. SERIOUSLY. WHAT COLOR IS THE SKY WHERE YOU COME FROM?
ONCE WE LURE HIM OUT WITH YOUR BLOOD SCENT, WE'LL GET THE JUMP ON HIM AND IT SHOULD BE OVER QUICKLY.
WAIT. WHAT BLOOD SCENT?
PULLED IT WHEN YOU WERE OUT.
OKAY, THIS IS FUN AND ALL, BUT I SHOULD REALLY CALL MY...
...MOTHER.

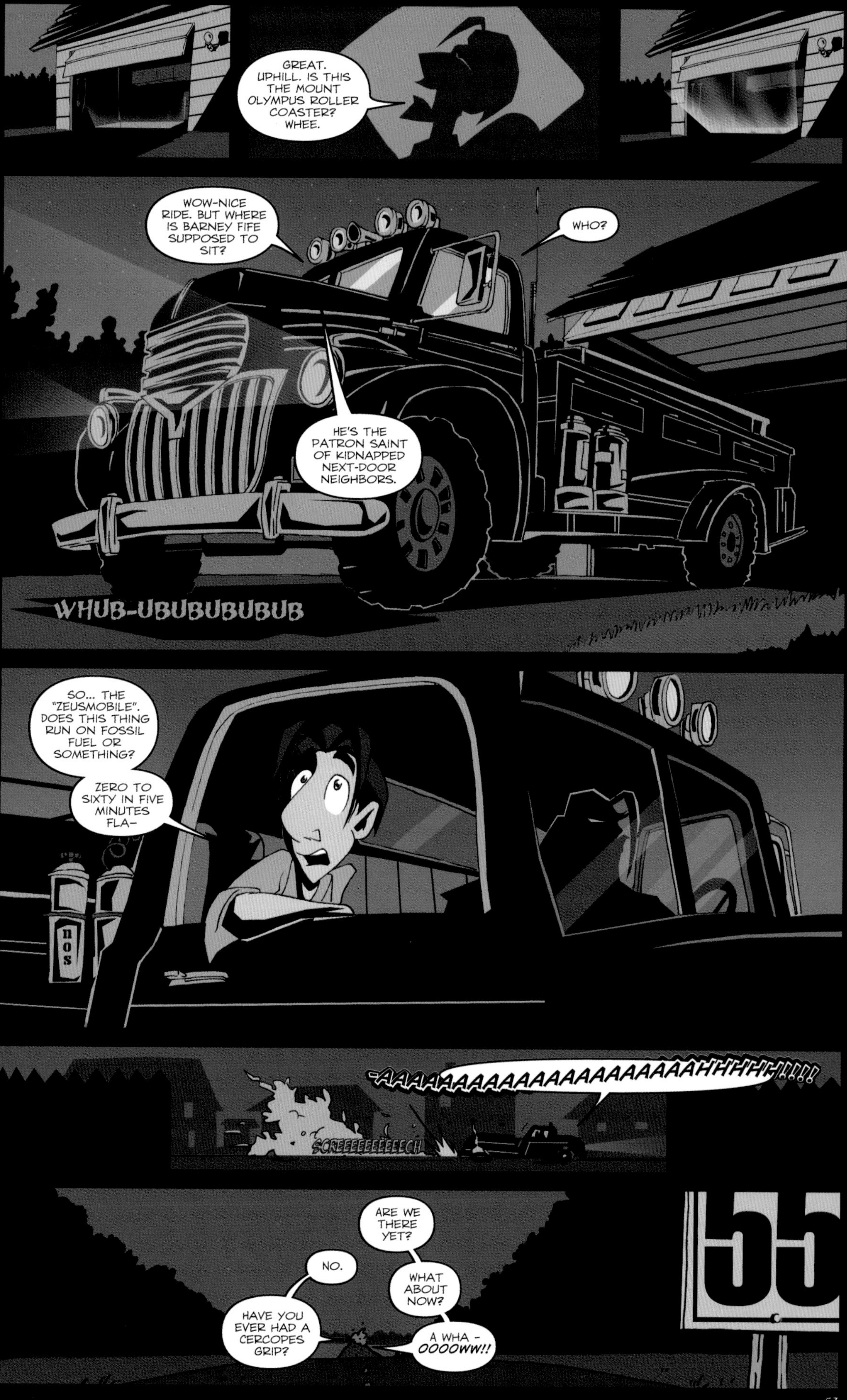
GREAT. UPHILL. IS THIS THE MOUNT OLYMPUS ROLLER COASTER? WHEE.
WOW-NICE RIDE. BUT WHERE IS BARNEY FIFE SUPPOSED TO SIT?
WHO?
HE'S THE PATRON SAINT OF KIDNAPPED NEXT-DOOR NEIGHBORS.
WHUB-UBUBUBUBUB
SO... THE "ZEUSMOBILE". DOES THIS THING RUN ON FOSSIL FUEL OR SOMETHING?
ZERO TO SIXTY IN FIVE MINUTES FLA-
NOS
-AAAAAAAAAAAAAAAAAAAAAAHHHHH!!!!
SCREEEEEEEEEEECH
ARE WE THERE YET?
NO.
WHAT ABOUT NOW?
HAVE YOU EVER HAD A CERCOPES GRIP?
A WHA - OOOOWW!!
55

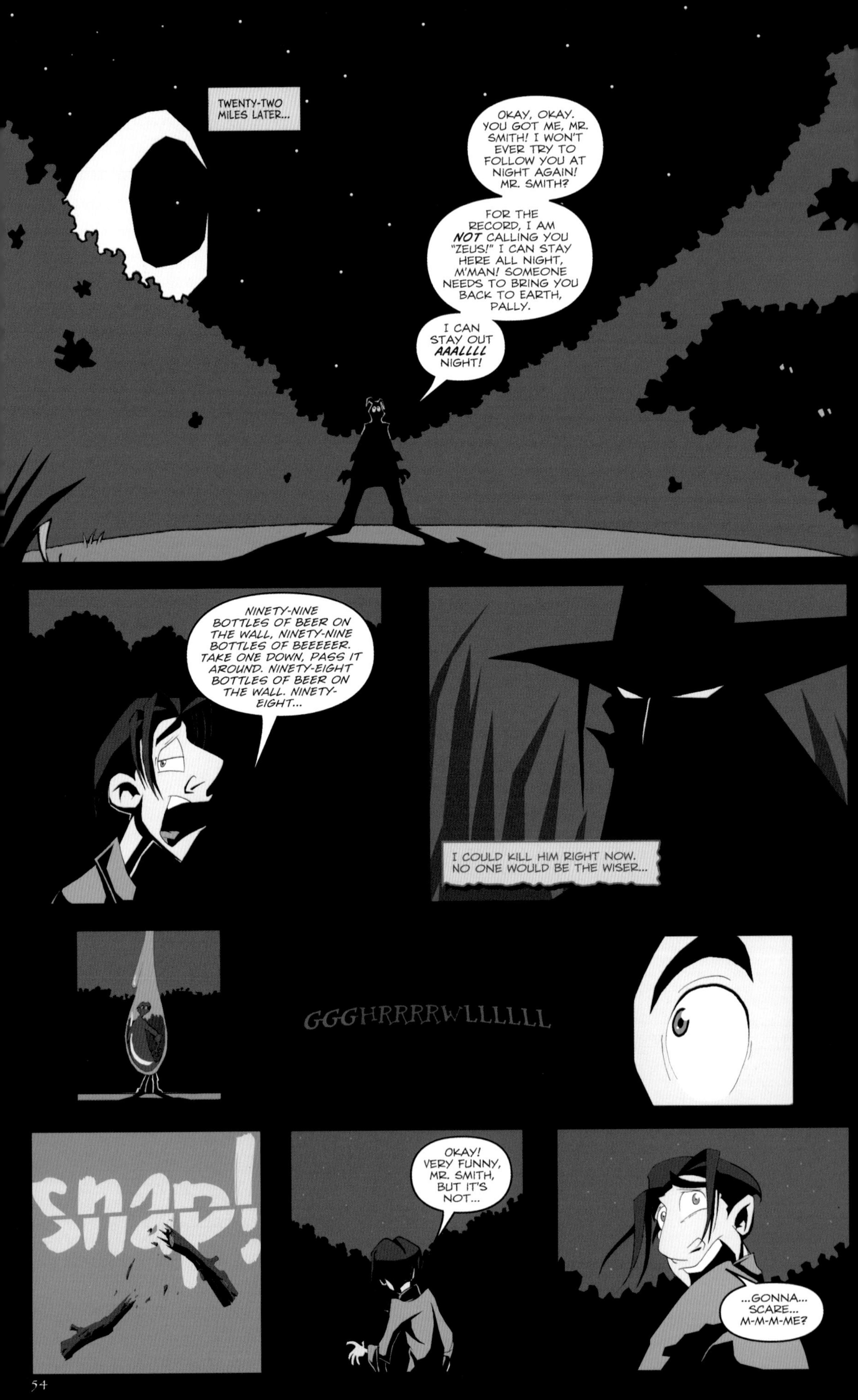

TWENTY-TWO MILES LATER...
OKAY, OKAY. YOU GOT ME, MR. SMITH! I WON'T EVER TRY TO FOLLOW YOU AT NIGHT AGAIN! MR. SMITH?
FOR THE RECORD, I AM NOT CALLING YOU "ZEUS!" I CAN STAY HERE ALL NIGHT, M'MAN! SOMEONE NEEDS TO BRING YOU BACK TO EARTH, PALLY.
I CAN STAY OUT AAALLLL NIGHT!
NINETY-NINE BOTTLES OF BEER ON THE WALL, NINETY-NINE BOTTLES OF BEEEEER. TAKE ONE DOWN, PASS IT AROUND. NINETY-EIGHT BOTTLES OF BEER ON THE WALL. NINETY-EIGHT...
I COULD KILL HIM RIGHT NOW. NO ONE WOULD BE THE WISER...
GGGHRRRRWLLLLLL
SNAP!
OKAY! VERY FUNNY, MR. SMITH, BUT IT'S NOT...
...GONNA... SCARE... M-M-M-ME?

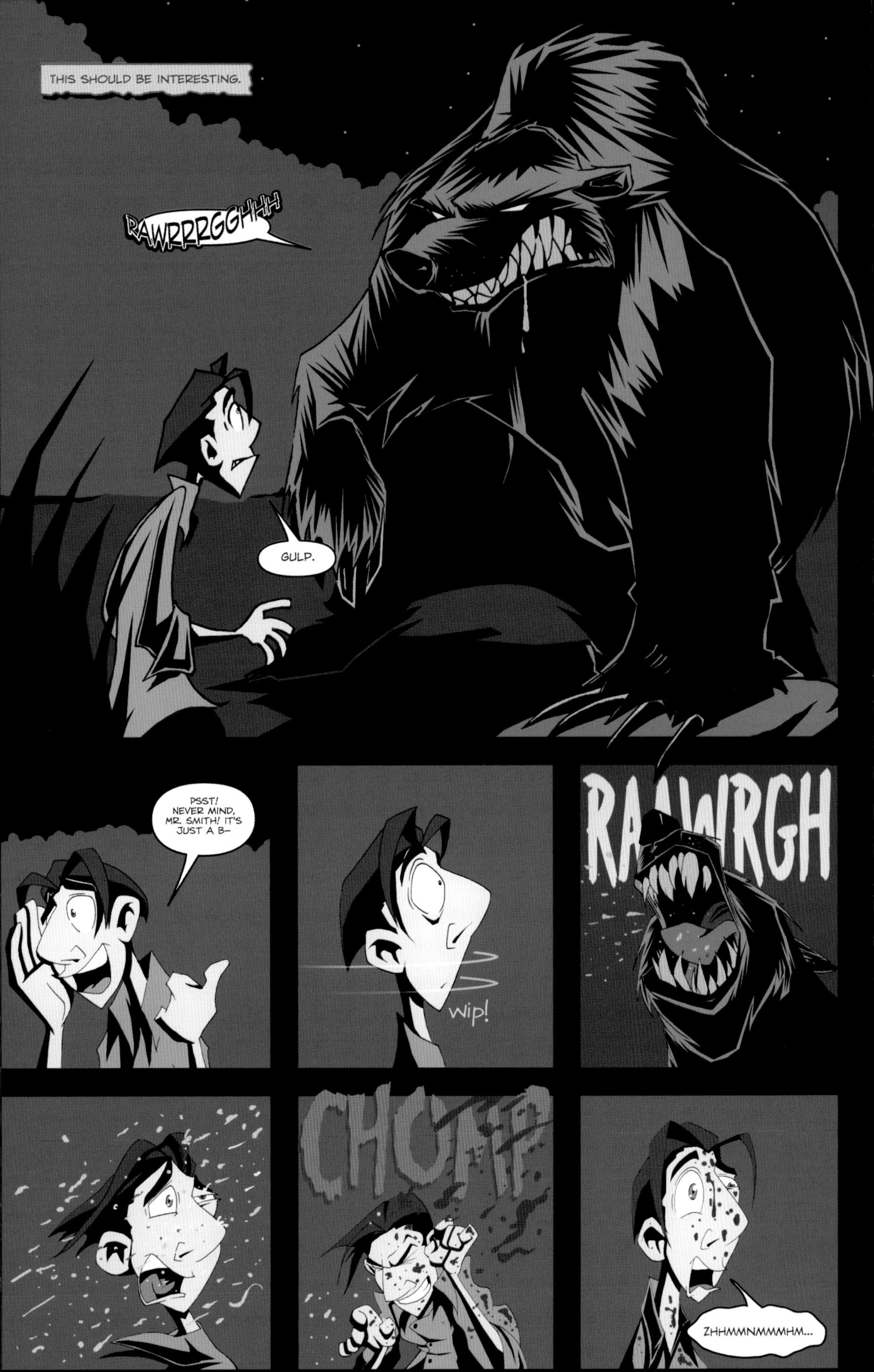

THIS SHOULD BE INTERESTING.
RAWRRRGGHHH
GULP.
PSST! NEVER MIND, MR. SMITH! IT'S JUST A B–
WIP!
RAAWRGH
CHOMP
ZHHMMNMMMHM...

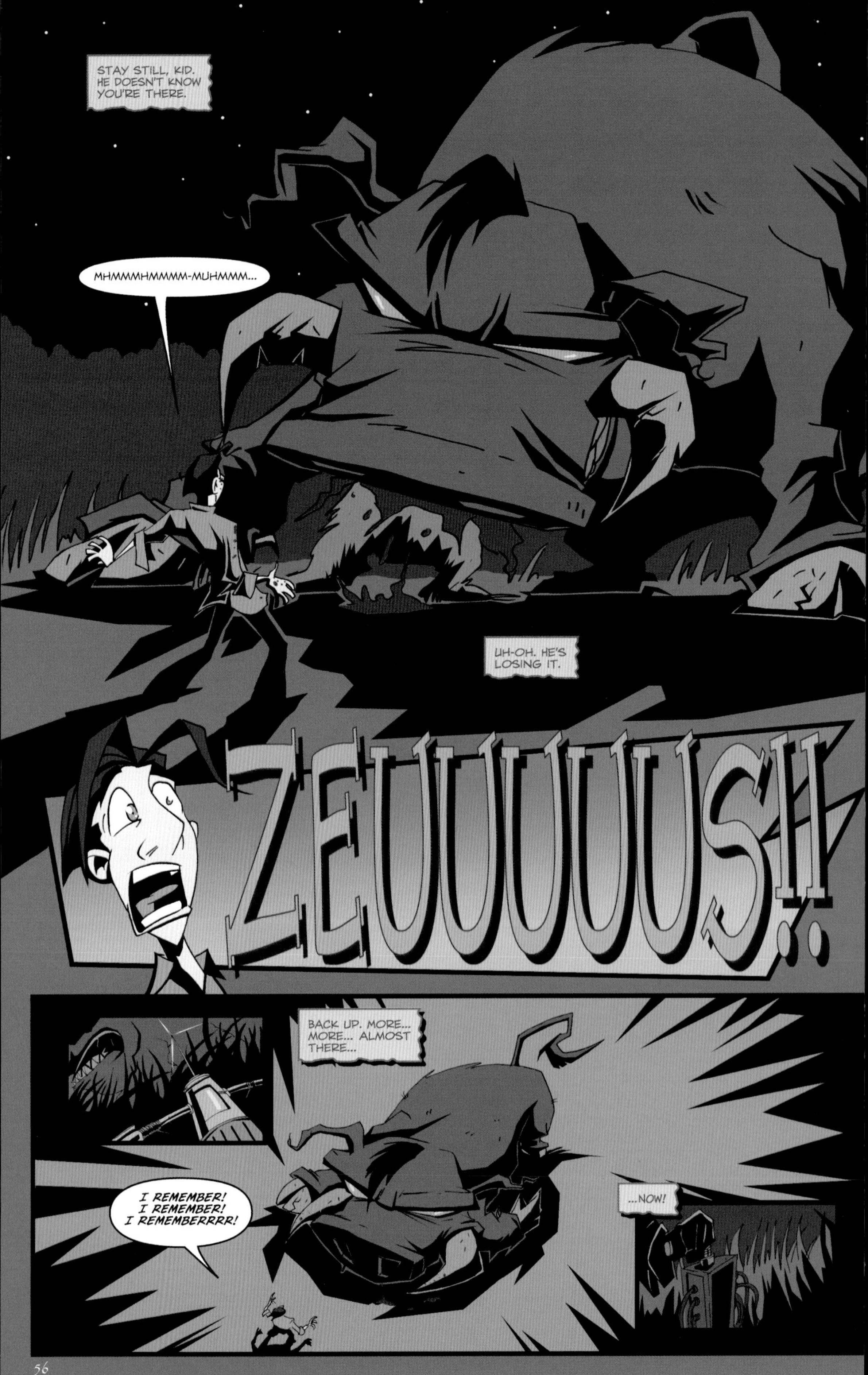
STAY STILL, KID. HE DOESN'T KNOW YOU'RE THERE.
MHMMMHMMMM-MUHMMM...
UH-OH. HE'S LOSING IT.
ZEUUUUUUS!!
BACK UP. MORE... MORE... ALMOST THERE...
I REMEMBER! I REMEMBER! I REMEMBERRRR!
...NOW!

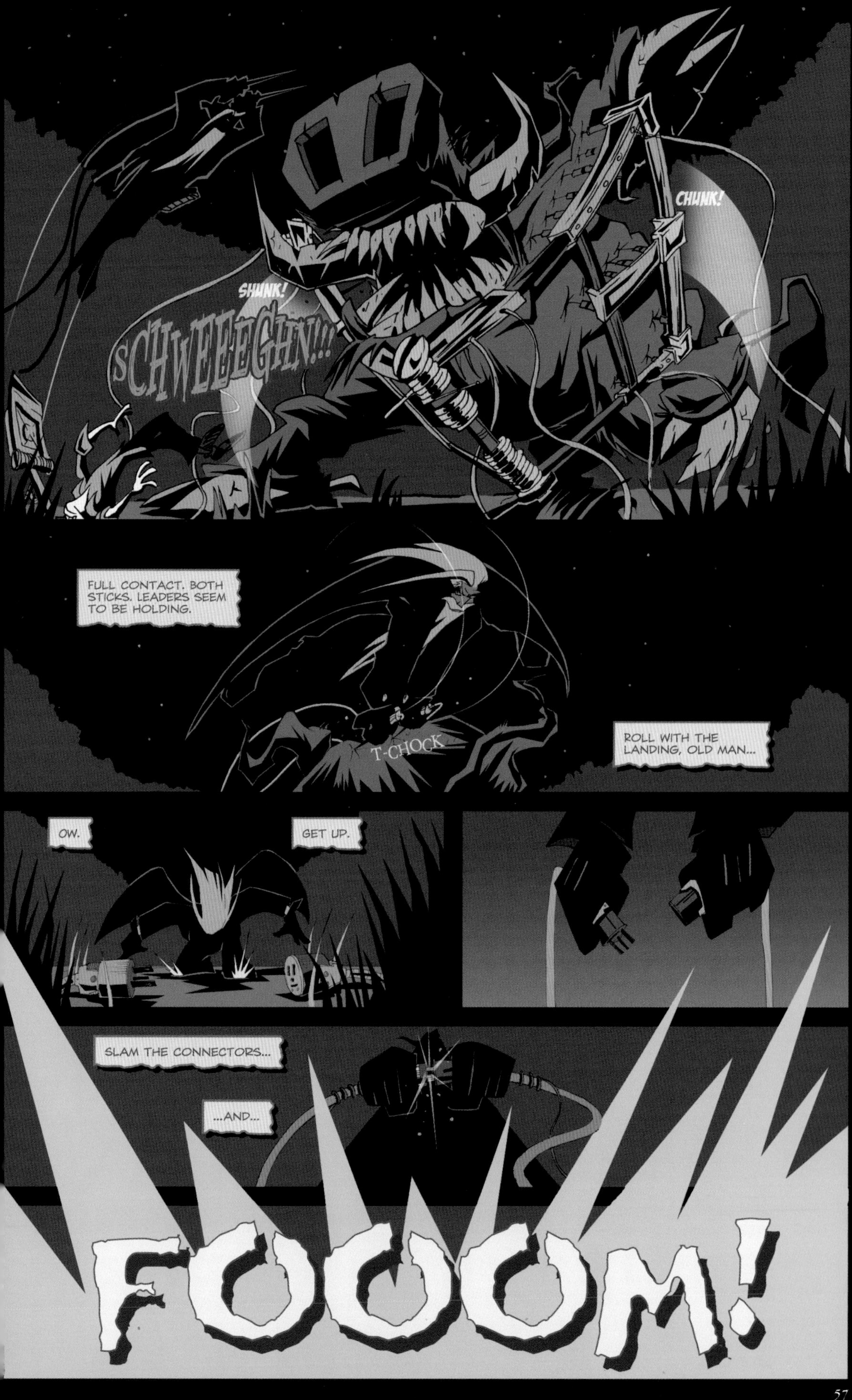
CHUNK!
SHUNK!
SCHWEEEGHN!!!
FULL CONTACT. BOTH STICKS. LEADERS SEEM TO BE HOLDING.
T-CHOCK
ROLL WITH THE LANDING, OLD MAN...
OW.
GET UP.
SLAM THE CONNECTORS...
...AND...
FOOOM!

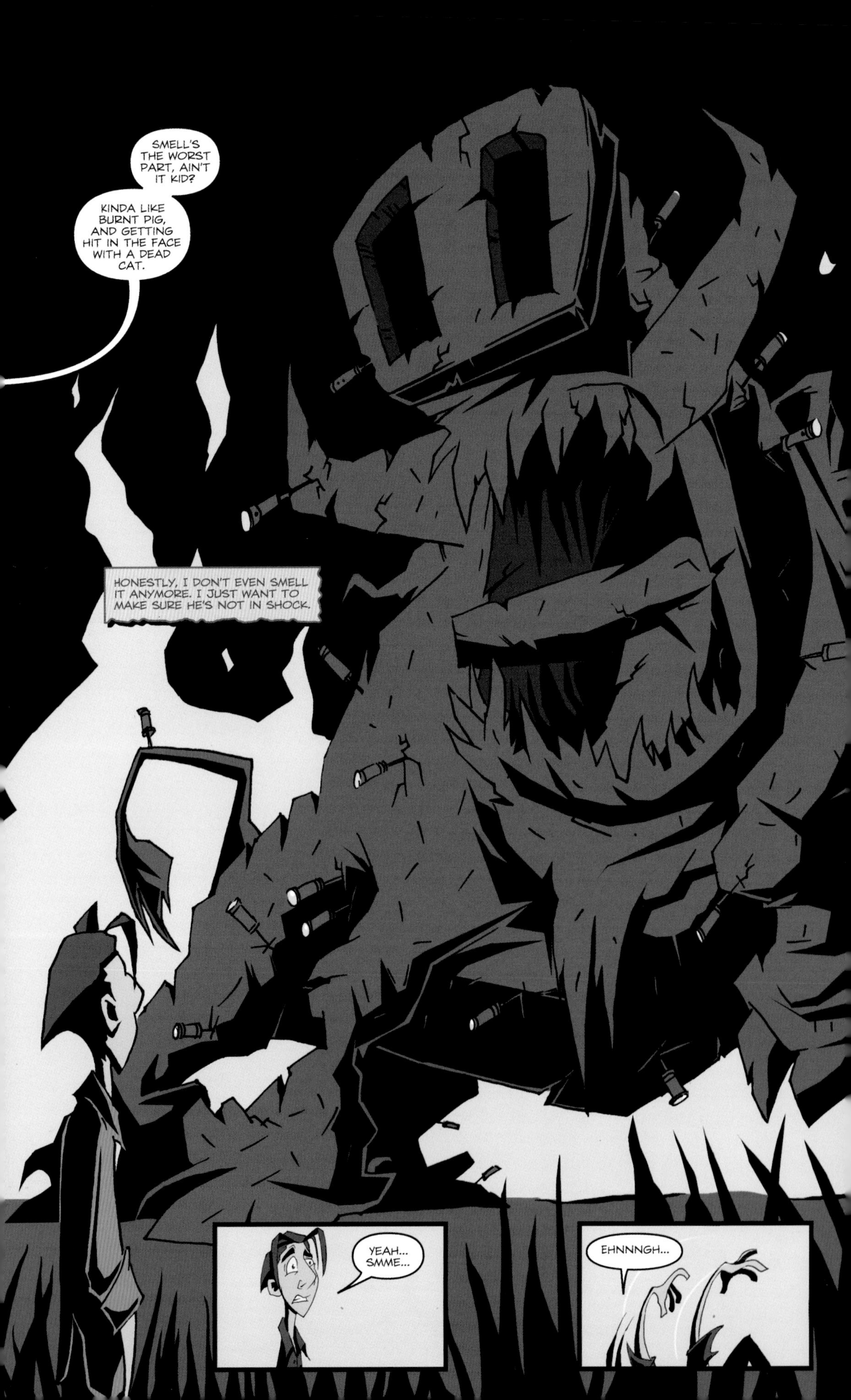
SMELL'S THE WORST PART, AIN'T IT KID?
KINDA LIKE BURNT PIG, AND GETTING HIT IN THE FACE WITH A DEAD CAT.
HONESTLY, I DON'T EVEN SMELL IT ANYMORE. I JUST WANT TO MAKE SURE HE'S NOT IN SHOCK.
YEAH... SMME...
EHNNNGH...

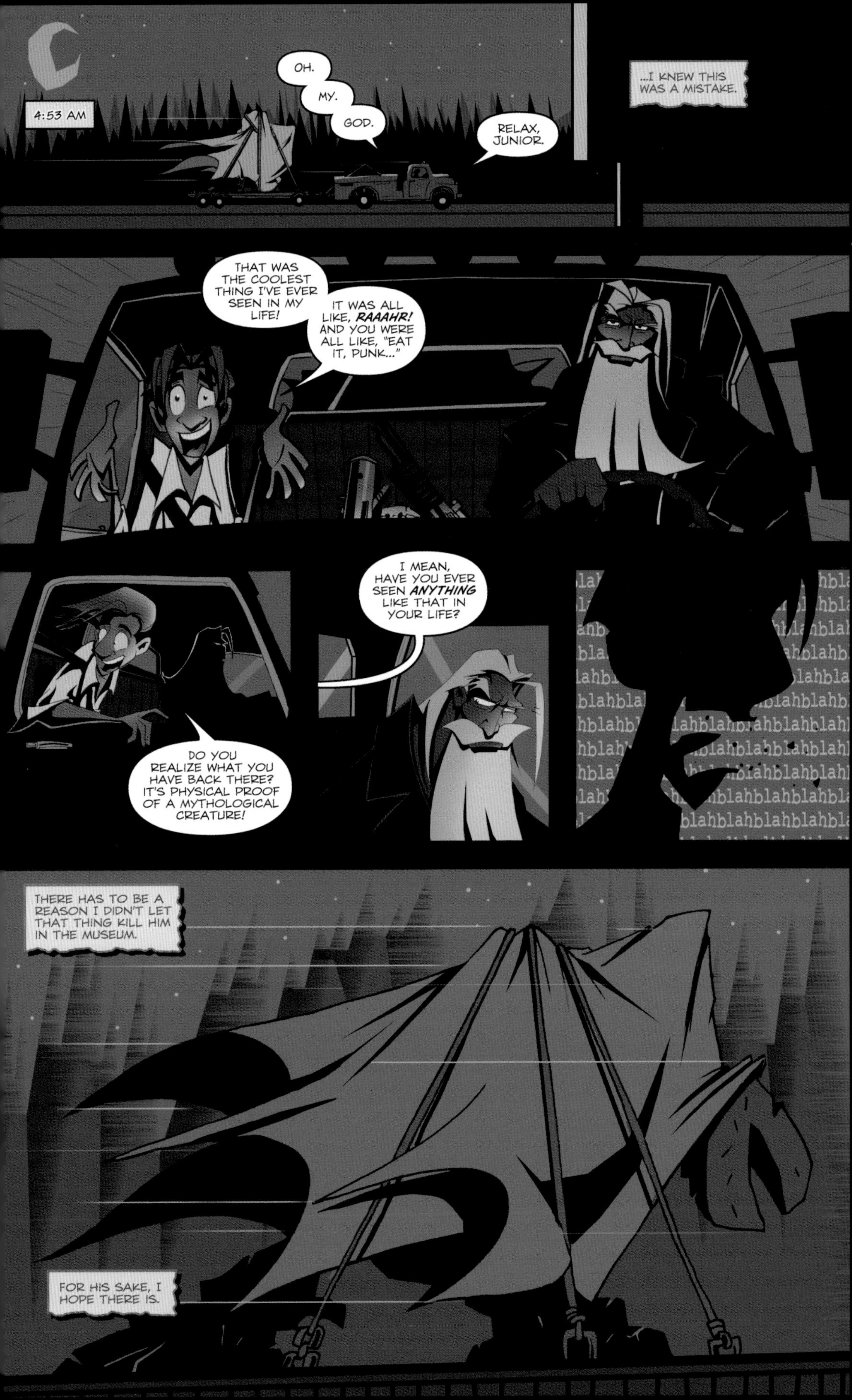
4:53 AM
OH.
MY.
GOD.
RELAX, JUNIOR.
...I KNEW THIS WAS A MISTAKE.
THAT WAS THE COOLEST THING I'VE EVER SEEN IN MY LIFE!
IT WAS ALL LIKE, RAAAHR! AND YOU WERE ALL LIKE, "EAT IT, PUNK..."
I MEAN, HAVE YOU EVER SEEN ANYTHING LIKE THAT IN YOUR LIFE?
DO YOU REALIZE WHAT YOU HAVE BACK THERE? IT'S PHYSICAL PROOF OF A MYTHOLOGICAL CREATURE!
THERE HAS TO BE A REASON I DIDN'T LET THAT THING KILL HIM IN THE MUSEUM.
FOR HIS SAKE, I HOPE THERE IS.

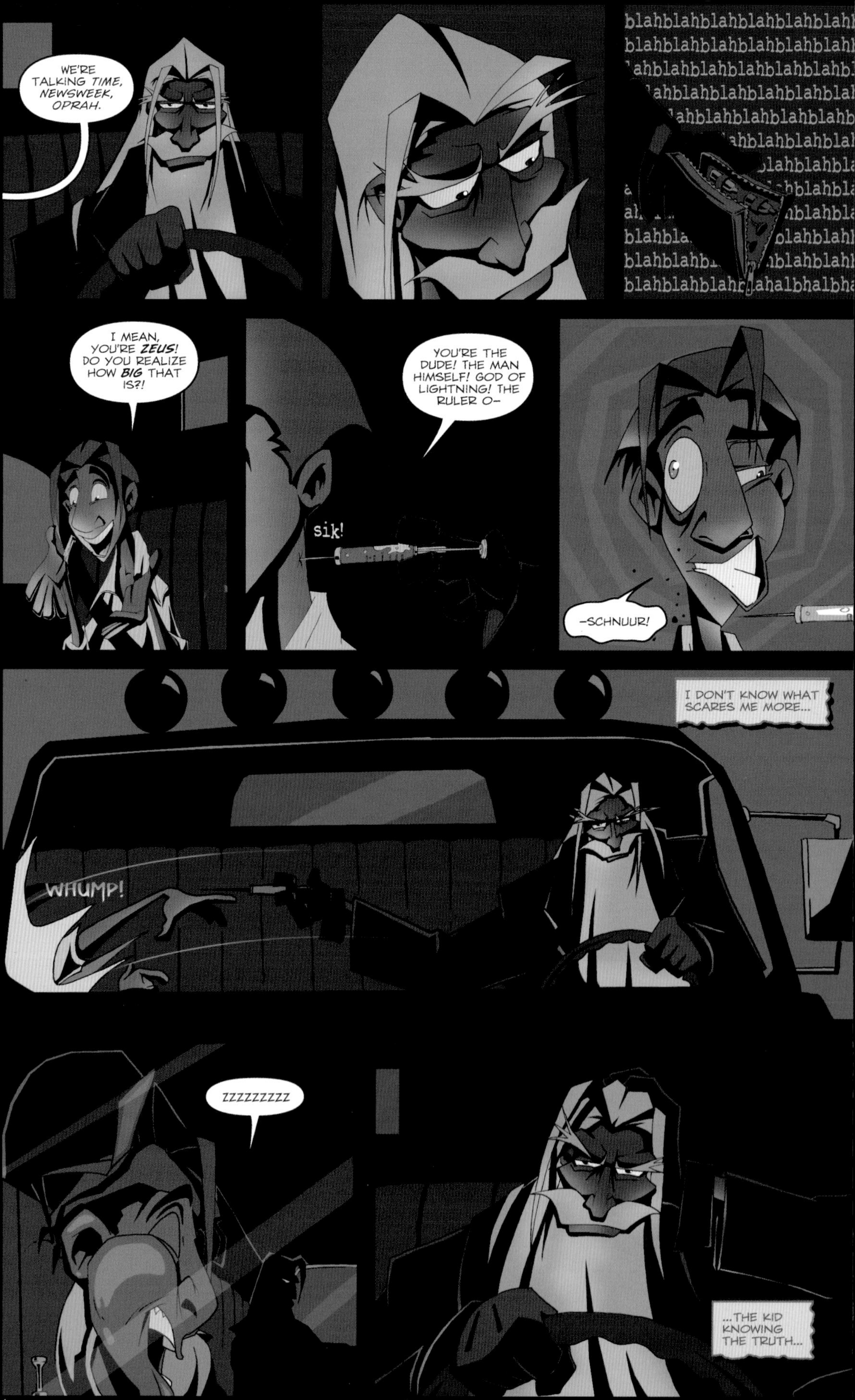

WE'RE TALKING *TIME*, *NEWSWEEK*, *OPRAH*.
blahblahblahblahblahblah
I MEAN, YOU'RE ***ZEUS***! DO YOU REALIZE HOW ***BIG*** THAT IS?!
YOU'RE THE DUDE! THE MAN HIMSELF! GOD OF LIGHTNING! THE RULER O–
sik!
–SCHNUUR!
I DON'T KNOW WHAT SCARES ME MORE...
WHUMP!
ZZZZZZZZZ
...THE KID KNOWING THE TRUTH...

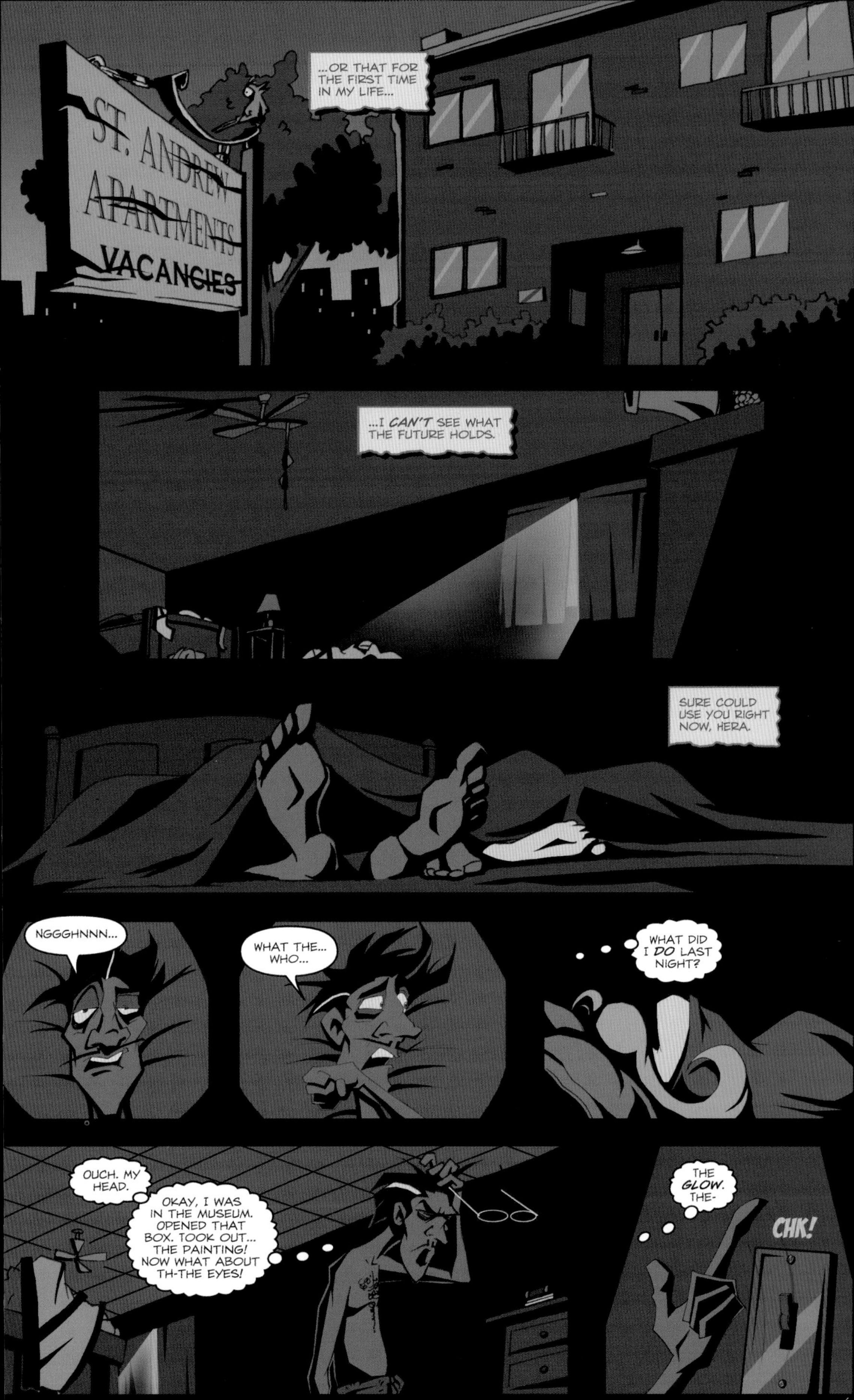
ST. ANDREW APARTMENTS
VACANCIES
...OR THAT FOR THE FIRST TIME IN MY LIFE...
...I CAN'T SEE WHAT THE FUTURE HOLDS.
SURE COULD USE YOU RIGHT NOW, HERA.
NGGGHNNN...
WHAT THE... WHO...
WHAT DID I DO LAST NIGHT?
OUCH. MY HEAD.
OKAY, I WAS IN THE MUSEUM. OPENED THAT BOX. TOOK OUT... THE PAINTING! NOW WHAT ABOUT TH-THE EYES!
THE GLOW. THE-
CHK!

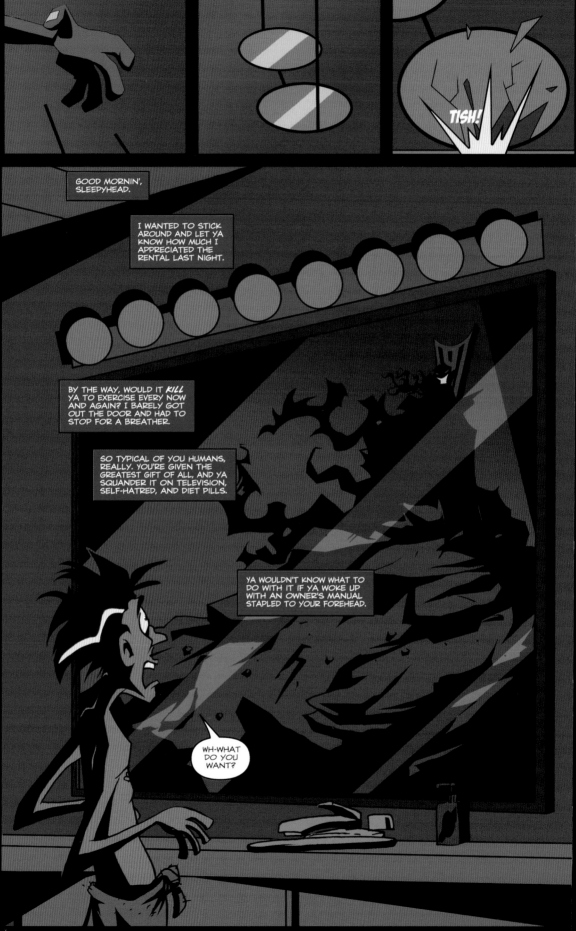

TISH!

GOOD MORNIN', SLEEPYHEAD.

I WANTED TO STICK AROUND AND LET YA KNOW HOW MUCH I APPRECIATED THE RENTAL LAST NIGHT.

BY THE WAY, WOULD IT *KILL* YA TO EXERCISE EVERY NOW AND AGAIN? I BARELY GOT OUT THE DOOR AND HAD TO STOP FOR A BREATHER.

SO TYPICAL OF YOU HUMANS, REALLY. YOU'RE GIVEN THE GREATEST GIFT OF ALL, AND YA SQUANDER IT ON TELEVISION, SELF-HATRED, AND DIET PILLS.

YA WOULDN'T KNOW WHAT TO DO WITH IT IF YA WOKE UP WITH AN OWNER'S MANUAL STAPLED TO YOUR FOREHEAD.

WH-WHAT DO YOU WANT?

WHAT DO I *WANT?* OHHH, SUCH A LOADED QUESTION.

I WANT MY LIFE BACK. I WANT TO WAKE UP AND NOT SMELL THE STENCH OF TEN-THOUSAND YEAR OLD TOOTH DECAY.

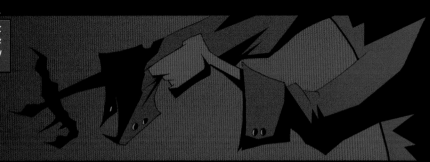

BUT MOST IMPORTANTLY, I WANT TO TAKE A BROKEN, POISONED, AND DECREPIT WORLD AND TEACH IT HOW TO LIVE ONCE AGAIN.

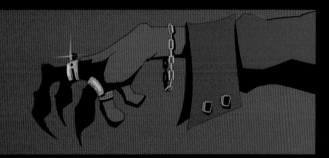

...LIKE IT SHOULD HAVE BEEN FROM THE START. YOU'VE BEEN A BAD BUNCH OF FLESHBAGS.

NOW IT'S TIME TO PAY THE BILL.

YOU 'N' ME ARE GONNA HAVE *SO MUCH* FUN, BUBBA.

OH YEAH, AND YA GOT COMPANY.

MORNIN', TIGER.

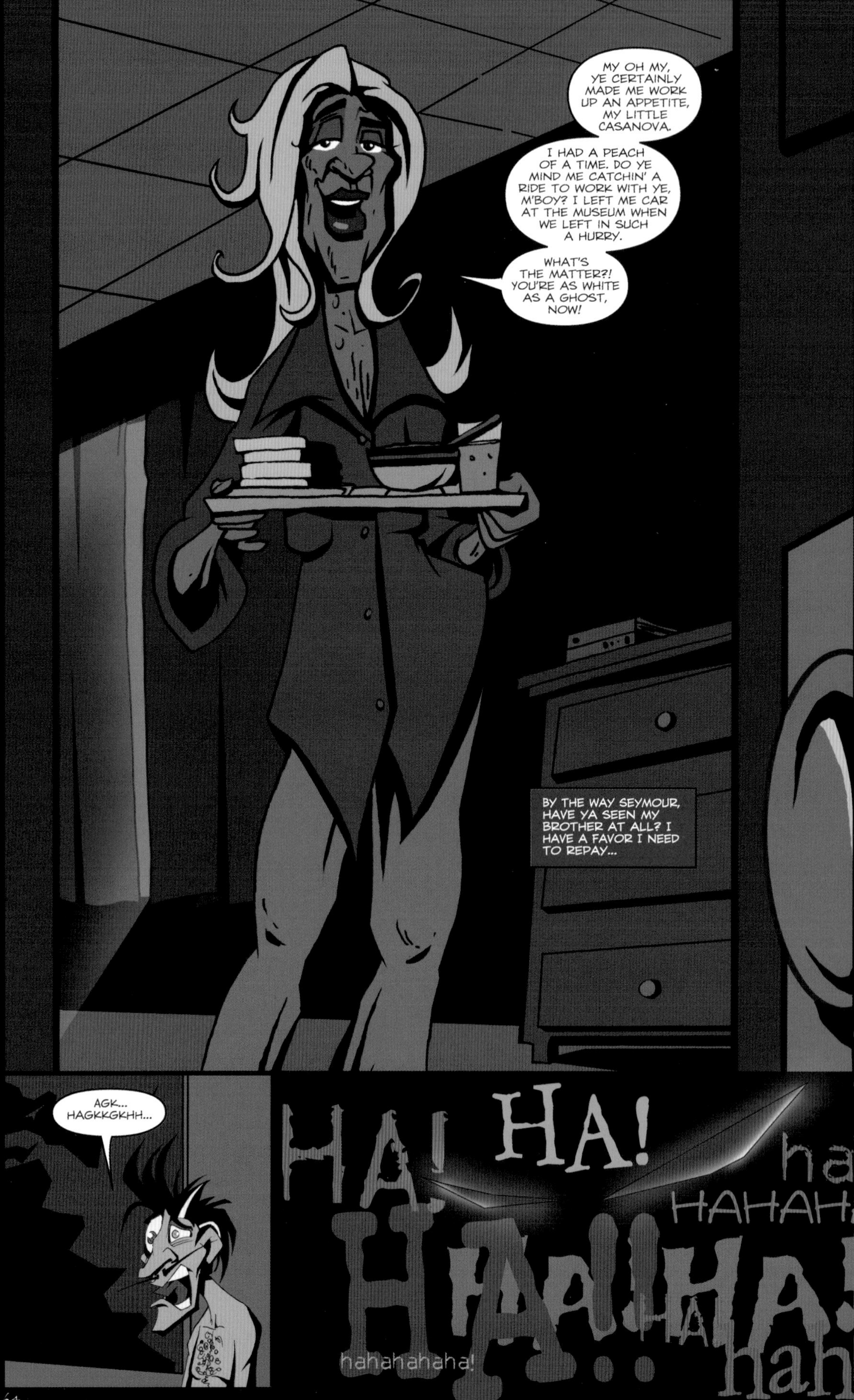
MY OH MY, YE CERTAINLY MADE ME WORK UP AN APPETITE, MY LITTLE CASANOVA.
I HAD A PEACH OF A TIME. DO YE MIND ME CATCHIN' A RIDE TO WORK WITH YE, M'BOY? I LEFT ME CAR AT THE MUSEUM WHEN WE LEFT IN SUCH A HURRY.
WHAT'S THE MATTER?! YOU'RE AS WHITE AS A GHOST, NOW!
BY THE WAY SEYMOUR, HAVE YA SEEN MY BROTHER AT ALL? I HAVE A FAVOR I NEED TO REPAY...
AGK... HAGKKGKHH...
HA!
HA!
HAHAHA
HA!
HA
HAHA!
hahahahaha!

THE BALLAD OF
SEYMOUR KENNEDY FITTS, ESQ.

The laughter swirled around Seymour's head. However, through it all, he was more appalled at his lost night with his elderly boss than the creature with the red glowing eyes camping out inside of his bathroom mirror. It became too much for him as he passed out on the linoleum... just as an automatic air freshener spritzed him in the face with Honeydew Lilac scent.

The Shape in the Mirror looked at Mrs. Mackenzie. Just as her wrinkled head turned to the mirror... the Shape was gone. She looked at it for a beat then back at Seymour... as she wryly smiled at her conquest. She dragged all 98 pounds of Seymour's limp body over to the bed and hoisted him on top. Tucking him in with a forehead kiss, she left a note.

"Thanks for the night, Fittsy. Can't wait to see ya at work today. Love, P"

And with that, Mrs. Mackenzie walked out of his apartment. But definitely not out of his life.

Seymour's eyes fluttered open. He strained to see where he was. He was still in his apartment, only now the sun had set. There wasn't a sign of Mrs. Mackenzie anymore. Was it all a dream? The bathroom was immaculate as usual. A normal mirror. Then why was his throat sore like he had been screaming?

...and why did he smell like lilac?

Seymour quickly got dressed, opting for tan khakis for the first time in his life. He climbed into his sensible German hatchback and puttered off to the Olympus Heights Museum. Once there, he was almost relieved to find that it was empty. The previous mysterious damage was nearly repaired, and yet still there was no sign of his favorite punching bag, Oliver.

Seymour walked to his office only to find it completely destroyed, along with the rest of the museum. So he spent the next three hours carting his desk, pencils, travel currency converter, and other such prized possessions into the miraculously preserved filing room just down the hall. Sitting back with his feet on his desk, his stomach began to cramp. He suddenly felt the need to dash to the bathroom. But before Seymour could do the clench-run down the hall, he dropped to his knees. He moaned... his voice lowering to a guttural growl.

And then he stood up.

His hair was tussled. The slightest of grins and cocked eyebrow grew on his face. Seymour didn't walk–rather, he swaggered out the door and into the night. The rest of the evening was a blur to him. Why? Again, he'll never know.

With the events framed in fuzz, Seymour seemed to remember meeting a beautiful woman with fire-red hair. He remembered a dinner of oysters and fine wine... and then a karaoke bar filled with the muzak stylings of John Denver.

When Seymour finally woke up the next morning he was in a strange bed... in a stranger bedroom. It was the most expensive suite in the swankiest hotel in nearby Indianapolis. His head ached and his body could barely move. Seymour managed to get out of bed and stumble to the bathroom, too afraid to flip on the lights. He dove into a rolling somersault that landed him smack in front of the vanity.

Slowly, carefully, Seymour peered over the sink into the darkened mirror, half expecting the strange creature to still be there. With a burst of bravery, he stood up in front of the mirror, only to see...

...nothing. Well, "nothing" except for the shape and details of a knock-out, drop-dead gorgeous woman standing behind him! She put a hand on his shoulder. Seymour screamed like a six-year-old girl playing tag. He fainted. Again. And knocked over a tiny vial of mouthwash that dripped onto his still face.

When he woke up an hour later he was alone and smelled strangely of peppermint. No other trace of another being remained in the room expect for a note left on a hotel notepad It merely had a heart drawn on it with the letter "P" scrolled underneath it. On the floor he found one single item: a long, wavy strand of hair...

...that was gray.

And thus, Seymour vowed to never leave his apartment nor sleep again.

Chapter Three

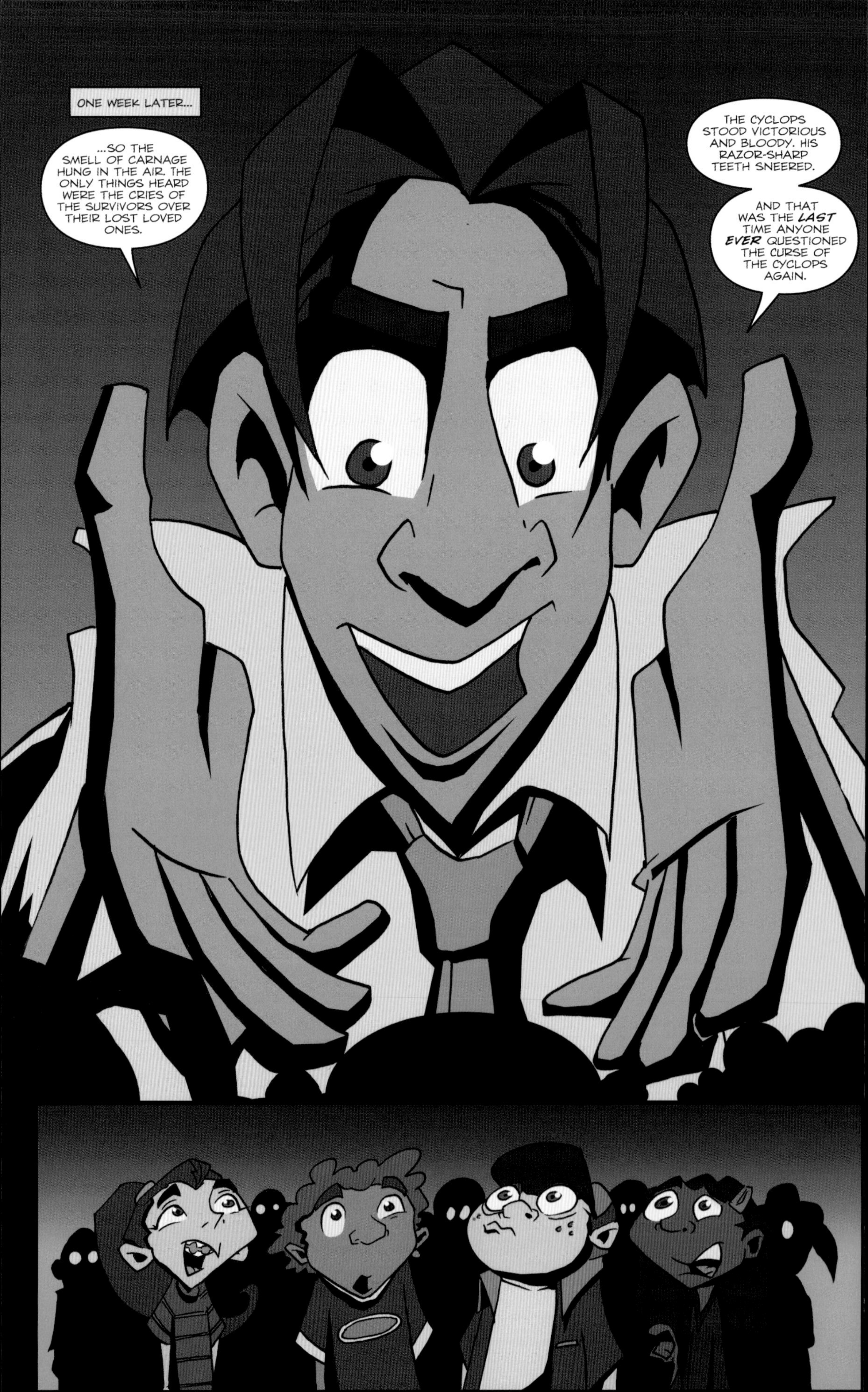
ONE WEEK LATER...
...SO THE SMELL OF CARNAGE HUNG IN THE AIR. THE ONLY THINGS HEARD WERE THE CRIES OF THE SURVIVORS OVER THEIR LOST LOVED ONES.
THE CYCLOPS STOOD VICTORIOUS AND BLOODY. HIS RAZOR-SHARP TEETH SNEERED.
AND THAT WAS THE LAST TIME ANYONE EVER QUESTIONED THE CURSE OF THE CYCLOPS AGAIN.

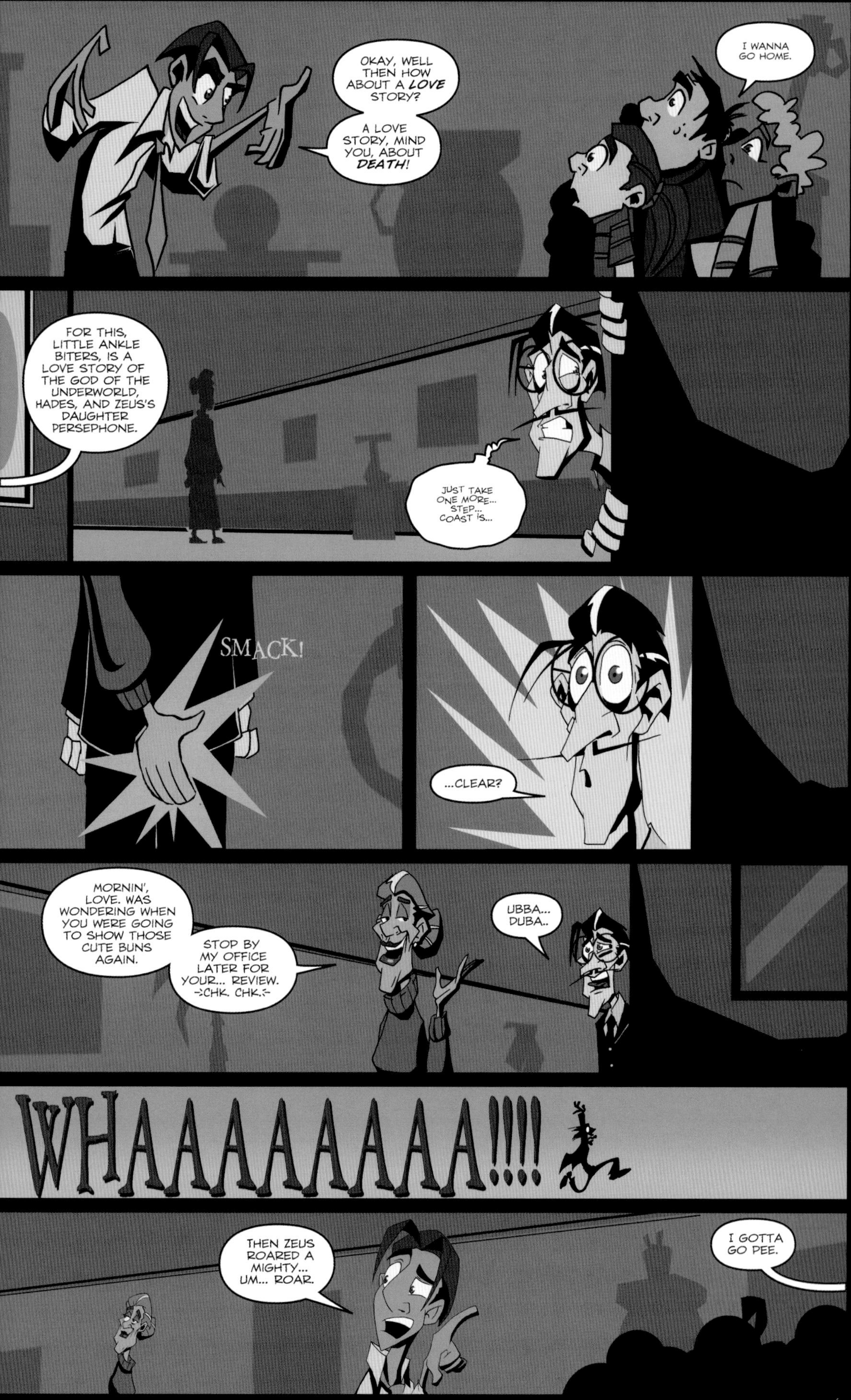
OKAY, WELL THEN HOW ABOUT A LOVE STORY?
A LOVE STORY, MIND YOU, ABOUT DEATH!
I WANNA GO HOME.
FOR THIS, LITTLE ANKLE BITERS, IS A LOVE STORY OF THE GOD OF THE UNDERWORLD, HADES, AND ZEUS'S DAUGHTER PERSEPHONE.
JUST TAKE ONE MORE... STEP... COAST IS...
SMACK!
...CLEAR?
MORNIN', LOVE. WAS WONDERING WHEN YOU WERE GOING TO SHOW THOSE CUTE BUNS AGAIN.
STOP BY MY OFFICE LATER FOR YOUR... REVIEW. CHK. CHK.
UBBA... DUBA..
WHAAAAAAAAA!!!!
THEN ZEUS ROARED A MIGHTY... UM... ROAR.
I GOTTA GO PEE.

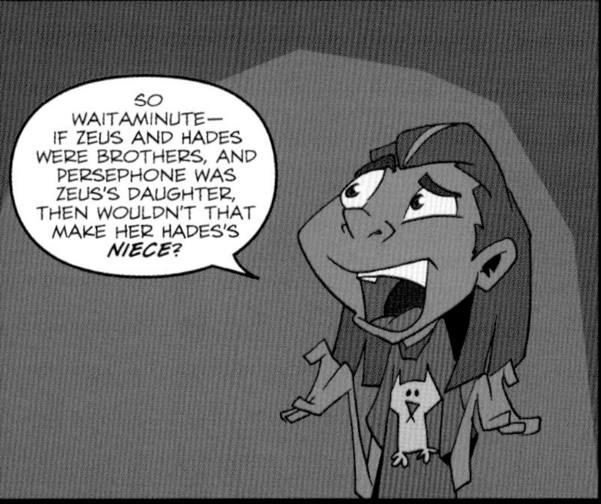
SO WAITAMINUTE— IF ZEUS AND HADES WERE BROTHERS, AND PERSEPHONE WAS ZEUS'S DAUGHTER, THEN WOULDN'T THAT MAKE HER HADES'S NIECE?

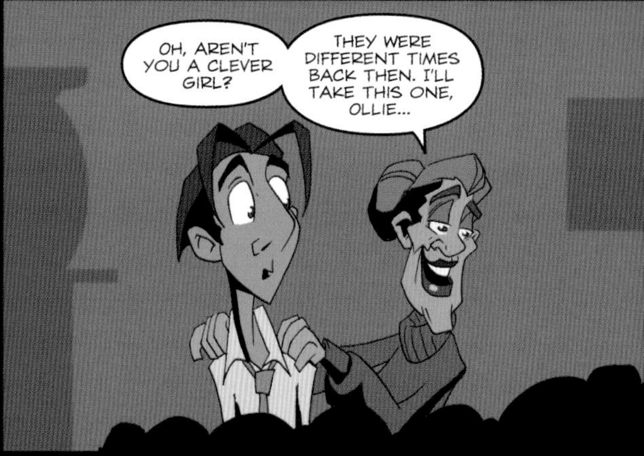
OH, AREN'T YOU A CLEVER GIRL?
THEY WERE DIFFERENT TIMES BACK THEN. I'LL TAKE THIS ONE, OLLIE...

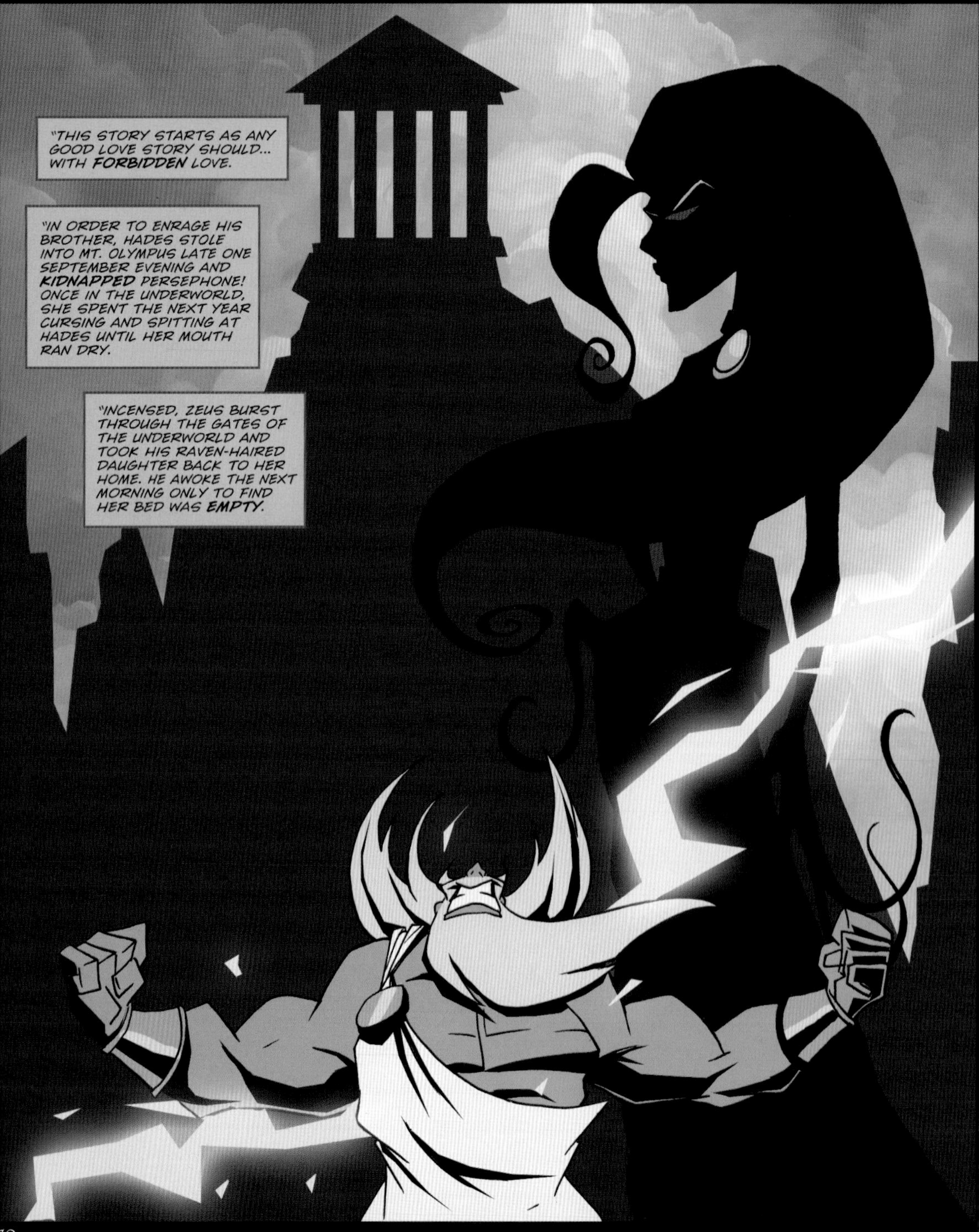
"THIS STORY STARTS AS ANY GOOD LOVE STORY SHOULD... WITH FORBIDDEN LOVE.
"IN ORDER TO ENRAGE HIS BROTHER, HADES STOLE INTO MT. OLYMPUS LATE ONE SEPTEMBER EVENING AND KIDNAPPED PERSEPHONE! ONCE IN THE UNDERWORLD, SHE SPENT THE NEXT YEAR CURSING AND SPITTING AT HADES UNTIL HER MOUTH RAN DRY.
"INCENSED, ZEUS BURST THROUGH THE GATES OF THE UNDERWORLD AND TOOK HIS RAVEN-HAIRED DAUGHTER BACK TO HER HOME. HE AWOKE THE NEXT MORNING ONLY TO FIND HER BED WAS EMPTY.

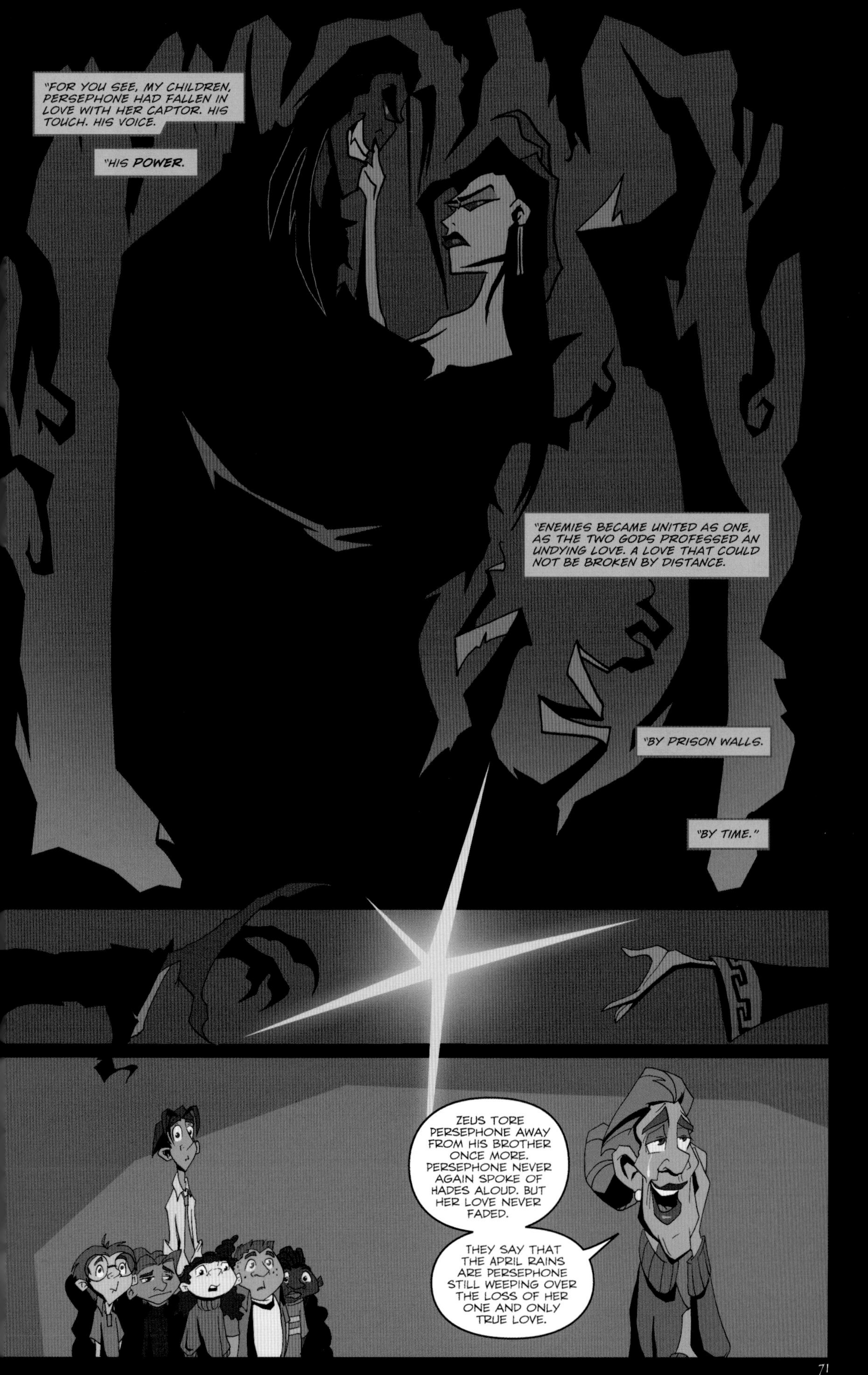
"FOR YOU SEE, MY CHILDREN, PERSEPHONE HAD FALLEN IN LOVE WITH HER CAPTOR. HIS TOUCH. HIS VOICE.
"HIS POWER.
"ENEMIES BECAME UNITED AS ONE, AS THE TWO GODS PROFESSED AN UNDYING LOVE. A LOVE THAT COULD NOT BE BROKEN BY DISTANCE.
"BY PRISON WALLS.
"BY TIME."
ZEUS TORE PERSEPHONE AWAY FROM HIS BROTHER ONCE MORE. PERSEPHONE NEVER AGAIN SPOKE OF HADES ALOUD. BUT HER LOVE NEVER FADED.
THEY SAY THAT THE APRIL RAINS ARE PERSEPHONE STILL WEEPING OVER THE LOSS OF HER ONE AND ONLY TRUE LOVE.

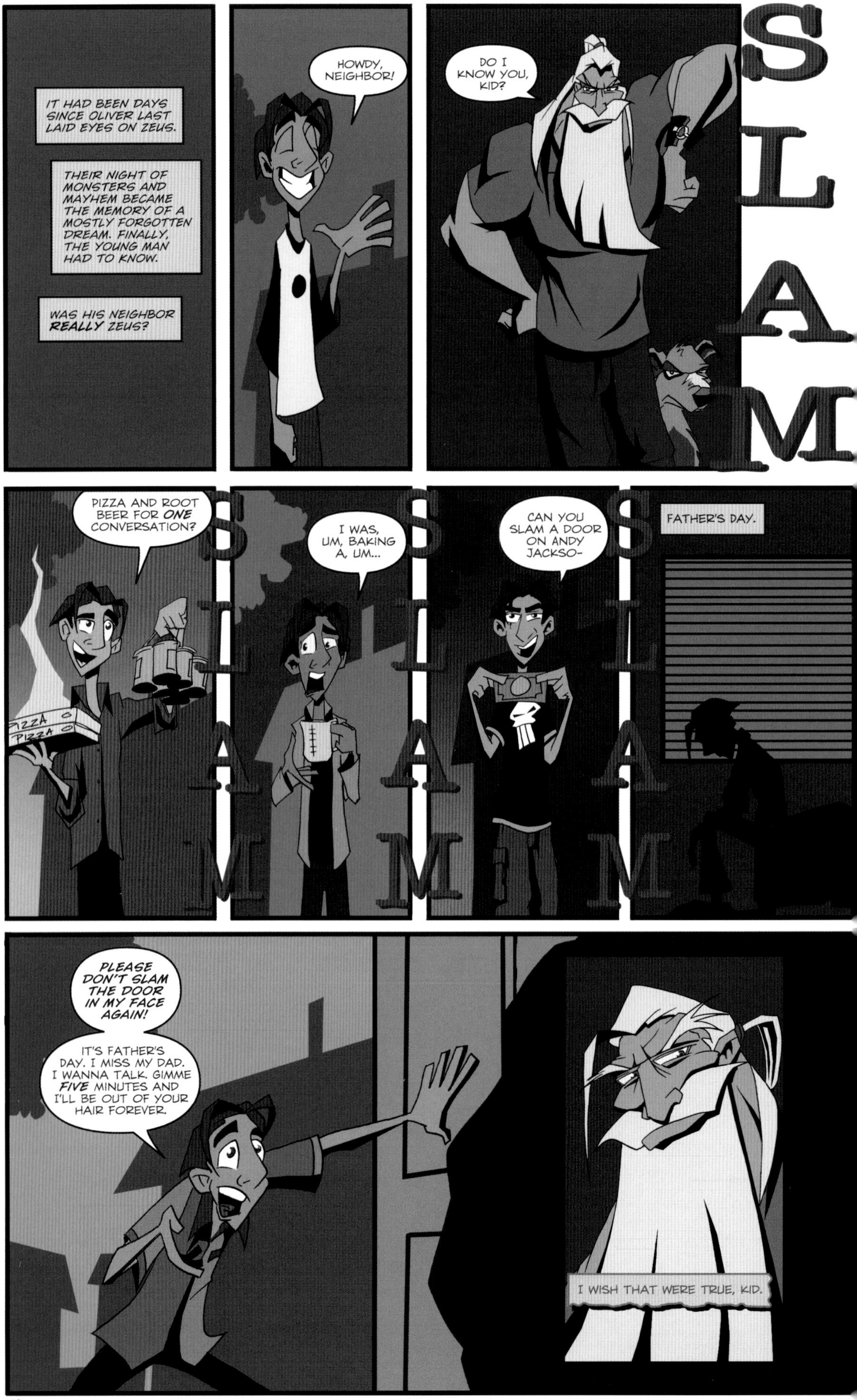
IT HAD BEEN DAYS SINCE OLIVER LAST LAID EYES ON ZEUS.
THEIR NIGHT OF MONSTERS AND MAYHEM BECAME THE MEMORY OF A MOSTLY FORGOTTEN DREAM. FINALLY, THE YOUNG MAN HAD TO KNOW.
WAS HIS NEIGHBOR REALLY ZEUS?
HOWDY, NEIGHBOR!
DO I KNOW YOU, KID?
SLAM
PIZZA AND ROOT BEER FOR ONE CONVERSATION?
PIZZA
PIZZA
SLAM
I WAS, UM, BAKING A, UM...
SLAM
CAN YOU SLAM A DOOR ON ANDY JACKSO-
SLAM
FATHER'S DAY.
PLEASE DON'T SLAM THE DOOR IN MY FACE AGAIN!
IT'S FATHER'S DAY. I MISS MY DAD. I WANNA TALK. GIMME FIVE MINUTES AND I'LL BE OUT OF YOUR HAIR FOREVER.
I WISH THAT WERE TRUE, KID.

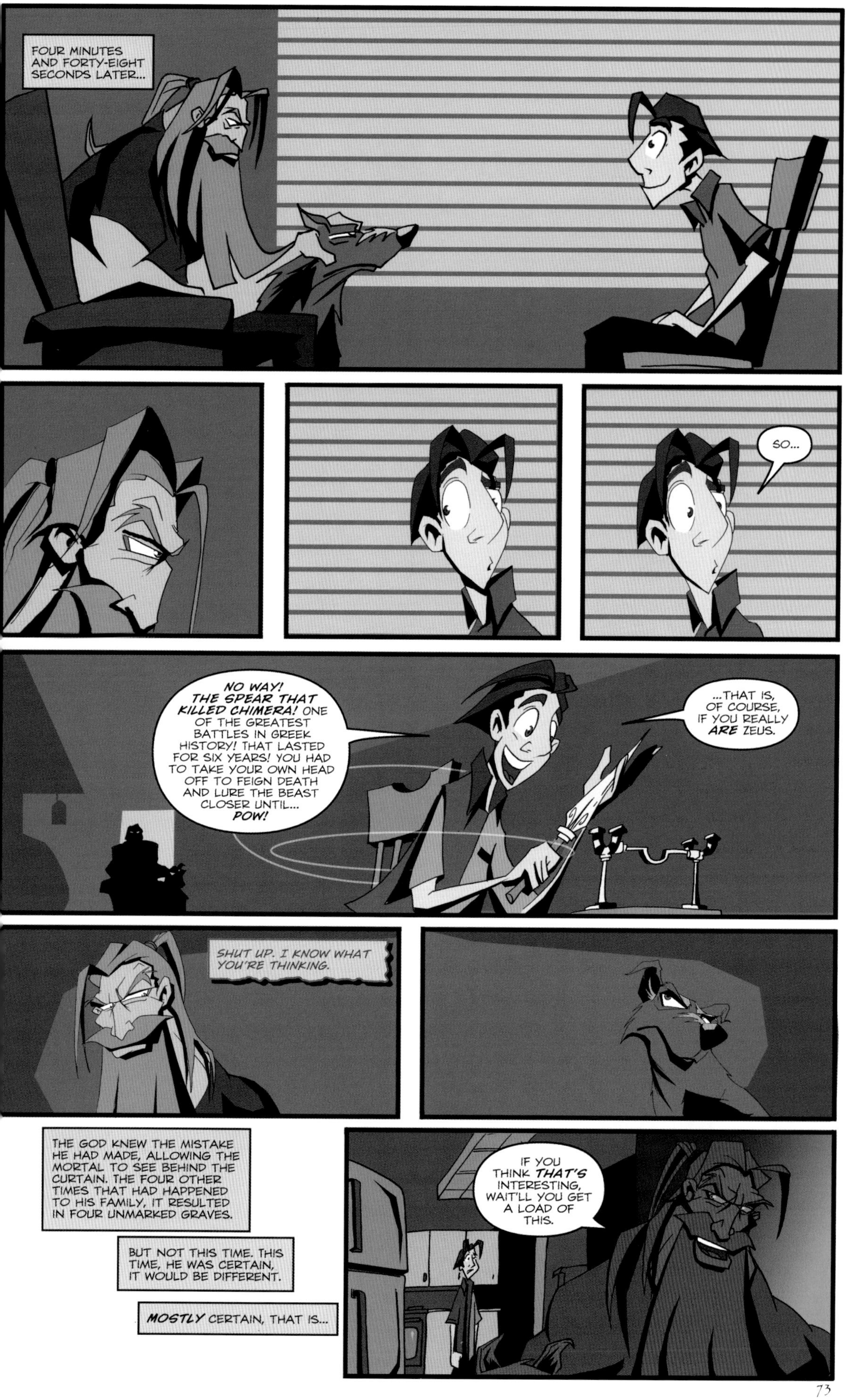
FOUR MINUTES AND FORTY-EIGHT SECONDS LATER...
SO...
NO WAY! THE SPEAR THAT KILLED CHIMERA! ONE OF THE GREATEST BATTLES IN GREEK HISTORY! THAT LASTED FOR SIX YEARS! YOU HAD TO TAKE YOUR OWN HEAD OFF TO FEIGN DEATH AND LURE THE BEAST CLOSER UNTIL... POW!
...THAT IS, OF COURSE, IF YOU REALLY ARE ZEUS.
SHUT UP. I KNOW WHAT YOU'RE THINKING.
THE GOD KNEW THE MISTAKE HE HAD MADE, ALLOWING THE MORTAL TO SEE BEHIND THE CURTAIN. THE FOUR OTHER TIMES THAT HAD HAPPENED TO HIS FAMILY, IT RESULTED IN FOUR UNMARKED GRAVES.
BUT NOT THIS TIME. THIS TIME, HE WAS CERTAIN, IT WOULD BE DIFFERENT.
MOSTLY CERTAIN, THAT IS...
IF YOU THINK THAT'S INTERESTING, WAIT'LL YOU GET A LOAD OF THIS.

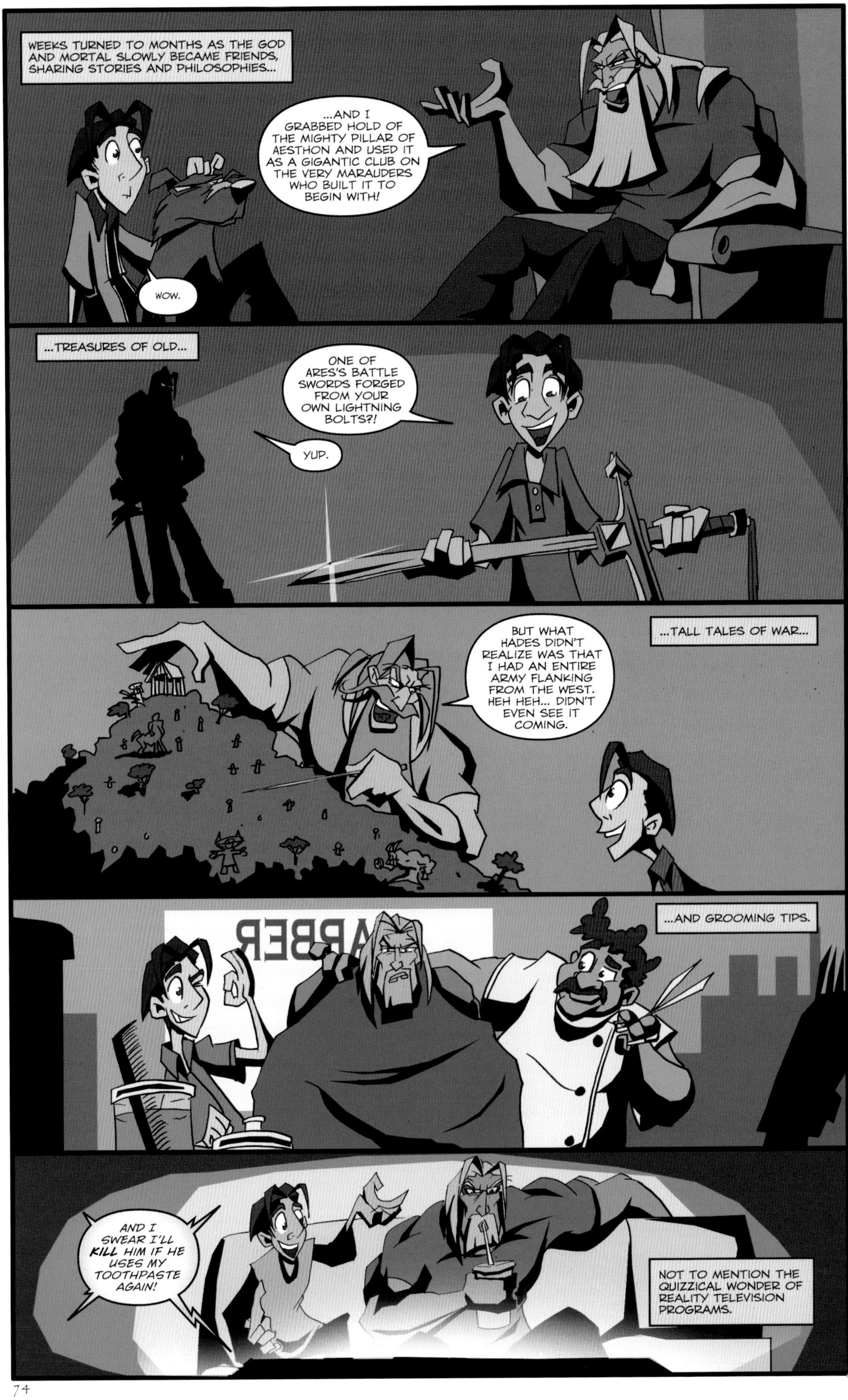
WEEKS TURNED TO MONTHS AS THE GOD AND MORTAL SLOWLY BECAME FRIENDS, SHARING STORIES AND PHILOSOPHIES...
...AND I GRABBED HOLD OF THE MIGHTY PILLAR OF AESTHON AND USED IT AS A GIGANTIC CLUB ON THE VERY MARAUDERS WHO BUILT IT TO BEGIN WITH!
WOW.
...TREASURES OF OLD...
ONE OF ARES'S BATTLE SWORDS FORGED FROM YOUR OWN LIGHTNING BOLTS?!
YUP.
...TALL TALES OF WAR...
BUT WHAT HADES DIDN'T REALIZE WAS THAT I HAD AN ENTIRE ARMY FLANKING FROM THE WEST. HEH HEH... DIDN'T EVEN SEE IT COMING.
...AND GROOMING TIPS.
ARBER
AND I SWEAR I'LL **KILL** HIM IF HE USES MY TOOTHPASTE AGAIN!
NOT TO MENTION THE QUIZZICAL WONDER OF REALITY TELEVISION PROGRAMS.

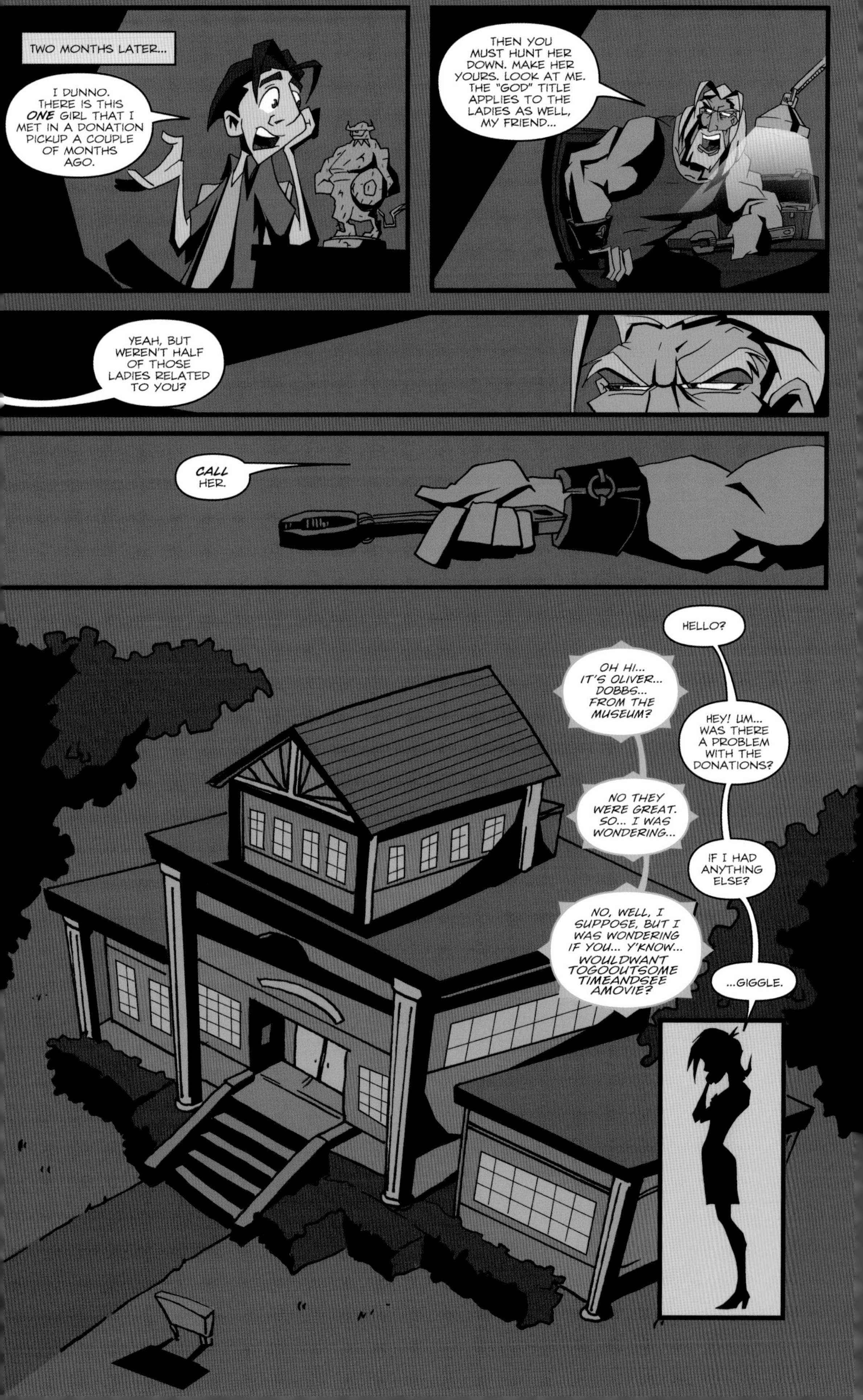
TWO MONTHS LATER...
I DUNNO. THERE IS THIS ONE GIRL THAT I MET IN A DONATION PICKUP A COUPLE OF MONTHS AGO.
THEN YOU MUST HUNT HER DOWN. MAKE HER YOURS. LOOK AT ME. THE "GOD" TITLE APPLIES TO THE LADIES AS WELL, MY FRIEND...
YEAH, BUT WEREN'T HALF OF THOSE LADIES RELATED TO YOU?
CALL HER.
HELLO?
OH HI... IT'S OLIVER... DOBBS... FROM THE MUSEUM?
HEY! UM... WAS THERE A PROBLEM WITH THE DONATIONS?
NO THEY WERE GREAT. SO... I WAS WONDERING...
IF I HAD ANYTHING ELSE?
NO, WELL, I SUPPOSE, BUT I WAS WONDERING IF YOU... Y'KNOW... WOULDWANT TOGOOUTSOME TIMEANDSEE AMOVIE?
...GIGGLE.

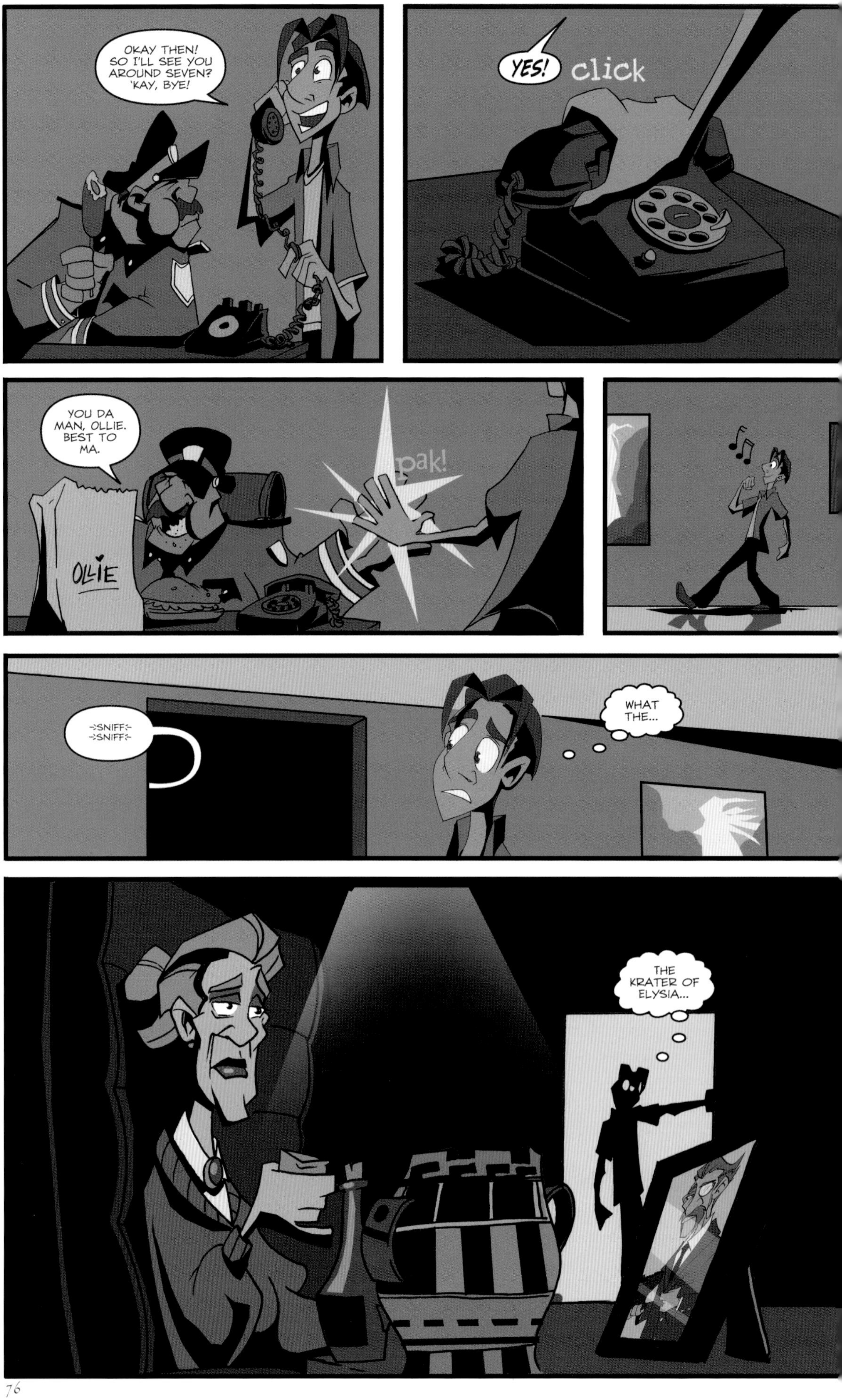
OKAY THEN! SO I'LL SEE YOU AROUND SEVEN? 'KAY, BYE!
YES!
click
YOU DA MAN, OLLIE. BEST TO MA.
OLLIE
pak!
SNIFF SNIFF
WHAT THE...
THE KRATER OF ELYSIA...

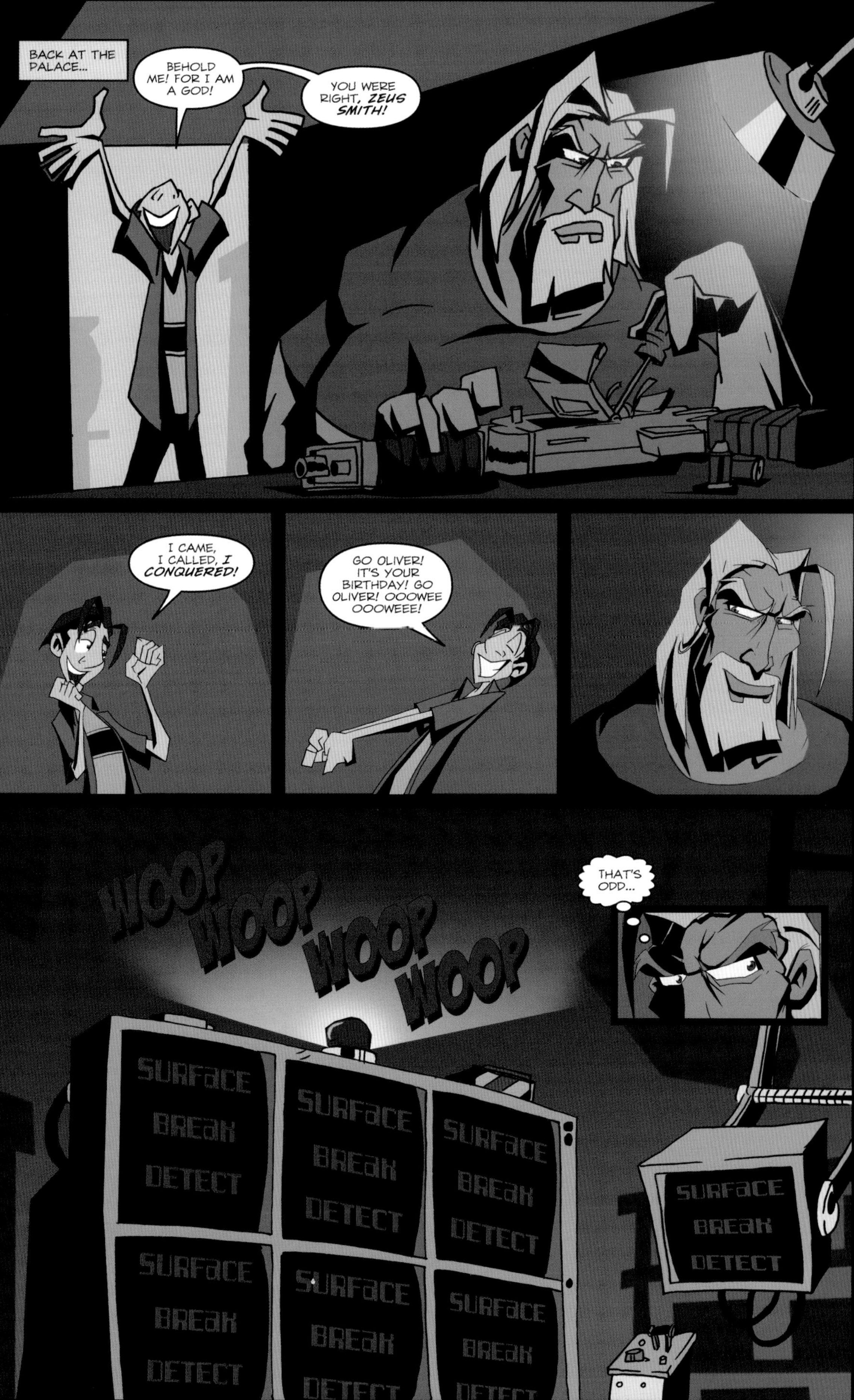
BACK AT THE PALACE...
BEHOLD ME! FOR I AM A GOD!
YOU WERE RIGHT, ZEUS SMITH!
I CAME, I CALLED, I CONQUERED!
GO OLIVER! IT'S YOUR BIRTHDAY! GO OLIVER! OOOWEE OOOWEEE!
WOOP WOOP WOOP WOOP
THAT'S ODD...
SURFACE BREAK DETECT
SURFACE BREAK DETECT
SURFACE BREAK DETECT
SURFACE BREAK DETECT
SURFACE BREAK DETECT
SURFACE BREAK DETECT
SURFACE BREAK DETECT

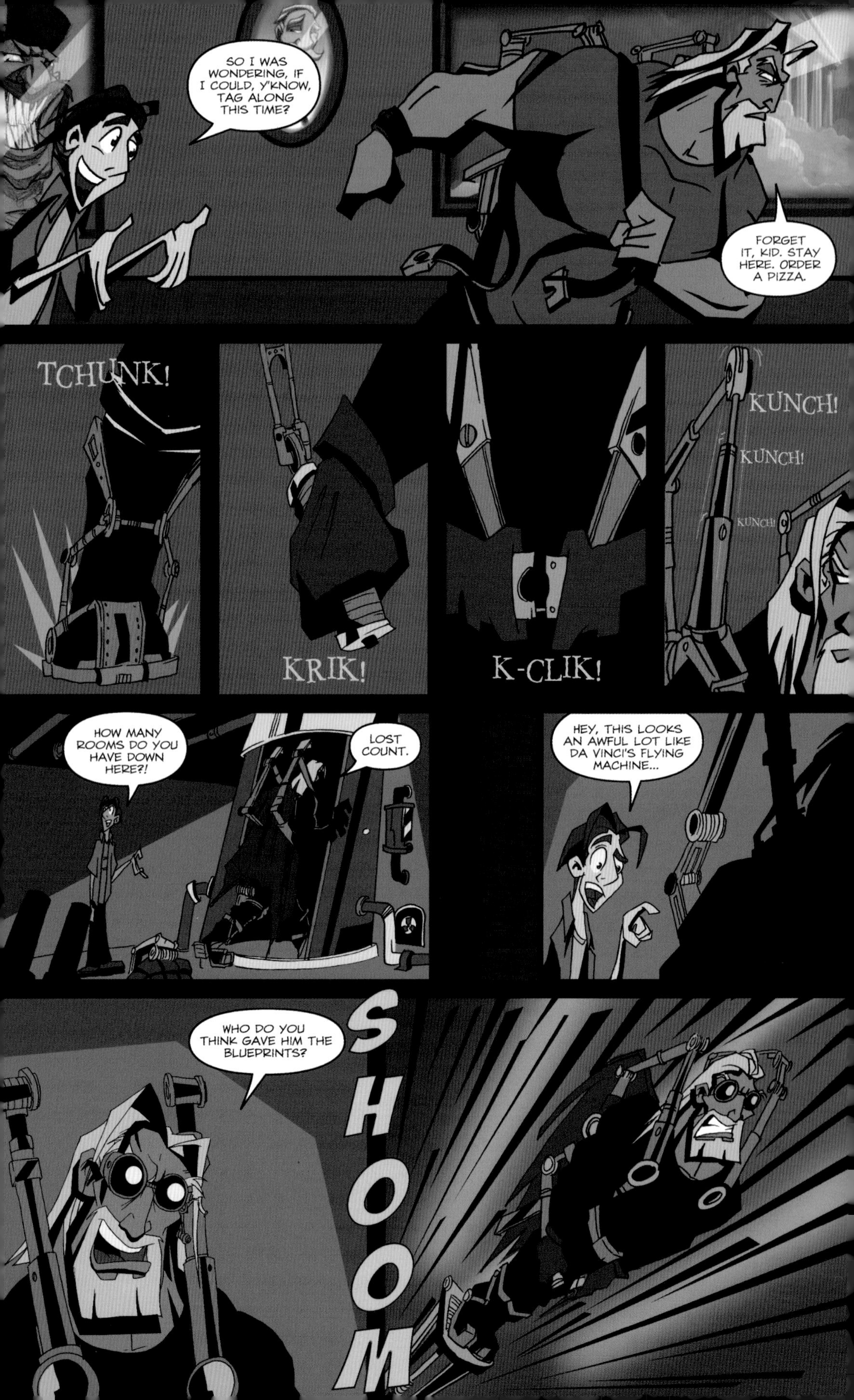
SO I WAS WONDERING, IF I COULD, Y'KNOW, TAG ALONG THIS TIME?
FORGET IT, KID. STAY HERE. ORDER A PIZZA.
TCHUNK!
KRIK!
K-CLIK!
KUNCH!
KUNCH!
KUNCH!
HOW MANY ROOMS DO YOU HAVE DOWN HERE?!
LOST COUNT.
HEY, THIS LOOKS AN AWFUL LOT LIKE DA VINCI'S FLYING MACHINE...
WHO DO YOU THINK GAVE HIM THE BLUEPRINTS?
SHOOM

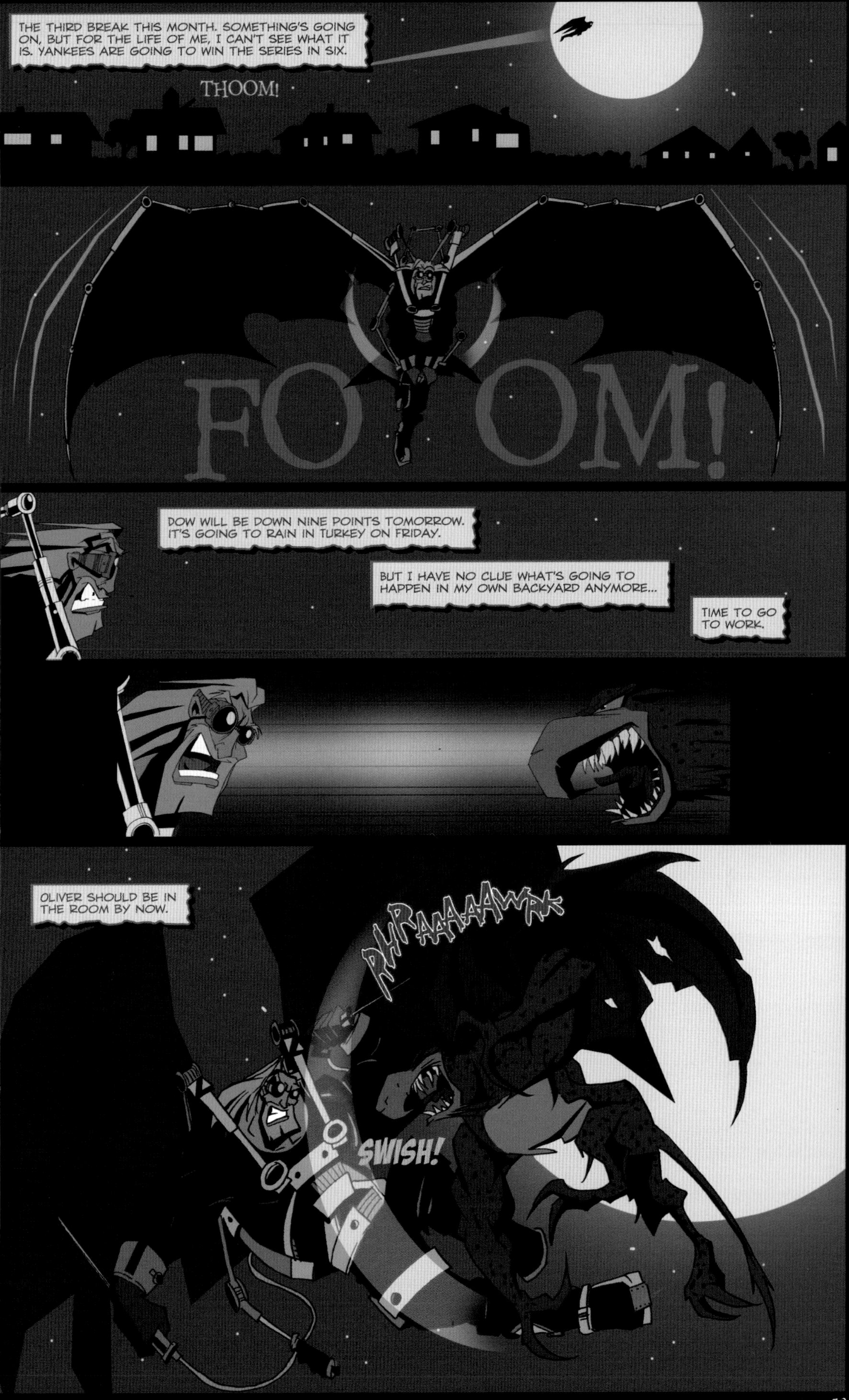
THE THIRD BREAK THIS MONTH. SOMETHING'S GOING ON, BUT FOR THE LIFE OF ME, I CAN'T SEE WHAT IT IS. YANKEES ARE GOING TO WIN THE SERIES IN SIX.
THOOM!
FOOOM!
DOW WILL BE DOWN NINE POINTS TOMORROW. IT'S GOING TO RAIN IN TURKEY ON FRIDAY.
BUT I HAVE NO CLUE WHAT'S GOING TO HAPPEN IN MY OWN BACKYARD ANYMORE...
TIME TO GO TO WORK.
OLIVER SHOULD BE IN THE ROOM BY NOW.
RHRAAAAAWRK
SWISH!

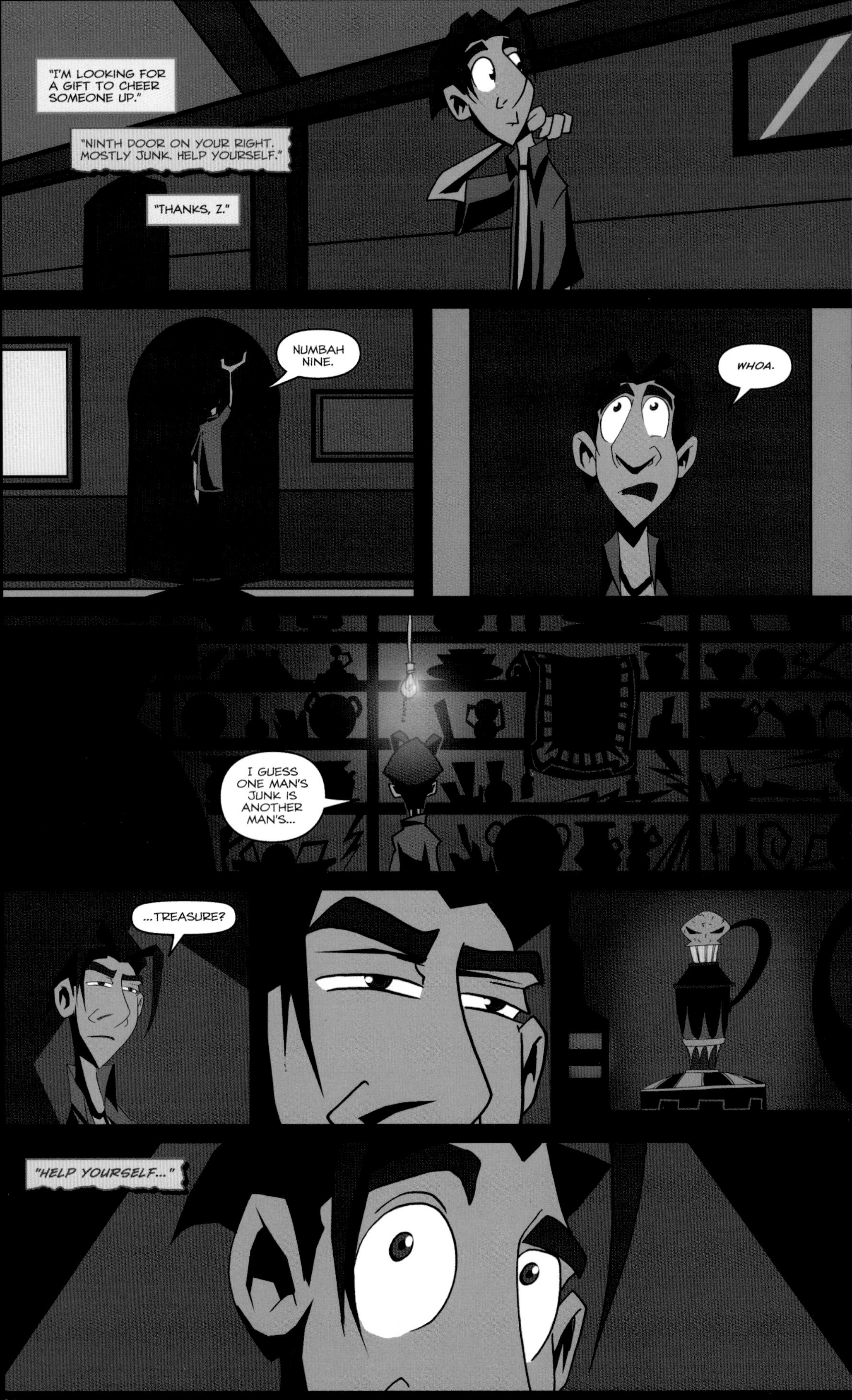
"I'M LOOKING FOR A GIFT TO CHEER SOMEONE UP."
"NINTH DOOR ON YOUR RIGHT. MOSTLY JUNK. HELP YOURSELF."
"THANKS, Z."
NUMBAH NINE.
WHOA.
I GUESS ONE MAN'S JUNK IS ANOTHER MAN'S...
...TREASURE?
"HELP YOURSELF..."

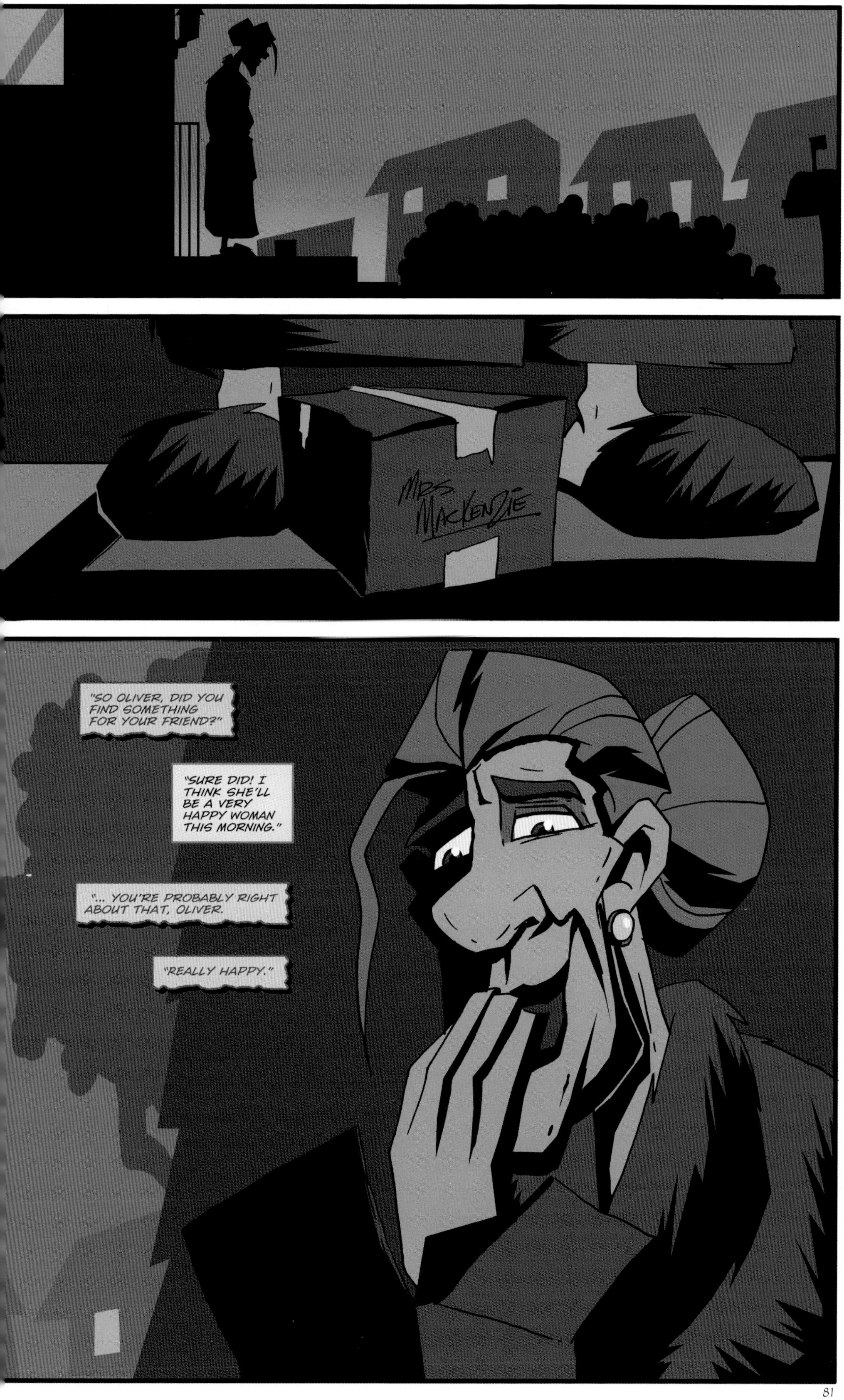
MRS. MACKENZIE
"SO OLIVER, DID YOU FIND SOMETHING FOR YOUR FRIEND?"
"SURE DID! I THINK SHE'LL BE A VERY HAPPY WOMAN THIS MORNING."
"... YOU'RE PROBABLY RIGHT ABOUT THAT, OLIVER.
"REALLY HAPPY."

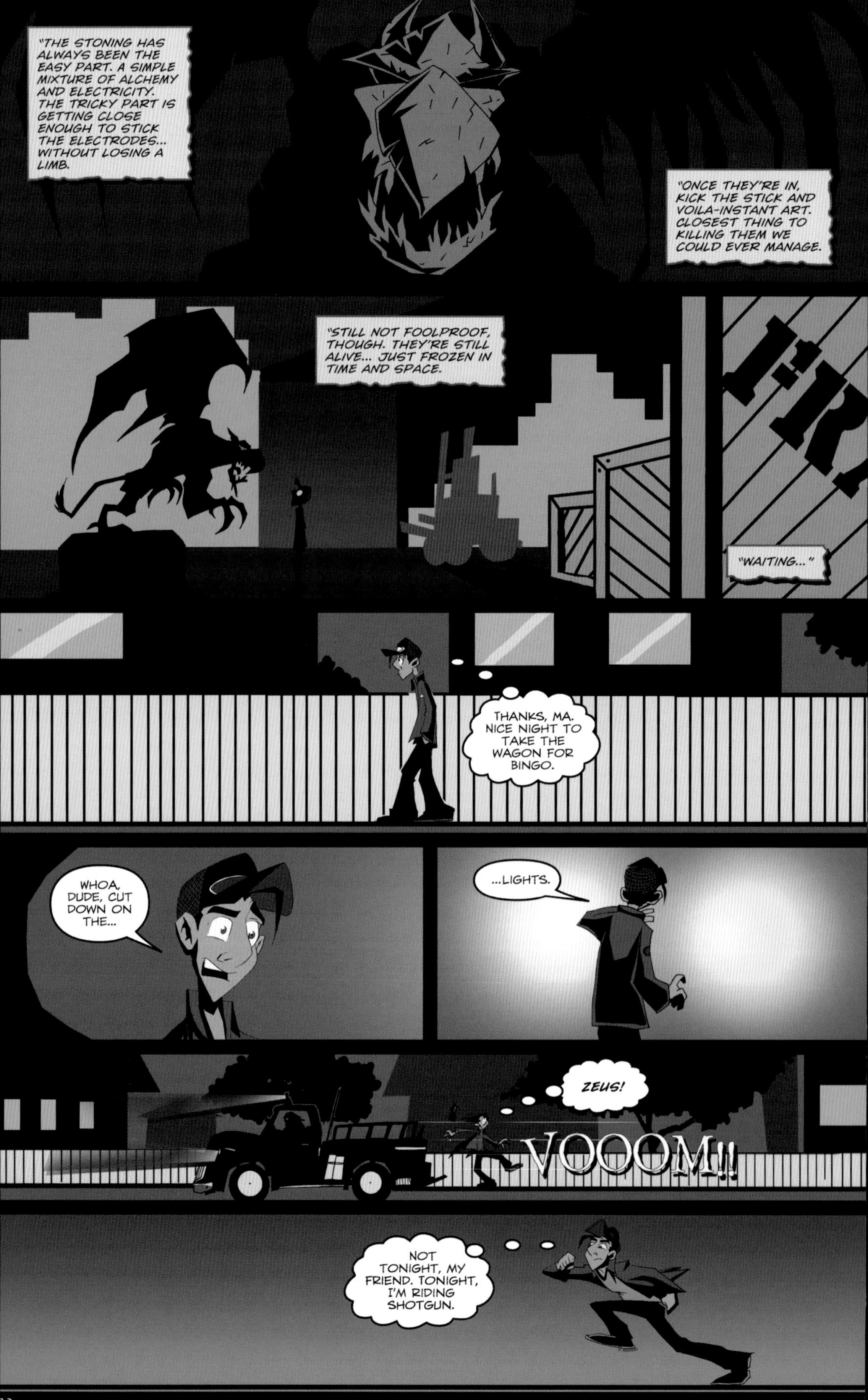
"THE STONING HAS ALWAYS BEEN THE EASY PART. A SIMPLE MIXTURE OF ALCHEMY AND ELECTRICITY. THE TRICKY PART IS GETTING CLOSE ENOUGH TO STICK THE ELECTRODES... WITHOUT LOSING A LIMB.
"ONCE THEY'RE IN, KICK THE STICK AND VOILA-INSTANT ART. CLOSEST THING TO KILLING THEM WE COULD EVER MANAGE.
"STILL NOT FOOLPROOF, THOUGH. THEY'RE STILL ALIVE... JUST FROZEN IN TIME AND SPACE.
"WAITING..."
THANKS, MA. NICE NIGHT TO TAKE THE WAGON FOR BINGO.
WHOA, DUDE, CUT DOWN ON THE...
...LIGHTS.
ZEUS!
VOOOM!!
NOT TONIGHT, MY FRIEND. TONIGHT, I'M RIDING SHOTGUN.

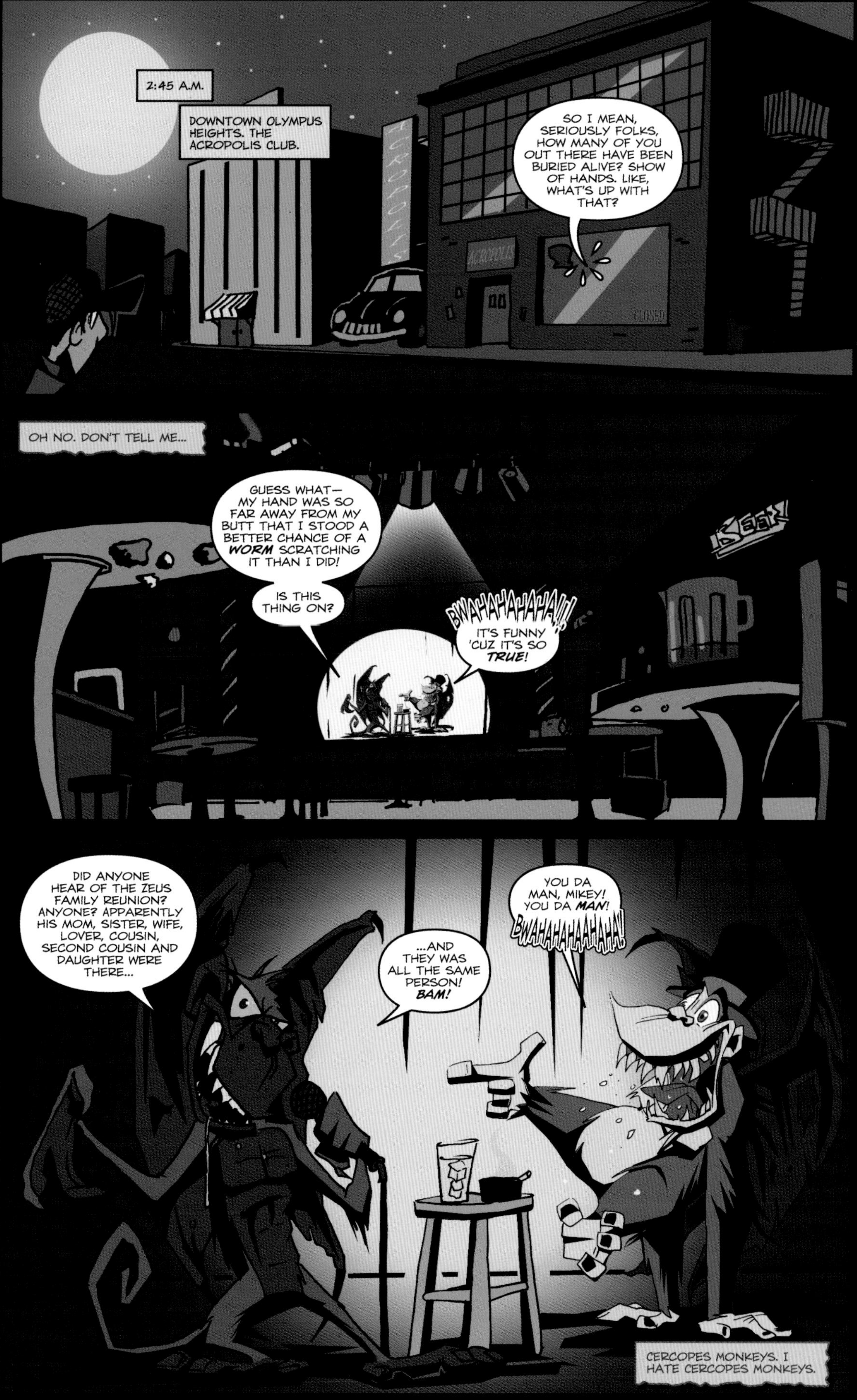
2:45 A.M.
DOWNTOWN OLYMPUS HEIGHTS. THE ACROPOLIS CLUB.
ACROPOLIS
SO I MEAN, SERIOUSLY FOLKS, HOW MANY OF YOU OUT THERE HAVE BEEN BURIED ALIVE? SHOW OF HANDS. LIKE, WHAT'S UP WITH THAT?
CLOSED
OH NO. DON'T TELL ME...
GUESS WHAT— MY HAND WAS SO FAR AWAY FROM MY BUTT THAT I STOOD A BETTER CHANCE OF A **WORM** SCRATCHING IT THAN I DID!
IS THIS THING ON?
BWAHAHAHAHA!!!
IT'S FUNNY 'CUZ IT'S SO ***TRUE!***
DID ANYONE HEAR OF THE ZEUS FAMILY REUNION? ANYONE? APPARENTLY HIS MOM, SISTER, WIFE, LOVER, COUSIN, SECOND COUSIN AND DAUGHTER WERE THERE...
...AND THEY WAS ALL THE SAME PERSON! ***BAM!***
YOU DA MAN, MIKEY! YOU DA ***MAN!***
BWAHAHAHAAHAHA!
CERCOPES MONKEYS. I HATE CERCOPES MONKEYS.

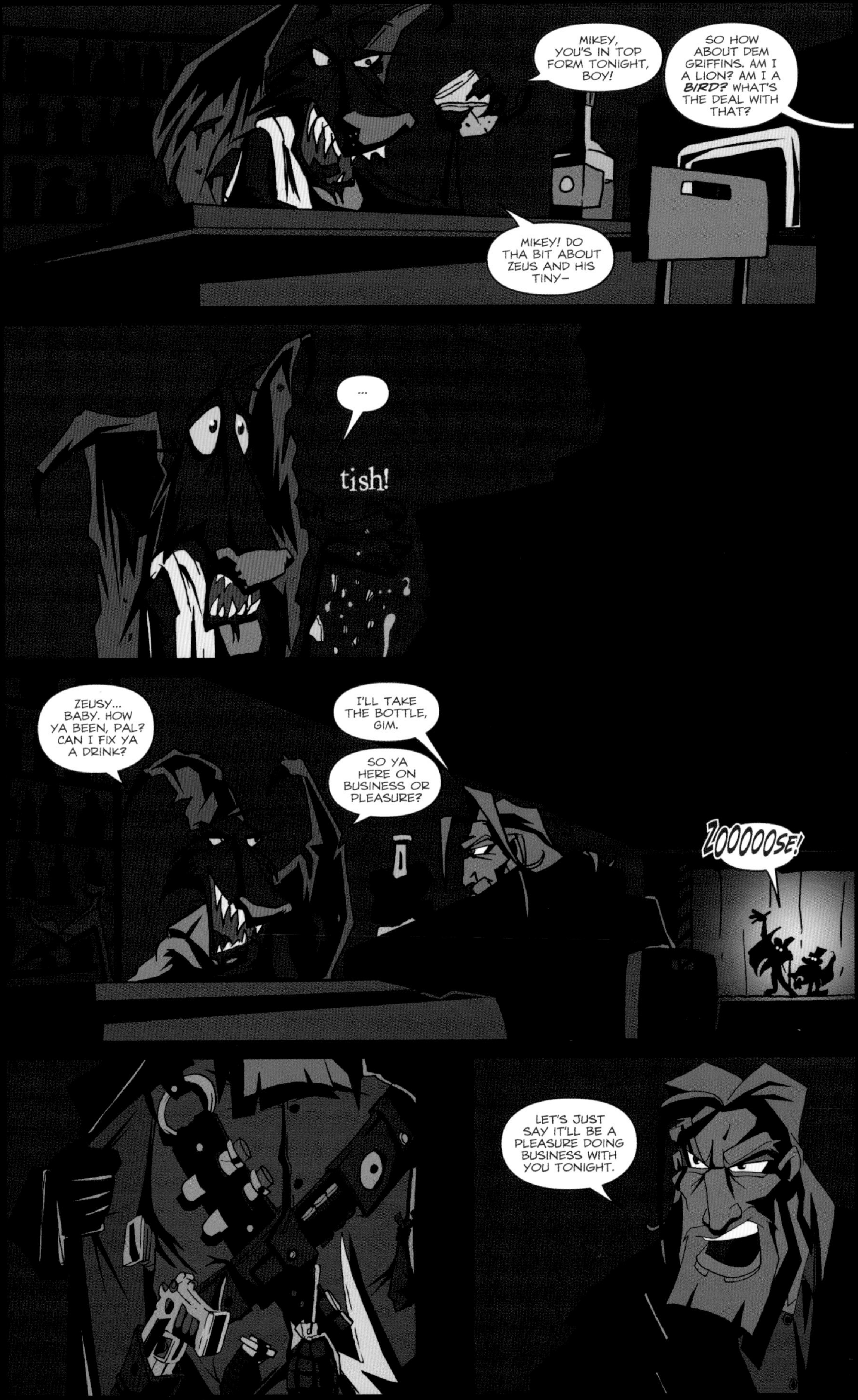
MIKEY, YOU'S IN TOP FORM TONIGHT, BOY!
SO HOW ABOUT DEM GRIFFINS. AM I A LION? AM I A BIRD? WHAT'S THE DEAL WITH THAT?
MIKEY! DO THA BIT ABOUT ZEUS AND HIS TINY–
...
tish!
ZEUSY... BABY. HOW YA BEEN, PAL? CAN I FIX YA A DRINK?
I'LL TAKE THE BOTTLE, GIM.
SO YA HERE ON BUSINESS OR PLEASURE?
ZOOOOOSE!
LET'S JUST SAY IT'LL BE A PLEASURE DOING BUSINESS WITH YOU TONIGHT.

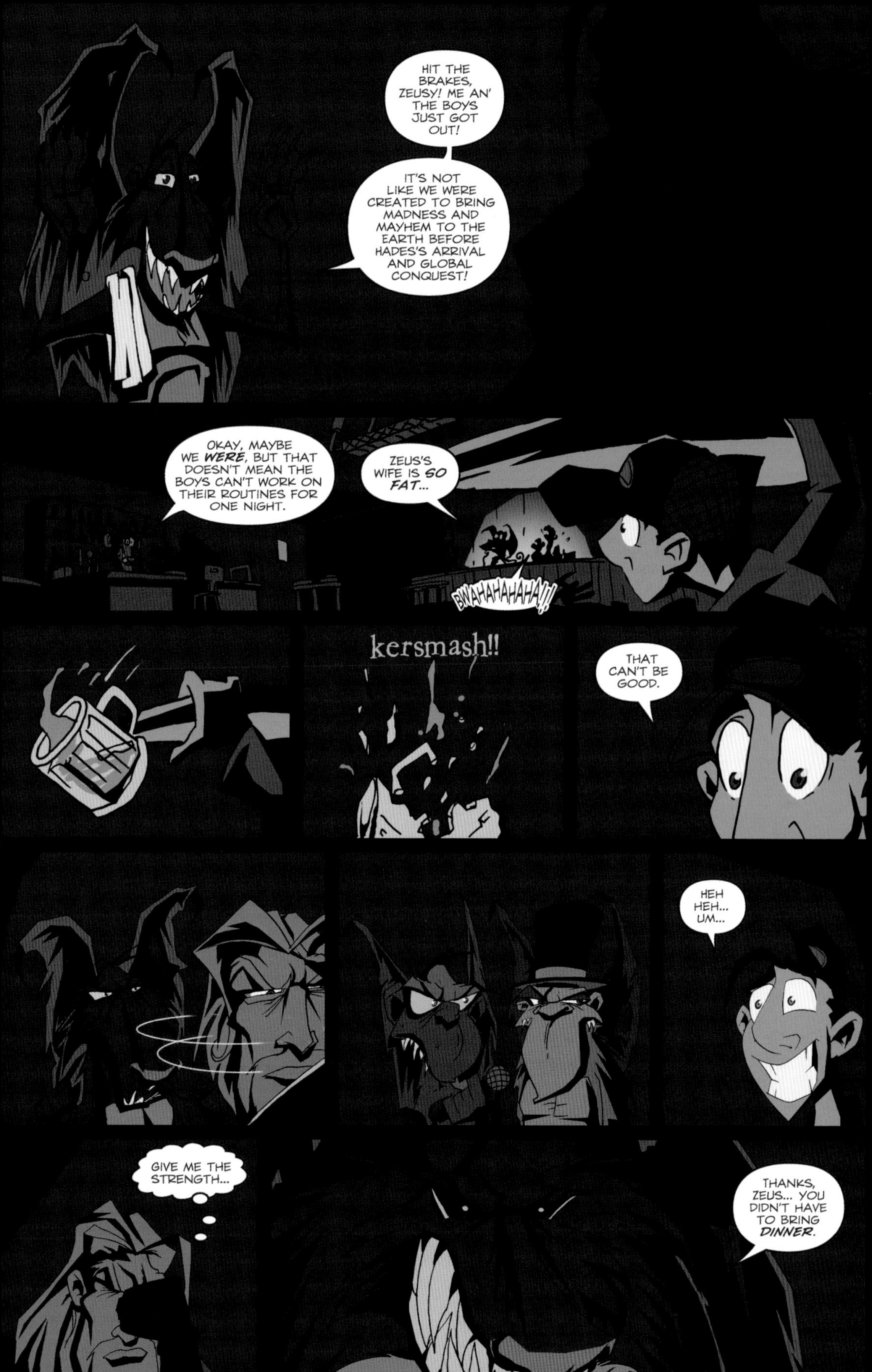
HIT THE BRAKES, ZEUSY! ME AN' THE BOYS JUST GOT OUT!
IT'S NOT LIKE WE WERE CREATED TO BRING MADNESS AND MAYHEM TO THE EARTH BEFORE HADES'S ARRIVAL AND GLOBAL CONQUEST!
OKAY, MAYBE WE WERE, BUT THAT DOESN'T MEAN THE BOYS CAN'T WORK ON THEIR ROUTINES FOR ONE NIGHT.
ZEUS'S WIFE IS SO FAT...
BWAHAHAHAHA!!!
kersmash!!
THAT CAN'T BE GOOD.
HEH HEH... UM...
GIVE ME THE STRENGTH...
THANKS, ZEUS... YOU DIDN'T HAVE TO BRING DINNER.

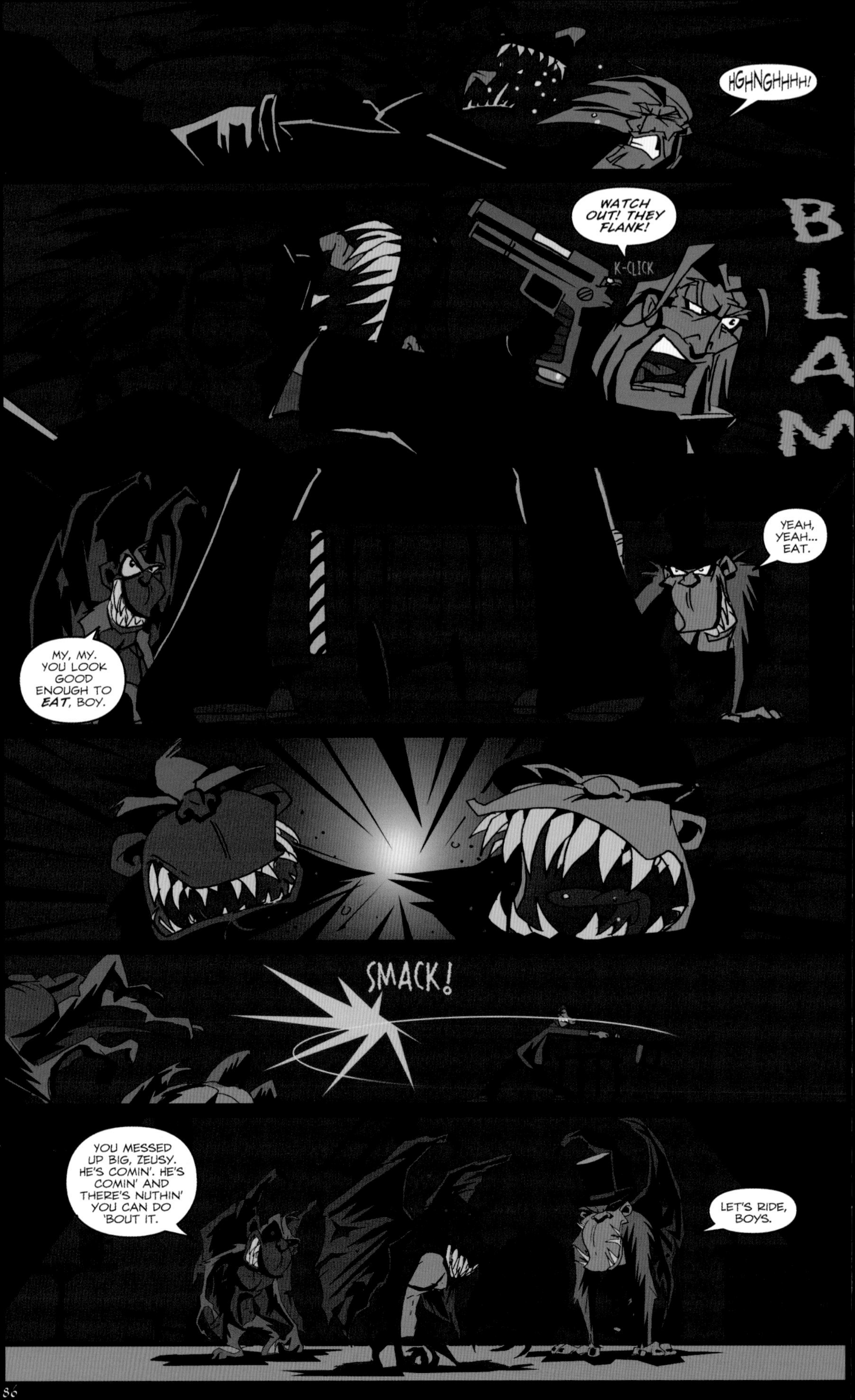
HGHNGHHHH!
WATCH OUT! THEY FLANK!
K-CLICK
BLAM
YEAH, YEAH... EAT.
MY, MY. YOU LOOK GOOD ENOUGH TO EAT, BOY.
SMACK!
YOU MESSED UP BIG, ZEUSY. HE'S COMIN'. HE'S COMIN' AND THERE'S NUTHIN' YOU CAN DO 'BOUT IT.
LET'S RIDE, BOYS.

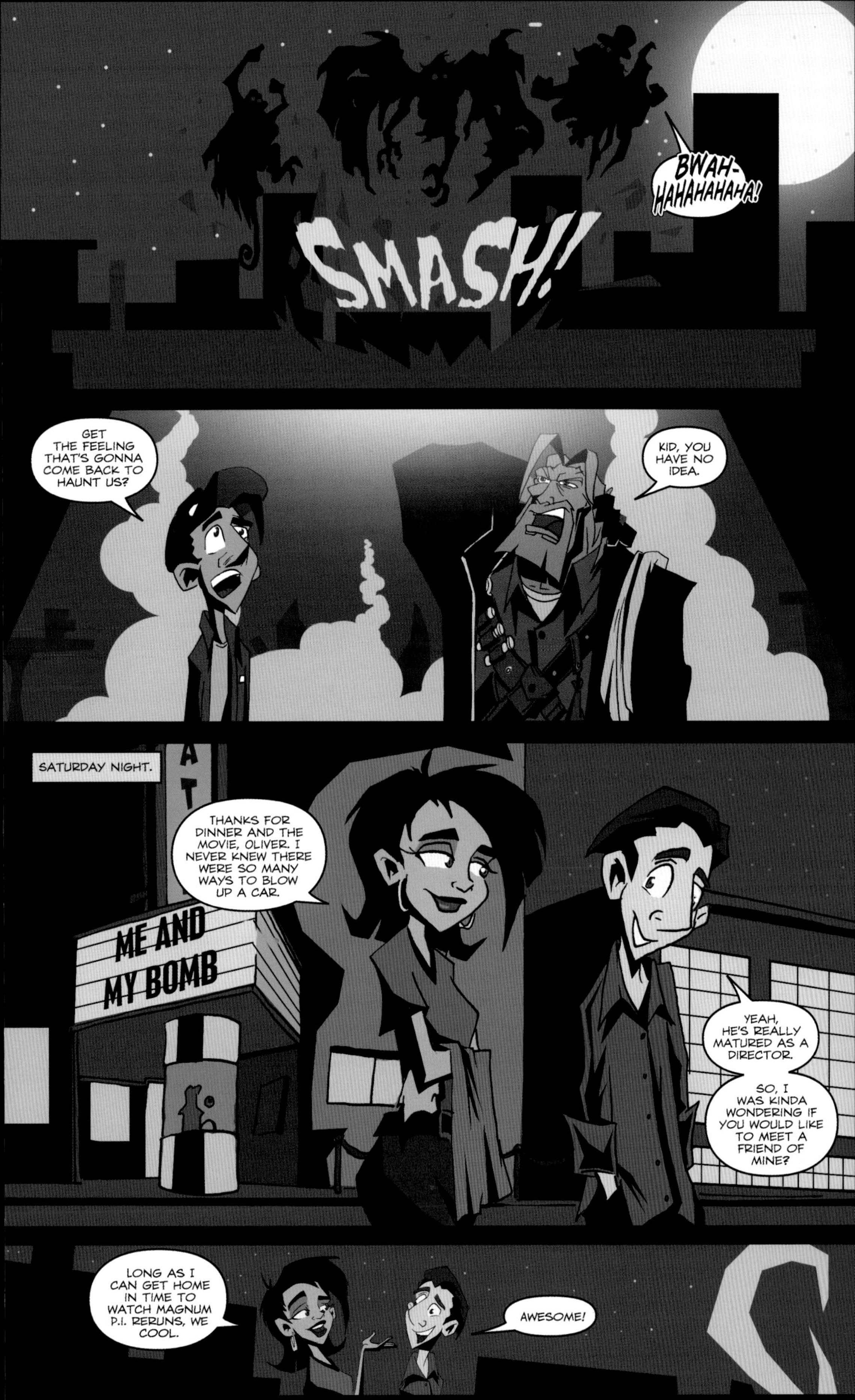
BWAH-HAHAHAHAHA!
SMASH!
GET THE FEELING THAT'S GONNA COME BACK TO HAUNT US?
KID, YOU HAVE NO IDEA.
SATURDAY NIGHT.
THANKS FOR DINNER AND THE MOVIE, OLIVER. I NEVER KNEW THERE WERE SO MANY WAYS TO BLOW UP A CAR.
ME AND MY BOMB
YEAH, HE'S REALLY MATURED AS A DIRECTOR.
SO, I WAS KINDA WONDERING IF YOU WOULD LIKE TO MEET A FRIEND OF MINE?
LONG AS I CAN GET HOME IN TIME TO WATCH MAGNUM P.I. RERUNS, WE COOL.
AWESOME!

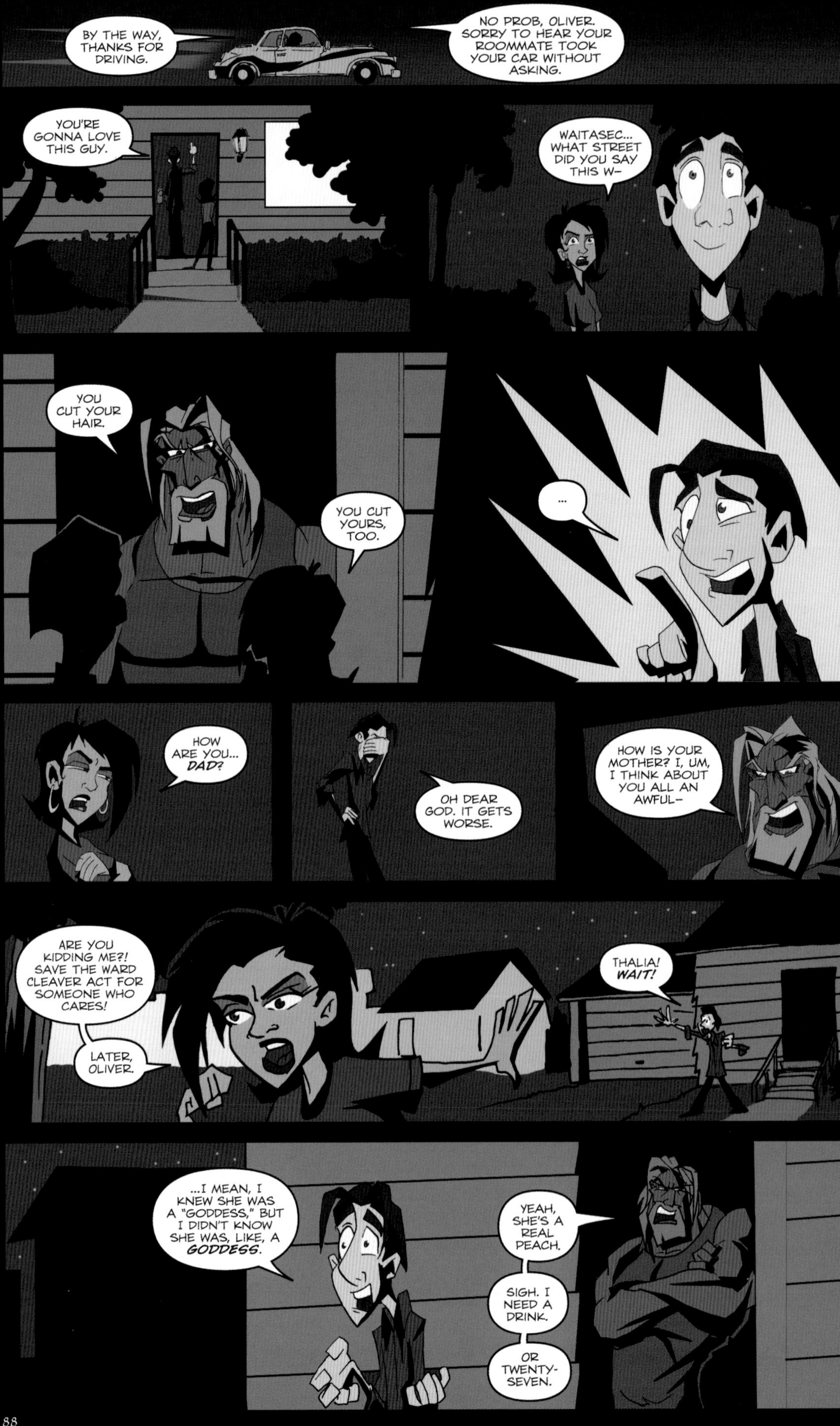
BY THE WAY, THANKS FOR DRIVING.
NO PROB, OLIVER. SORRY TO HEAR YOUR ROOMMATE TOOK YOUR CAR WITHOUT ASKING.
YOU'RE GONNA LOVE THIS GUY.
WAITASEC... WHAT STREET DID YOU SAY THIS W—
YOU CUT YOUR HAIR.
YOU CUT YOURS, TOO.
...
HOW ARE YOU... ***DAD?***
OH DEAR GOD. IT GETS WORSE.
HOW IS YOUR MOTHER? I, UM, I THINK ABOUT YOU ALL AN AWFUL—
ARE YOU KIDDING ME?! SAVE THE WARD CLEAVER ACT FOR SOMEONE WHO CARES!
LATER, OLIVER.
THALIA! ***WAIT!***
...I MEAN, I KNEW SHE WAS A "GODDESS," BUT I DIDN'T KNOW SHE WAS, LIKE, A ***GODDESS***.
YEAH, SHE'S A REAL PEACH.
SIGH. I NEED A DRINK.
OR TWENTY-SEVEN.

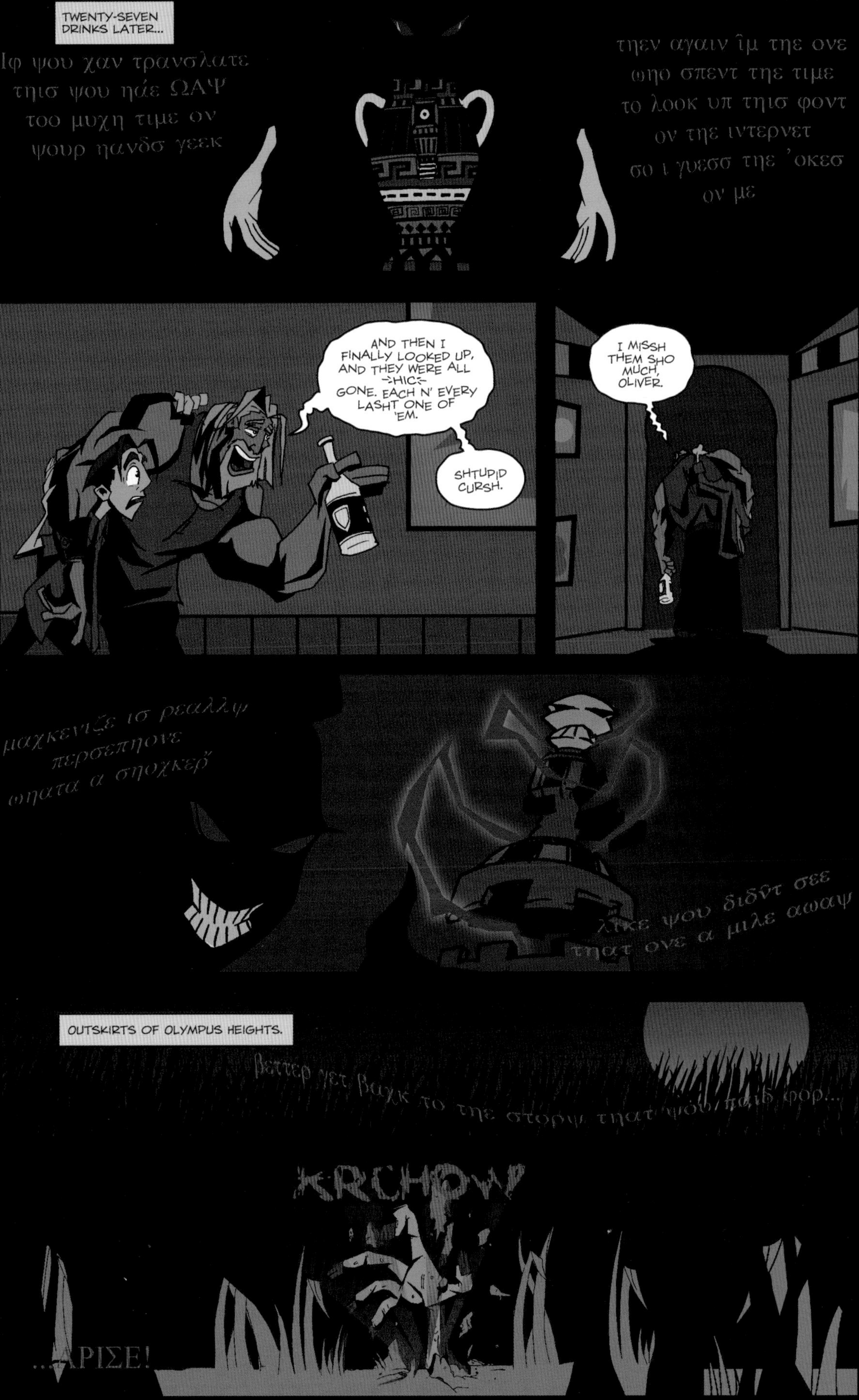
TWENTY-SEVEN DRINKS LATER...
Ιφ ψου χαν τρανσλατε τηισ ψου ηάε ΩΑΨ τοο μυχη τιμε ον ψουρ ηανδσ γεεκ
τηεν αγαιν î μ τηε ονε ωηο σπεντ τηε τιμε το λοοκ υπ τηισ φοντ ον τηε ιντερνετ σο ι γυεσσ τηε ’οκεσ ον με
AND THEN I FINALLY LOOKED UP, AND THEY WERE ALL -HIC- GONE. EACH N' EVERY LASHT ONE OF 'EM.
SHTUPID CURSH.
I MISSH THEM SHO MUCH, OLIVER.
μαχκενιζε ισ ρεαλλψ περσεπηονε ωηατα α σηοχκερ
λικε ψου διδν̂τ σεε τηατ ονε α μιλε αωαψ
OUTSKIRTS OF OLYMPUS HEIGHTS.
βεττερ γετ βαχκ το τηε στορψ τηατ ψου παιδ φορ...
KRCHOW
...ΑΡΙΣΕ!

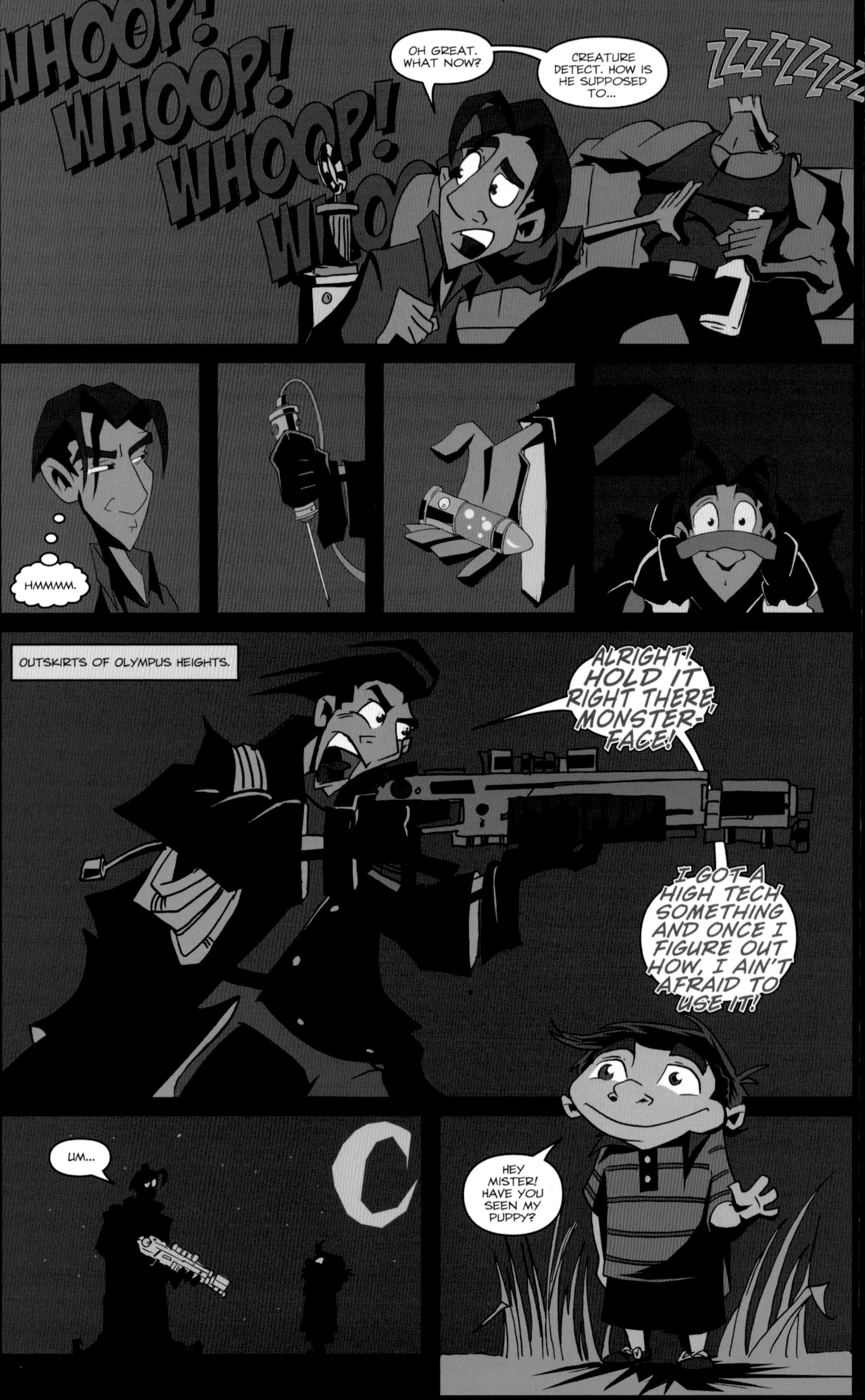
WHOOP! WHOOP! WHOOP! WHOO
OH GREAT. WHAT NOW?
CREATURE DETECT. HOW IS HE SUPPOSED TO...
ZZZZZZZZZ
HMMMM.
OUTSKIRTS OF OLYMPUS HEIGHTS.
ALRIGHT! HOLD IT RIGHT THERE, MONSTER-FACE!
I GOT A HIGH TECH SOMETHING AND ONCE I FIGURE OUT HOW, I AIN'T AFRAID TO USE IT!
UM...
HEY MISTER! HAVE YOU SEEN MY PUPPY?

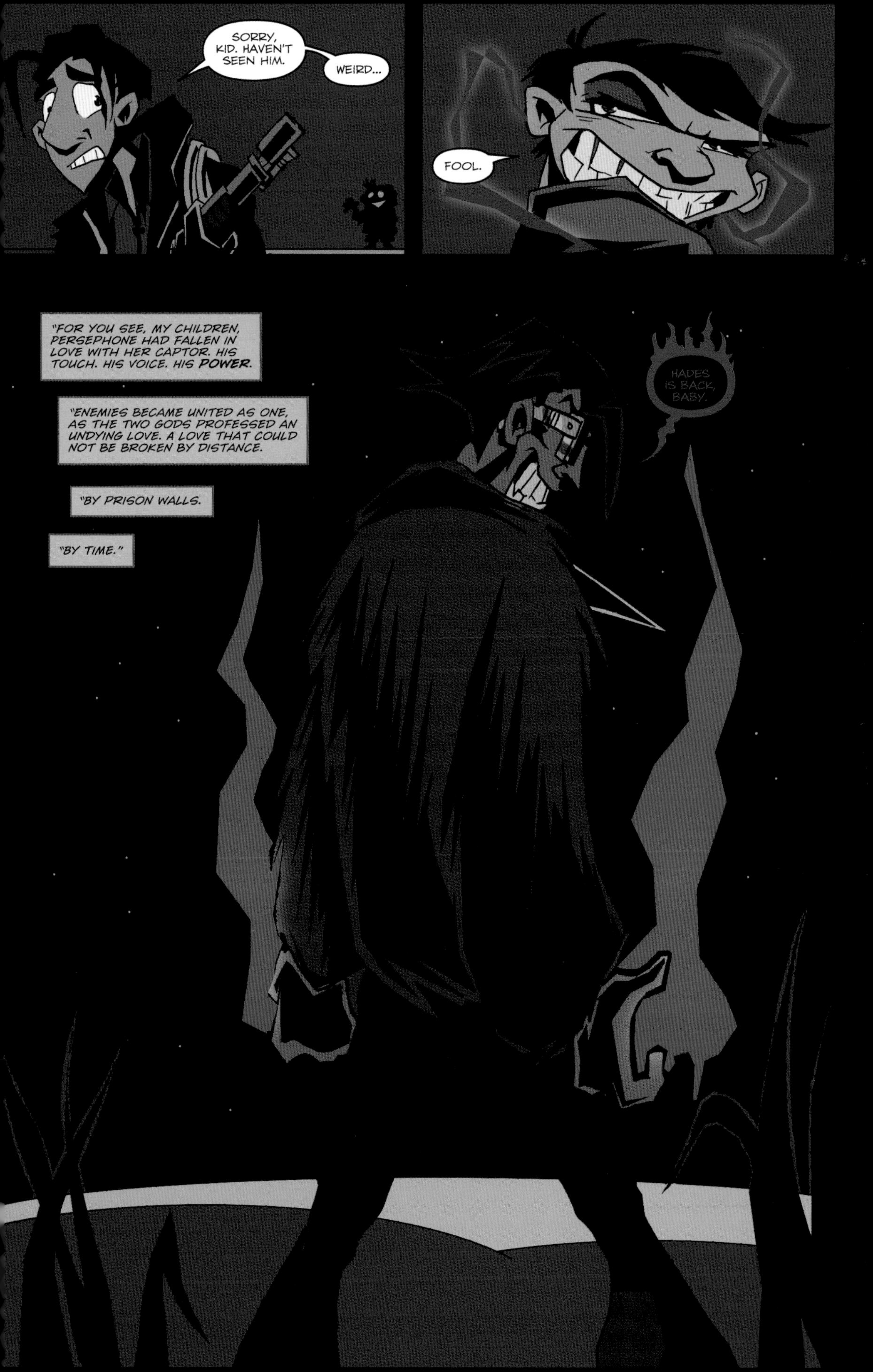
SORRY, KID. HAVEN'T SEEN HIM.
WEIRD...
FOOL.
"FOR YOU SEE, MY CHILDREN, PERSEPHONE HAD FALLEN IN LOVE WITH HER CAPTOR. HIS TOUCH. HIS VOICE. HIS POWER.
"ENEMIES BECAME UNITED AS ONE, AS THE TWO GODS PROFESSED AN UNDYING LOVE. A LOVE THAT COULD NOT BE BROKEN BY DISTANCE.
"BY PRISON WALLS.
"BY TIME."
HADES IS BACK, BABY.

THE DEVIL KNOWN

Oliver walked away, unaware of the beast he had just allowed into this world. He was finally free now, after centuries of climbing through the thick dirt and rock of Earth's crust. Hades, now fully formed, watched as the beat up station wagon disappeared over the horizon. He cricked his neck, fluffed his fur collar, and walked toward the small town of Olympus Heights.

As he swaggered down the dirt road, his feet began to hurt. So with a wave of his hand and a crackle of red electricity, his snake-skin boots changed into comfortable three-stripe running shoes straight out of an '80s rap video.

Once in the sleepy town, Hades strutted down the silent streets. Only a few houses had the familiar blue glow of late night television bouncing off the walls. However, as he passed each one, they momentarily switched to crackling static with strange demonic faces seeming to form when the couch potatoes weren't looking. And then Hades reached his destination:

...43 Mockingbird Lane.

The doorbell chimed as a familiar shape approached the screen door. It opened. Hades smiled, taking off his gold Elvis shades. Mrs. Mackenzie stood in her cotton night shirt and thick terrycloth robe with the ugly flowers. A single tear rolling down her cheek and her bottom lip quivered.

And then they kissed. Like they hadn't kissed in 5000 years.

Hades grinned. "I'll need to know where I can get a truck... and a ton of explosives." He lifted his hand to his mouth, hocked up a demonic loogie, and then dropped the hairball-sized droplet into Mackenzie's sprinkler drain. They kissed again as the loogie slithered into the drain hole and picked up its own momentum, tearing through the yard pipes.

The loogie didn't stop there. It wound its way through the copper piping, and then into the main sewer system, zigging and zagging its way past mice, turtles, and things no one else thought could be flushed down a toilet.

As the loogie rolled along, strange things began to happen. Nubs began to appear, eventually forming tiny arms that clamored as the shape moved faster and faster. Suddenly, two tiny horns appeared. As it banked upwards through an impossibly high series of pipes, its yellow eyes blinked open!

Elsewhere, driving into a high-rise apartment building in Indianapolis, Andrew Parker had just finished a long, hard day filing corporate audit records. As he climbed out of the sunroof of his sedan in the narrow-spaced parking garage, he couldn't help but think that his dreams had become lost orphans in a sea of fluorescent-lit cubicles. His dreams of running his own accounting firm were all but dead.

He could barely hear the screams of terrified neighbors as he got into the elevator with only one working light. He counted himself lucky that the one that smelled like pee didn't arrive at the garage first. All he could think of was the promise he made the kids—they could finally get a dog. The apartment super probably wouldn't look fondly upon it, but he figured that if they didn't care about a smelly elevator, they probably wouldn't notice the dog.

But there was a problem. As if a yappy Yorkshire Terrier wasn't enough of a cost, the price of shots, neutering, food, and training for the little beast surely made him think twice. But, fortunately, the rumor was that his company was going to promote Andrew to senior account executive.

So the kids went to that place in the mall that swears they're not cruel to the dogs and picked one out. But there were two more problems...

Andrew didn't get the raise. And tonight was the night he was supposed to bring the dog home.

Quinn and Adam ran to see Daddy as Andrew snuck in the door. When asked about the dog, he stammered, his wife Lise knowing full well that he got screwed over at work again.

But then a growling came from the bathroom. A playful animal grunt that made the kids laugh, knowing that Daddy was being silly again. He already had the dog in the apartment to trick them! Andrew and Lise looked at each other, trying to figure out who was behind it.

The kids ran to the knob as the scratching started behind the cheap, molded door. They squealed. Even the cat, Jules, broke his twenty-two hour nap to check it out. The kids turned to look at Andrew. "We love you, Daddy!" Even if he felt like crap, Andrew couldn't help but smile back.

They opened the door. Their faces fell. Jules hissed. Then they all screamed...

Chapter Four

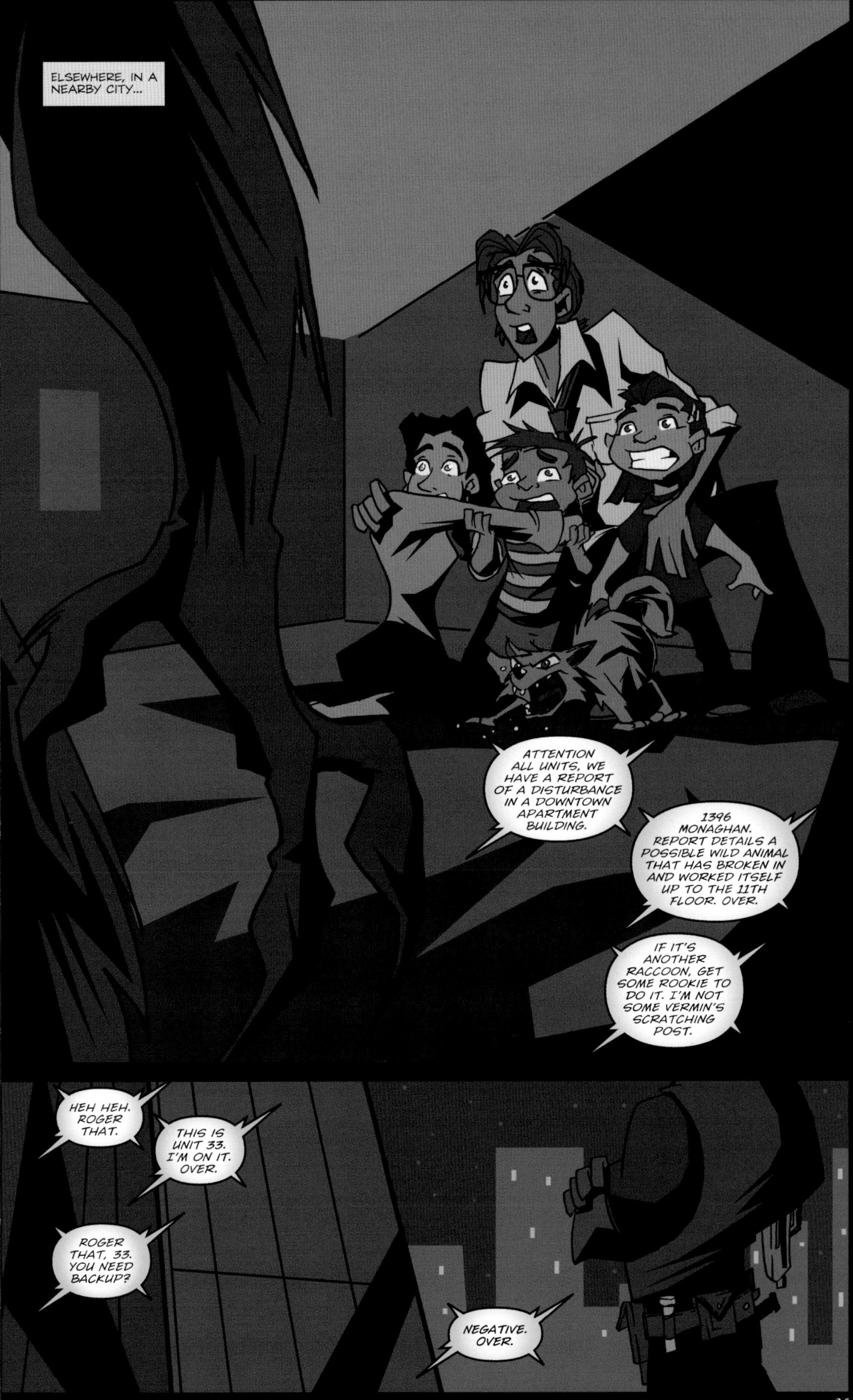
ELSEWHERE, IN A NEARBY CITY...
ATTENTION ALL UNITS, WE HAVE A REPORT OF A DISTURBANCE IN A DOWNTOWN APARTMENT BUILDING.
1396 MONAGHAN. REPORT DETAILS A POSSIBLE WILD ANIMAL THAT HAS BROKEN IN AND WORKED ITSELF UP TO THE 11TH FLOOR. OVER.
IF IT'S ANOTHER RACCOON, GET SOME ROOKIE TO DO IT. I'M NOT SOME VERMIN'S SCRATCHING POST.
HEH HEH. ROGER THAT.
THIS IS UNIT 33. I'M ON IT. OVER.
ROGER THAT, 33. YOU NEED BACKUP?
NEGATIVE. OVER.

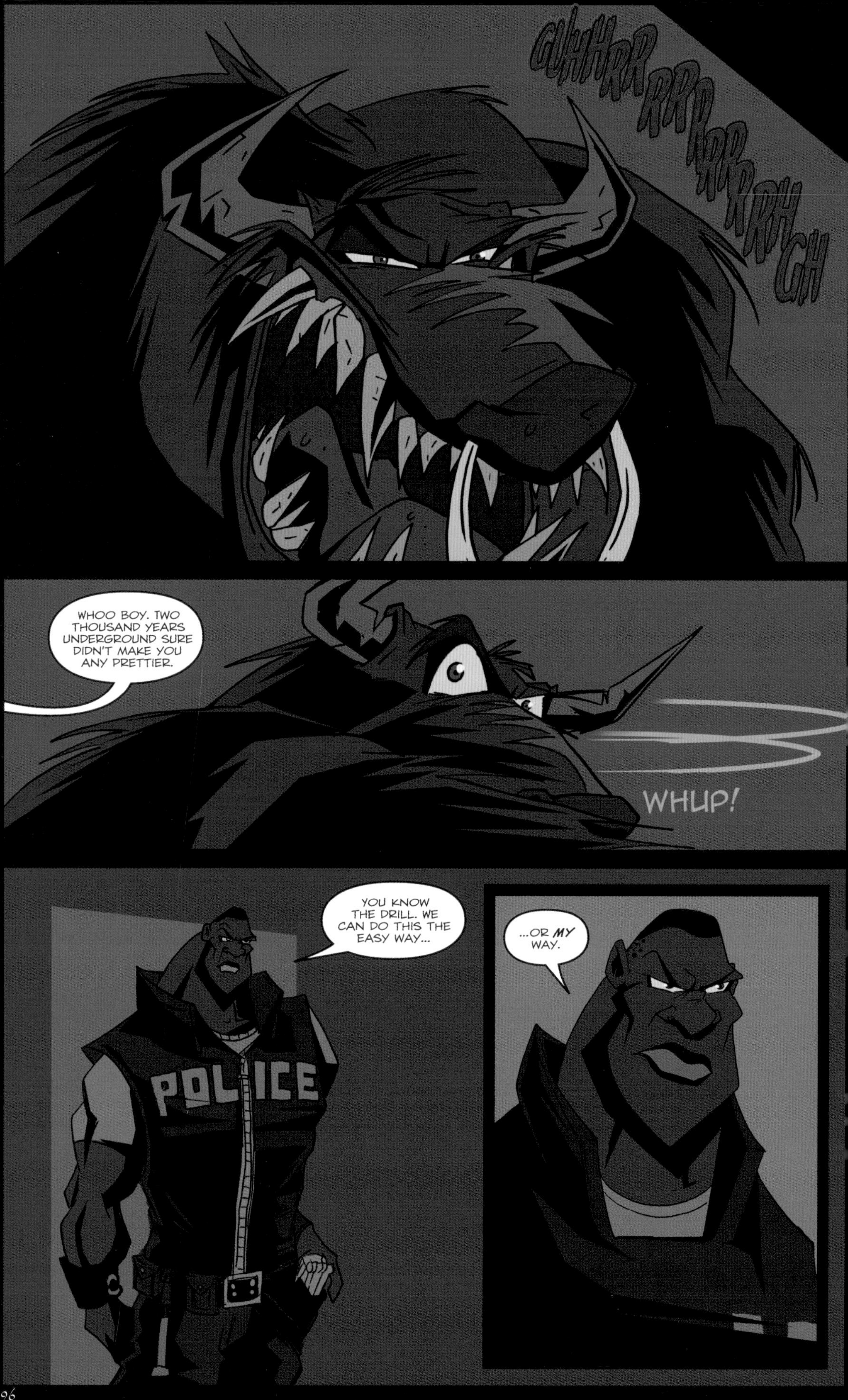
GUHHRRRRRRRRRRRRRHGH
WHOO BOY. TWO THOUSAND YEARS UNDERGROUND SURE DIDN'T MAKE YOU ANY PRETTIER.
WHUP!
YOU KNOW THE DRILL. WE CAN DO THIS THE EASY WAY...
...OR *MY* WAY.

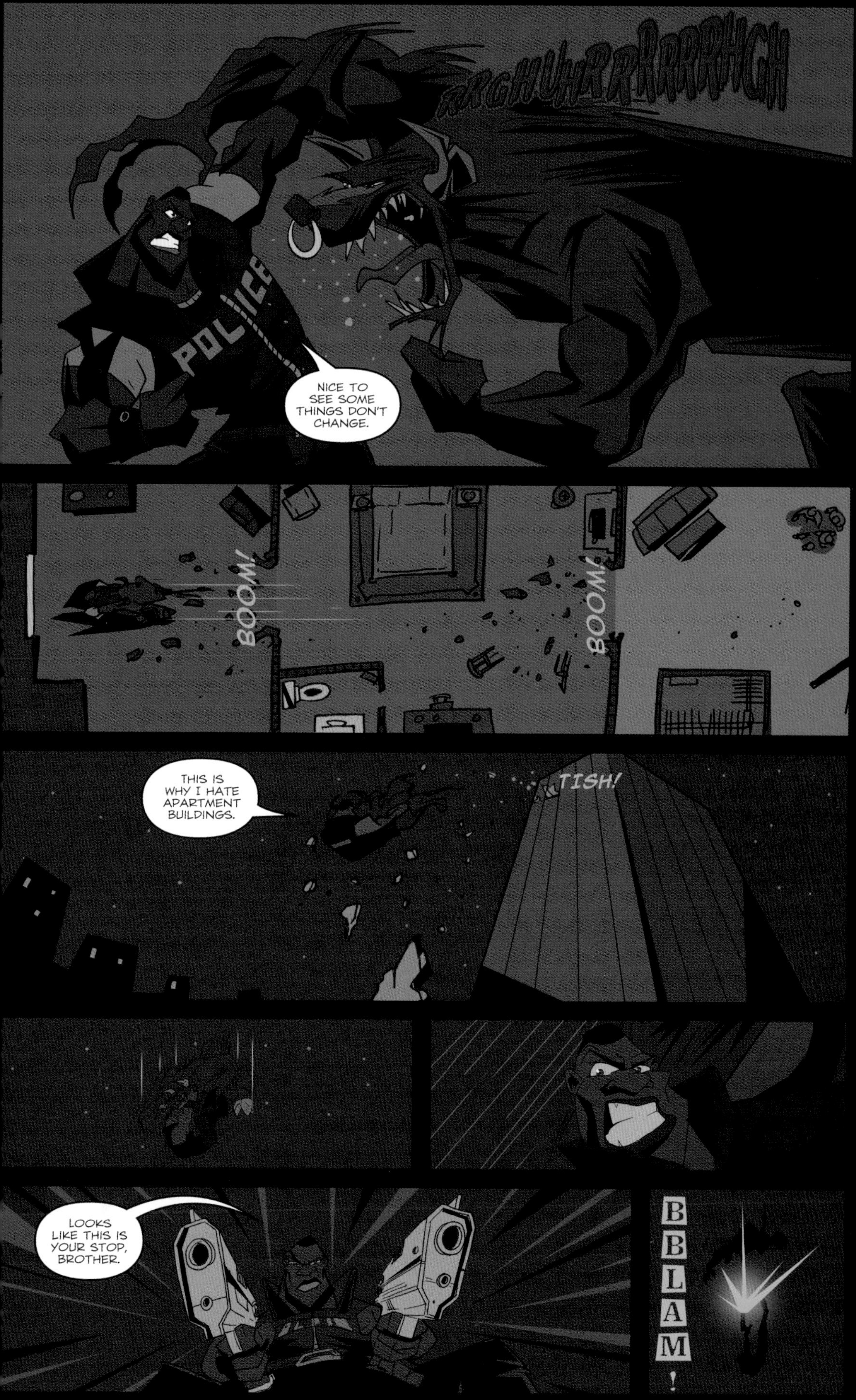
RRGHUHRRRRRRHGH
NICE TO SEE SOME THINGS DON'T CHANGE.
BOOM!
BOOM!
THIS IS WHY I HATE APARTMENT BUILDINGS.
TISH!
LOOKS LIKE THIS IS YOUR STOP, BROTHER.
BBLAM!

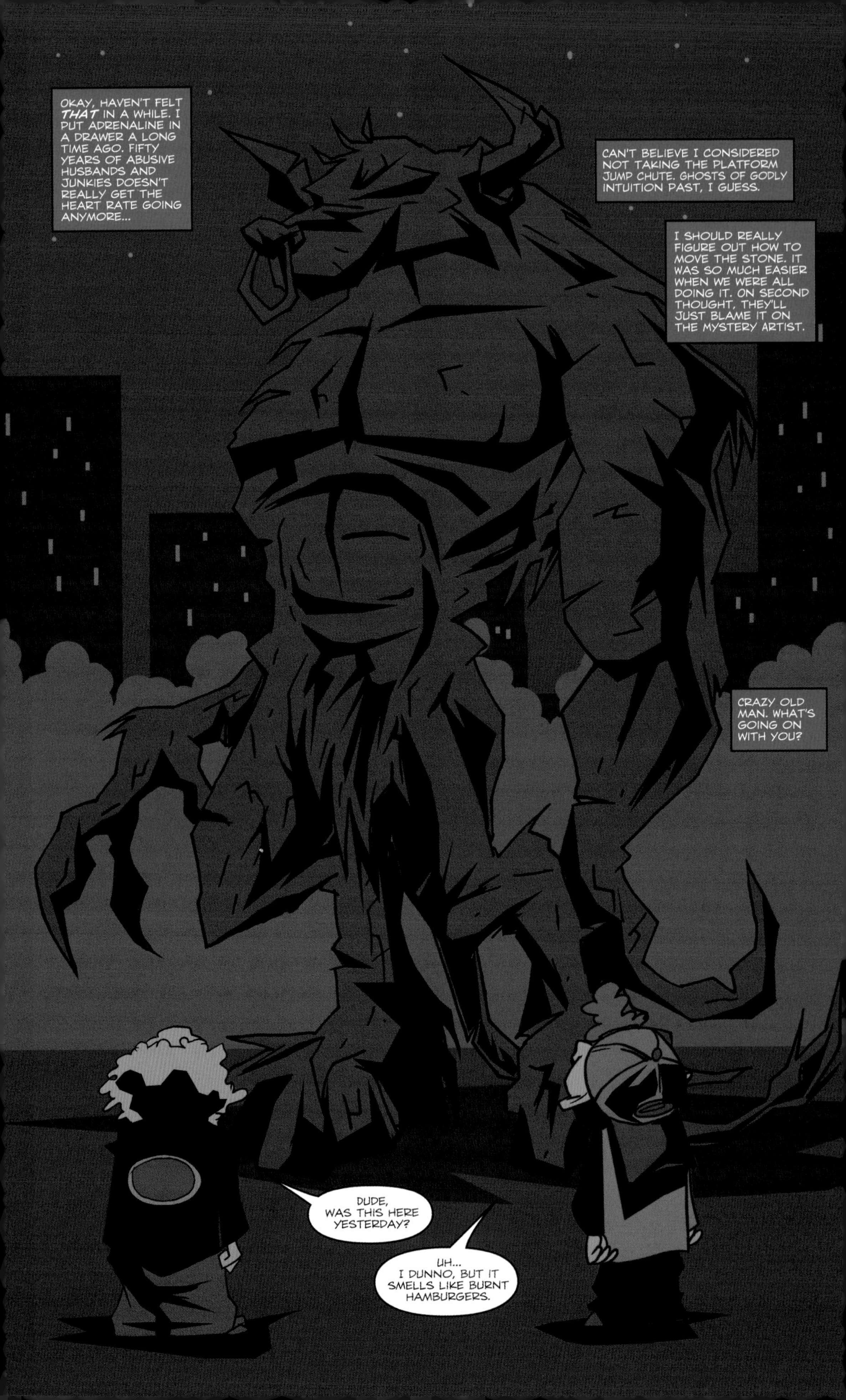
OKAY, HAVEN'T FELT *THAT* IN A WHILE. I PUT ADRENALINE IN A DRAWER A LONG TIME AGO. FIFTY YEARS OF ABUSIVE HUSBANDS AND JUNKIES DOESN'T REALLY GET THE HEART RATE GOING ANYMORE...
CAN'T BELIEVE I CONSIDERED NOT TAKING THE PLATFORM JUMP CHUTE. GHOSTS OF GODLY INTUITION PAST, I GUESS.
I SHOULD REALLY FIGURE OUT HOW TO MOVE THE STONE. IT WAS SO MUCH EASIER WHEN WE WERE ALL DOING IT. ON SECOND THOUGHT, THEY'LL JUST BLAME IT ON THE MYSTERY ARTIST.
CRAZY OLD MAN. WHAT'S GOING ON WITH YOU?
DUDE, WAS THIS HERE YESTERDAY?
UH... I DUNNO, BUT IT SMELLS LIKE BURNT HAMBURGERS.

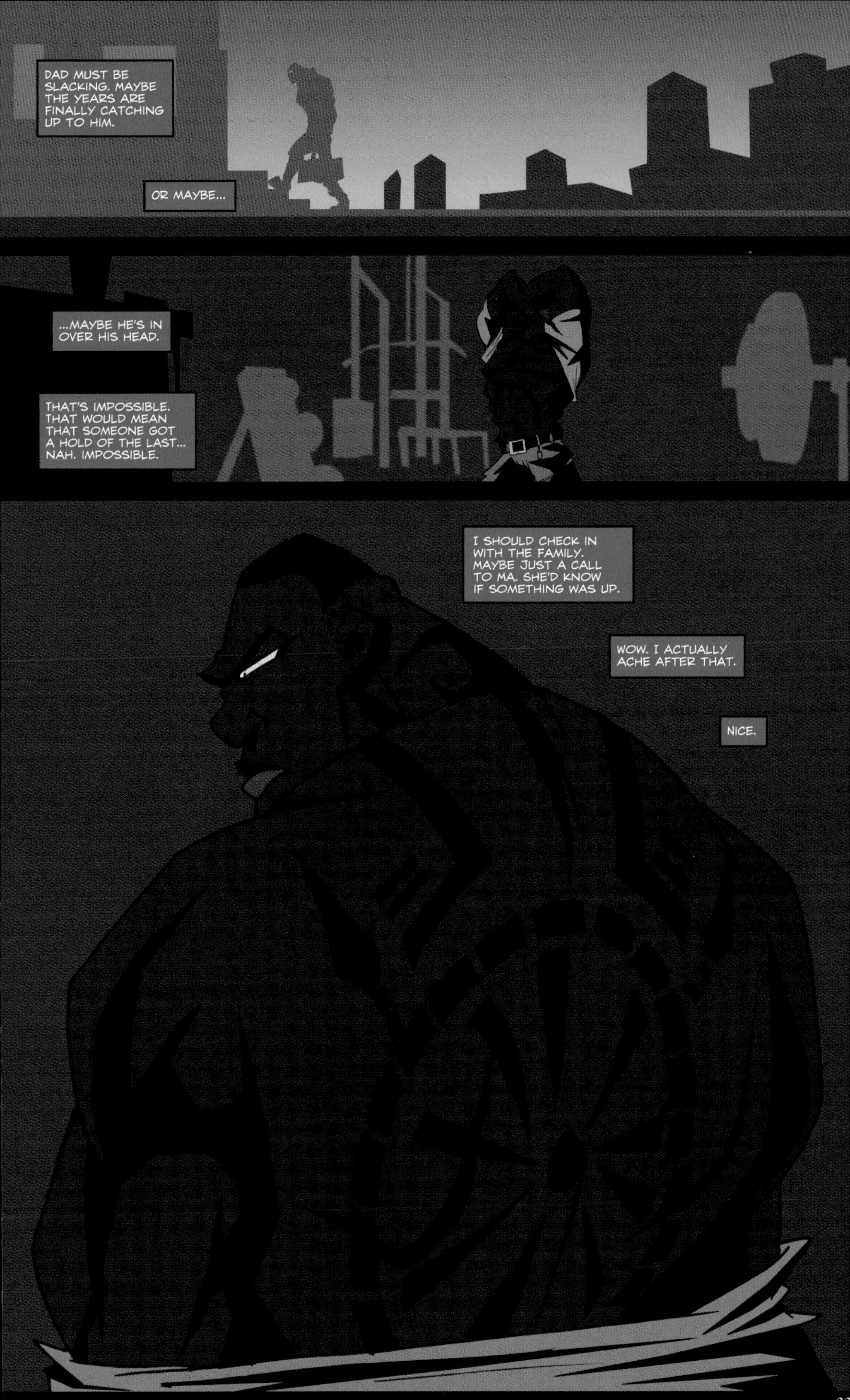
DAD MUST BE SLACKING. MAYBE THE YEARS ARE FINALLY CATCHING UP TO HIM.
OR MAYBE...
...MAYBE HE'S IN OVER HIS HEAD.
THAT'S IMPOSSIBLE. THAT WOULD MEAN THAT SOMEONE GOT A HOLD OF THE LAST... NAH. IMPOSSIBLE.
I SHOULD CHECK IN WITH THE FAMILY. MAYBE JUST A CALL TO MA. SHE'D KNOW IF SOMETHING WAS UP.
WOW. I ACTUALLY ACHE AFTER THAT.
NICE.

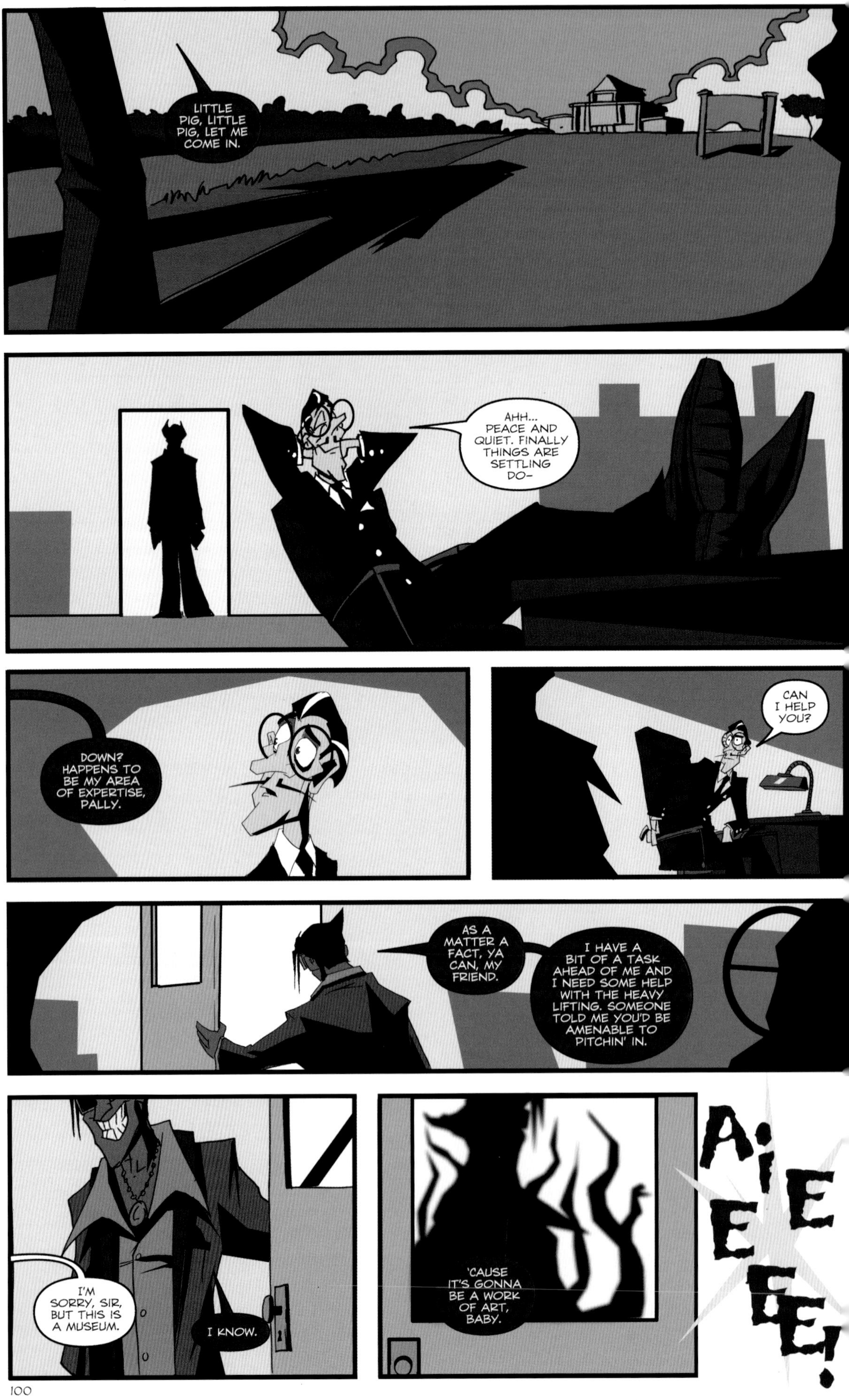
LITTLE PIG, LITTLE PIG, LET ME COME IN.
AHH... PEACE AND QUIET. FINALLY THINGS ARE SETTLING DO–
DOWN? HAPPENS TO BE MY AREA OF EXPERTISE, PALLY.
CAN I HELP YOU?
AS A MATTER A FACT, YA CAN, MY FRIEND.
I HAVE A BIT OF A TASK AHEAD OF ME AND I NEED SOME HELP WITH THE HEAVY LIFTING. SOMEONE TOLD ME YOU'D BE AMENABLE TO PITCHIN' IN.
I'M SORRY, SIR, BUT THIS IS A MUSEUM.
I KNOW.
'CAUSE IT'S GONNA BE A WORK OF ART, BABY.
AIEEEEE!

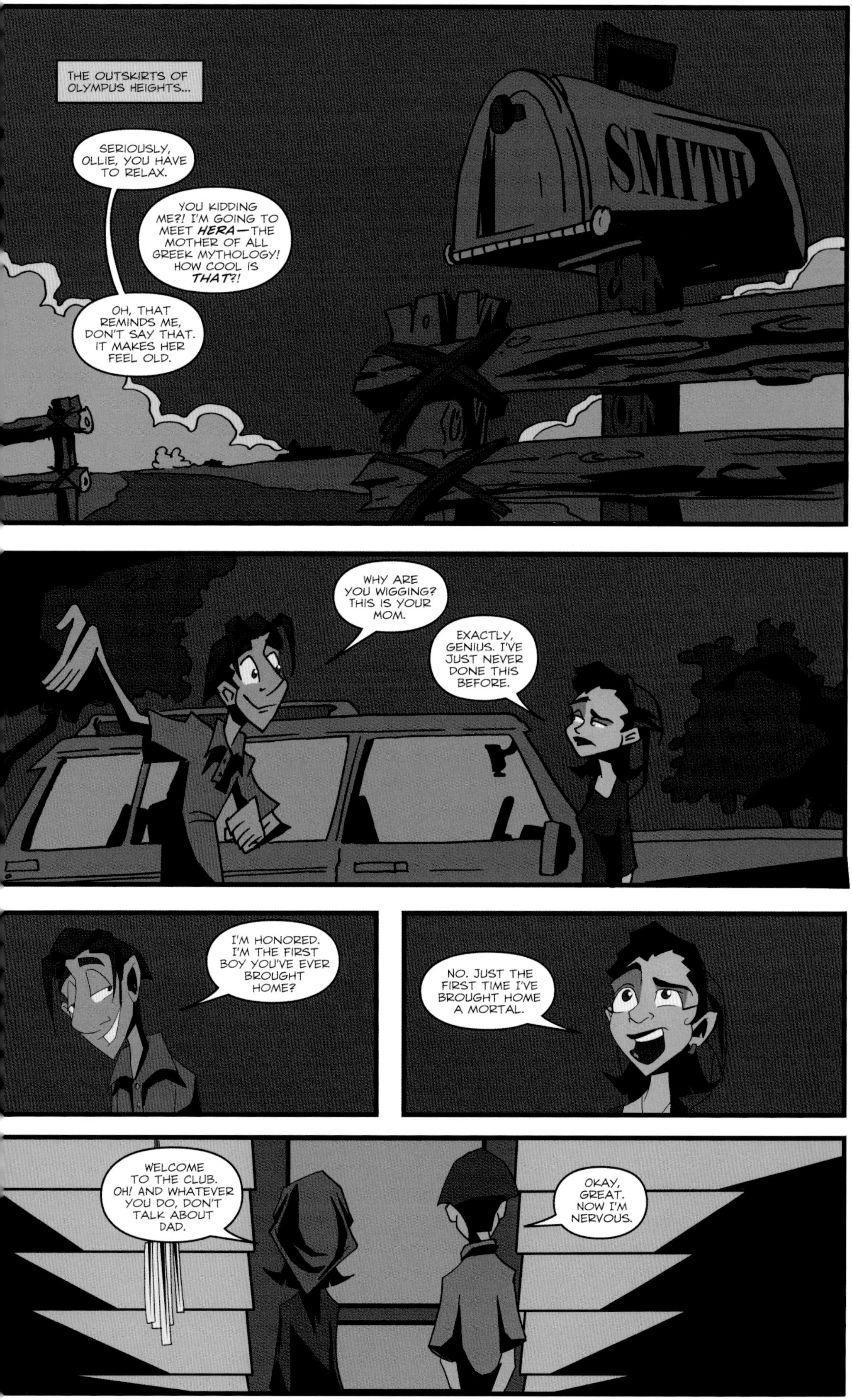
THE OUTSKIRTS OF OLYMPUS HEIGHTS...
SMITH
SERIOUSLY, OLLIE, YOU HAVE TO RELAX.
YOU KIDDING ME?! I'M GOING TO MEET HERA—THE MOTHER OF ALL GREEK MYTHOLOGY! HOW COOL IS THAT?!
OH, THAT REMINDS ME, DON'T SAY THAT. IT MAKES HER FEEL OLD.
WHY ARE YOU WIGGING? THIS IS YOUR MOM.
EXACTLY, GENIUS. I'VE JUST NEVER DONE THIS BEFORE.
I'M HONORED. I'M THE FIRST BOY YOU'VE EVER BROUGHT HOME?
NO. JUST THE FIRST TIME I'VE BROUGHT HOME A MORTAL.
WELCOME TO THE CLUB. OH! AND WHATEVER YOU DO, DON'T TALK ABOUT DAD.
OKAY, GREAT. NOW I'M NERVOUS.

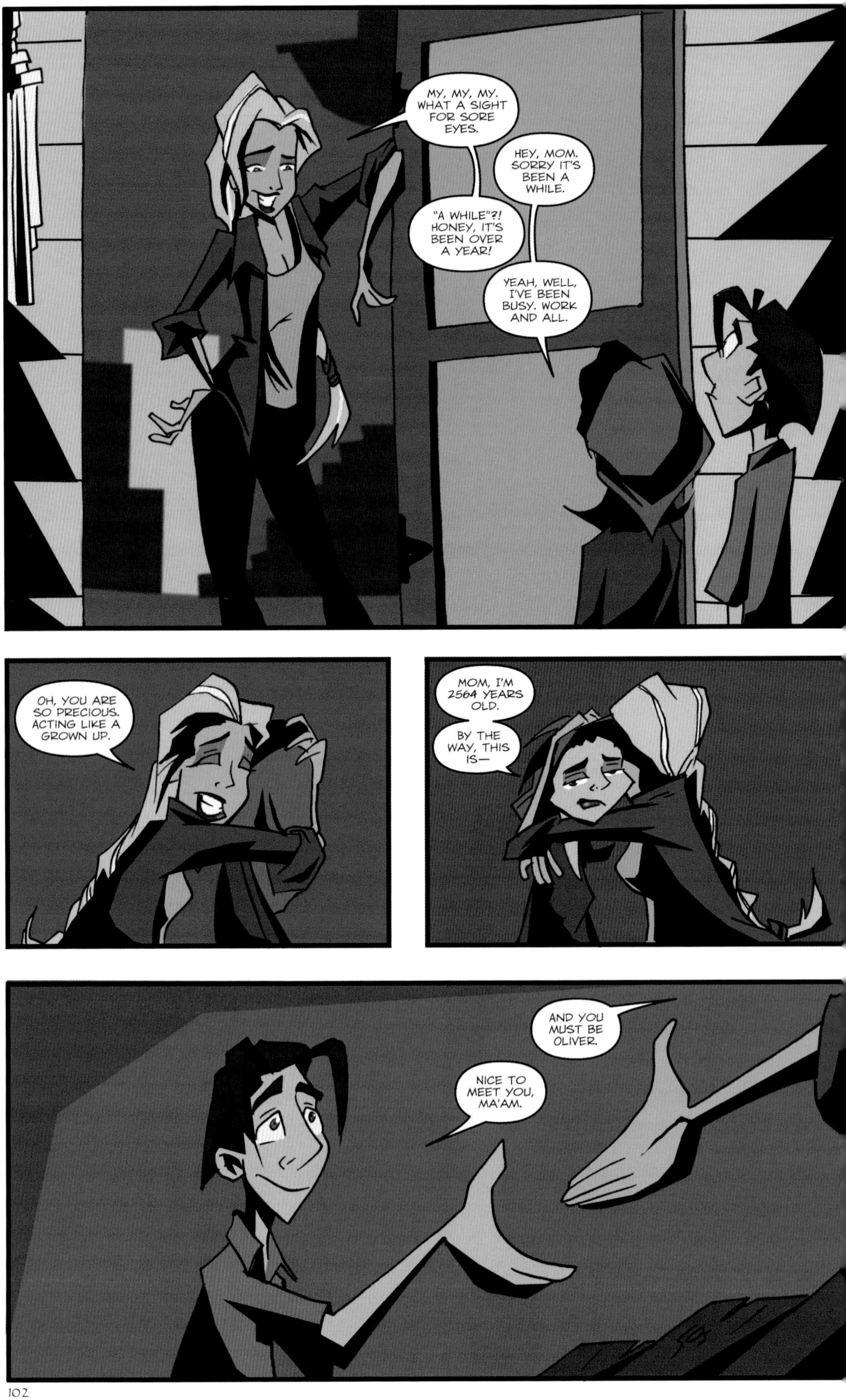
MY, MY, MY. WHAT A SIGHT FOR SORE EYES.
HEY, MOM. SORRY IT'S BEEN A WHILE.
"A WHILE"?! HONEY, IT'S BEEN OVER A YEAR!
YEAH, WELL, I'VE BEEN BUSY. WORK AND ALL.
OH, YOU ARE SO PRECIOUS. ACTING LIKE A GROWN UP.
MOM, I'M 2564 YEARS OLD.
BY THE WAY, THIS IS—
AND YOU MUST BE OLIVER.
NICE TO MEET YOU, MA'AM.

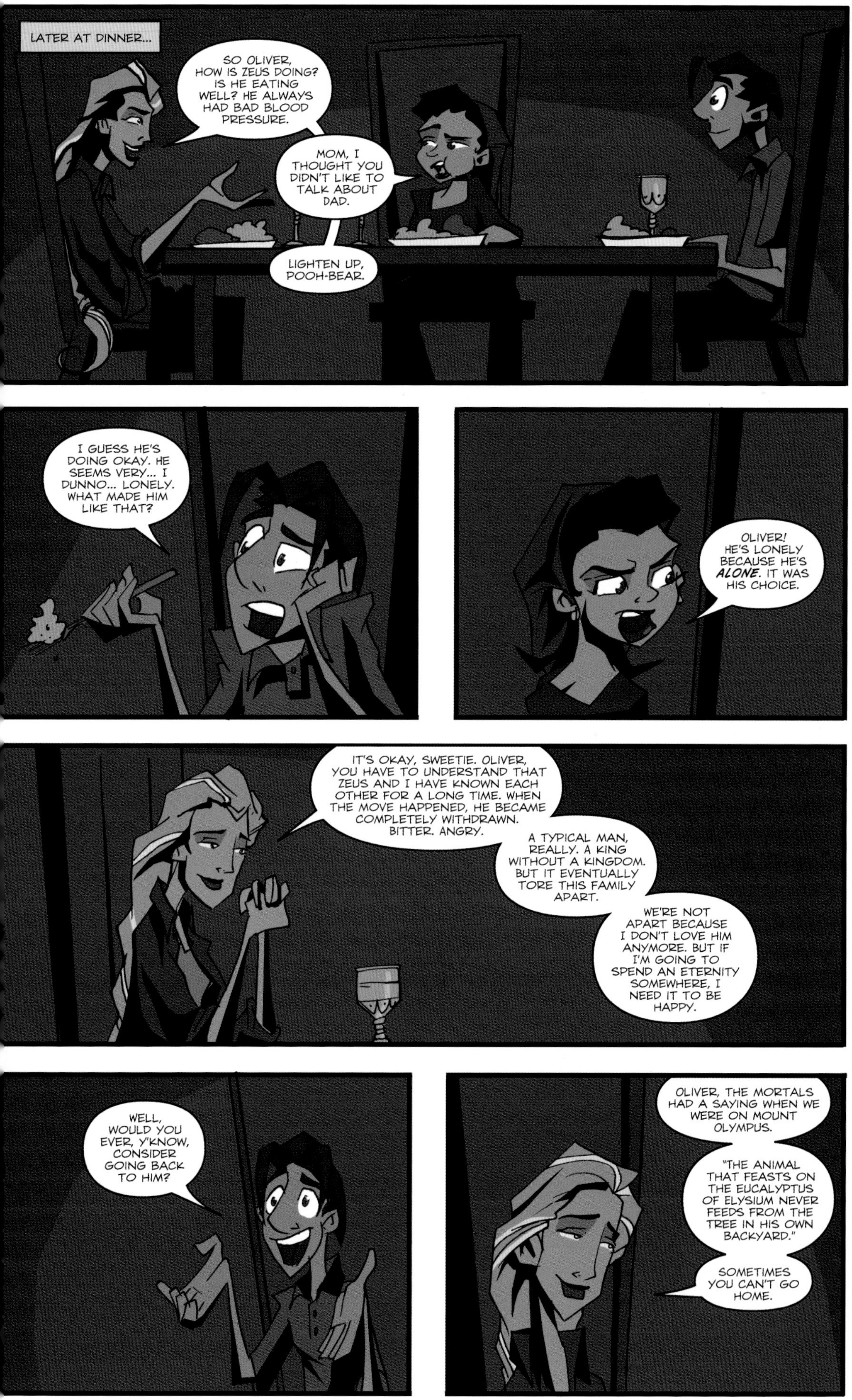
LATER AT DINNER...
SO OLIVER, HOW IS ZEUS DOING? IS HE EATING WELL? HE ALWAYS HAD BAD BLOOD PRESSURE.
MOM, I THOUGHT YOU DIDN'T LIKE TO TALK ABOUT DAD.
LIGHTEN UP, POOH-BEAR.
I GUESS HE'S DOING OKAY. HE SEEMS VERY... I DUNNO... LONELY. WHAT MADE HIM LIKE THAT?
OLIVER! HE'S LONELY BECAUSE HE'S *ALONE*. IT WAS HIS CHOICE.
IT'S OKAY, SWEETIE. OLIVER, YOU HAVE TO UNDERSTAND THAT ZEUS AND I HAVE KNOWN EACH OTHER FOR A LONG TIME. WHEN THE MOVE HAPPENED, HE BECAME COMPLETELY WITHDRAWN. BITTER. ANGRY.
A TYPICAL MAN, REALLY. A KING WITHOUT A KINGDOM. BUT IT EVENTUALLY TORE THIS FAMILY APART.
WE'RE NOT APART BECAUSE I DON'T LOVE HIM ANYMORE. BUT IF I'M GOING TO SPEND AN ETERNITY SOMEWHERE, I NEED IT TO BE HAPPY.
WELL, WOULD YOU EVER, Y'KNOW, CONSIDER GOING BACK TO HIM?
OLIVER, THE MORTALS HAD A SAYING WHEN WE WERE ON MOUNT OLYMPUS.
"THE ANIMAL THAT FEASTS ON THE EUCALYPTUS OF ELYSIUM NEVER FEEDS FROM THE TREE IN HIS OWN BACKYARD."
SOMETIMES YOU CAN'T GO HOME.

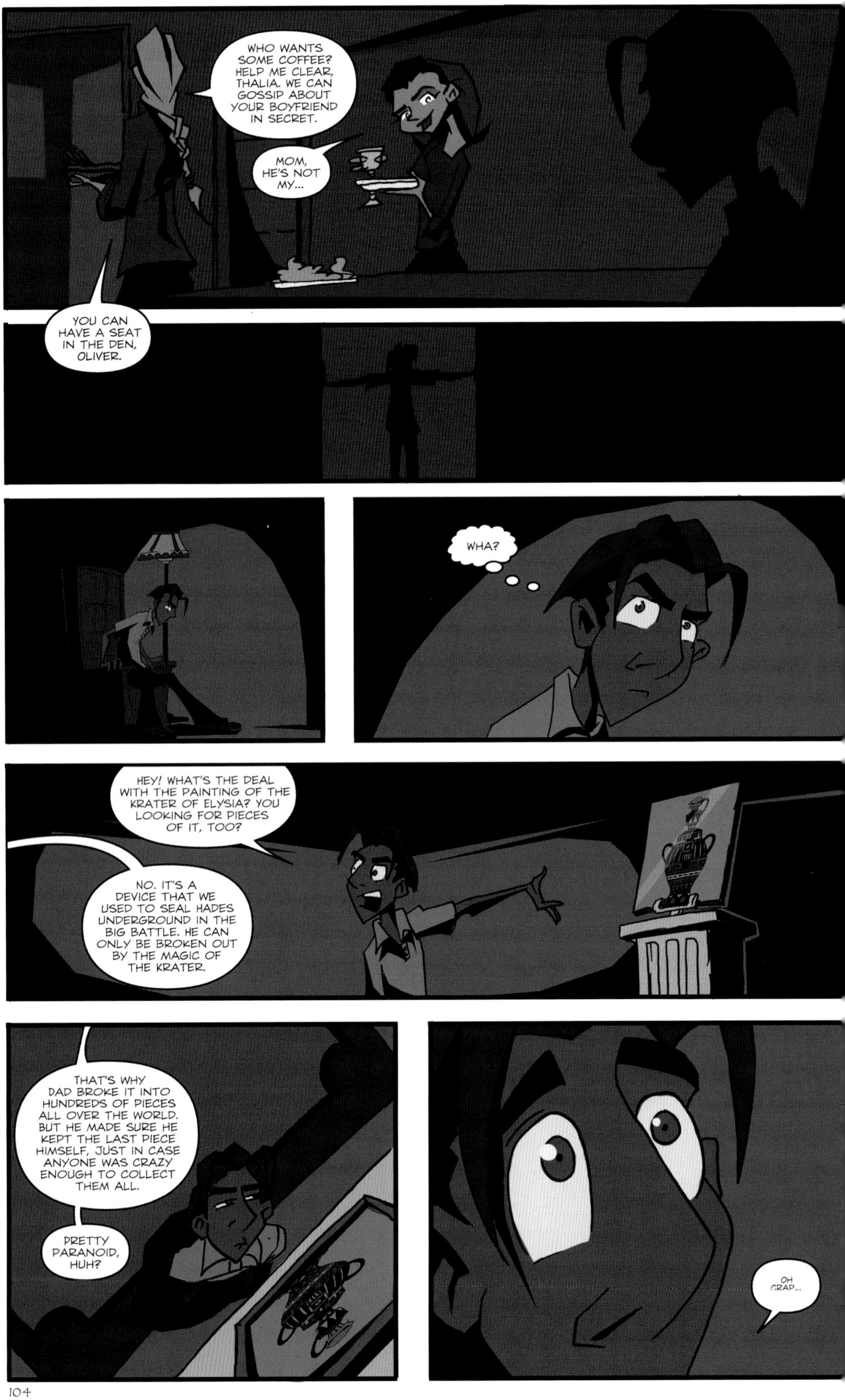
WHO WANTS SOME COFFEE? HELP ME CLEAR, THALIA. WE CAN GOSSIP ABOUT YOUR BOYFRIEND IN SECRET.
MOM, HE'S NOT MY...
YOU CAN HAVE A SEAT IN THE DEN, OLIVER.
WHA?
HEY! WHAT'S THE DEAL WITH THE PAINTING OF THE KRATER OF ELYSIA? YOU LOOKING FOR PIECES OF IT, TOO?
NO. IT'S A DEVICE THAT WE USED TO SEAL HADES UNDERGROUND IN THE BIG BATTLE. HE CAN ONLY BE BROKEN OUT BY THE MAGIC OF THE KRATER.
THAT'S WHY DAD BROKE IT INTO HUNDREDS OF PIECES ALL OVER THE WORLD. BUT HE MADE SURE HE KEPT THE LAST PIECE HIMSELF, JUST IN CASE ANYONE WAS CRAZY ENOUGH TO COLLECT THEM ALL.
PRETTY PARANOID, HUH?
OH CRAP...

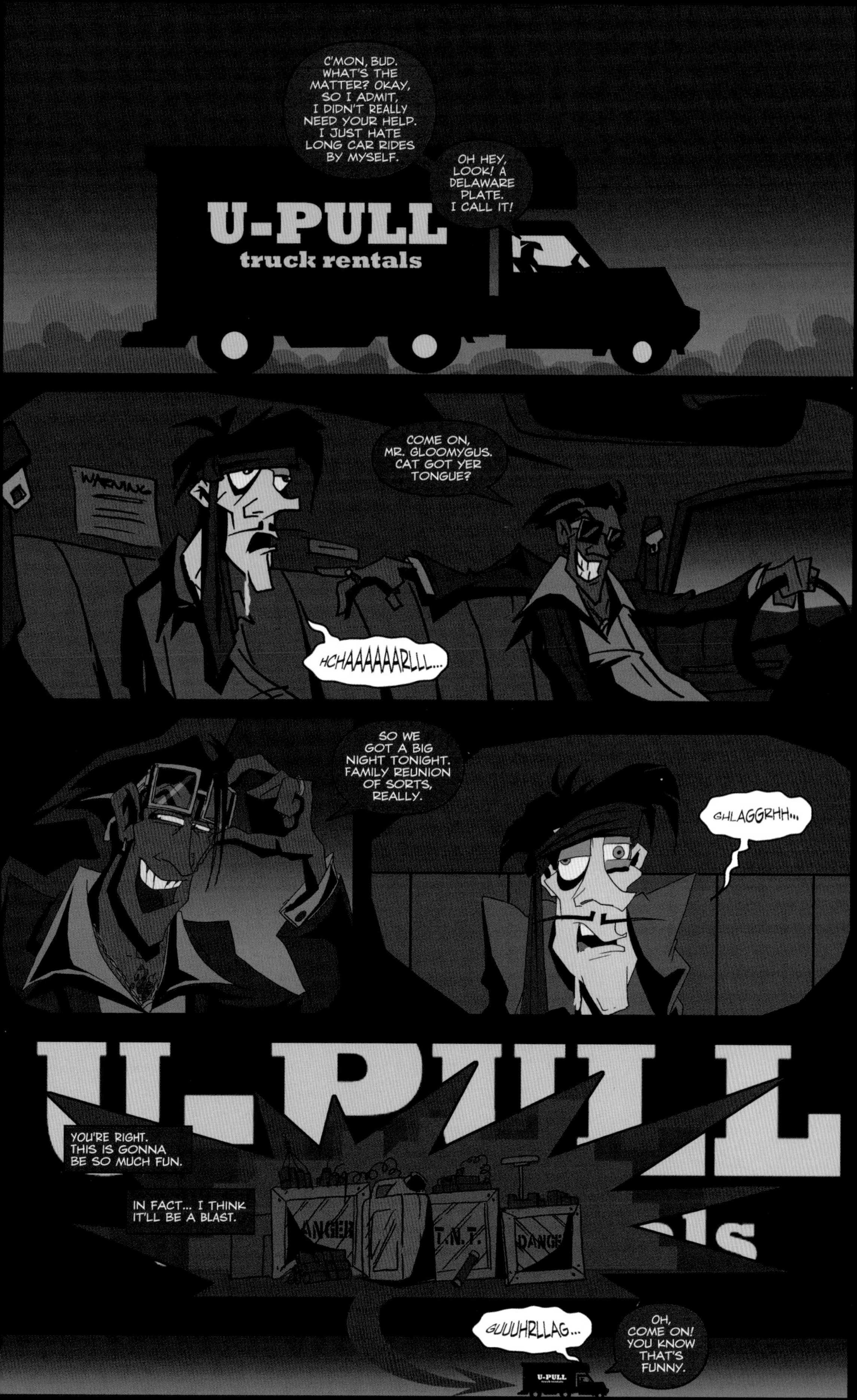
U-PULL
truck rentals
C'MON, BUD. WHAT'S THE MATTER? OKAY, SO I ADMIT, I DIDN'T REALLY NEED YOUR HELP. I JUST HATE LONG CAR RIDES BY MYSELF.
OH HEY, LOOK! A DELAWARE PLATE. I CALL IT!
COME ON, MR. GLOOMYGUS. CAT GOT YER TONGUE?
HCHAAAAAAARLLL...
SO WE GOT A BIG NIGHT TONIGHT. FAMILY REUNION OF SORTS, REALLY.
GHLAGGRHH...
YOU'RE RIGHT. THIS IS GONNA BE SO MUCH FUN.
IN FACT... I THINK IT'LL BE A BLAST.
T.N.T.
GUUUHRLLAG...
OH, COME ON! YOU KNOW THAT'S FUNNY.

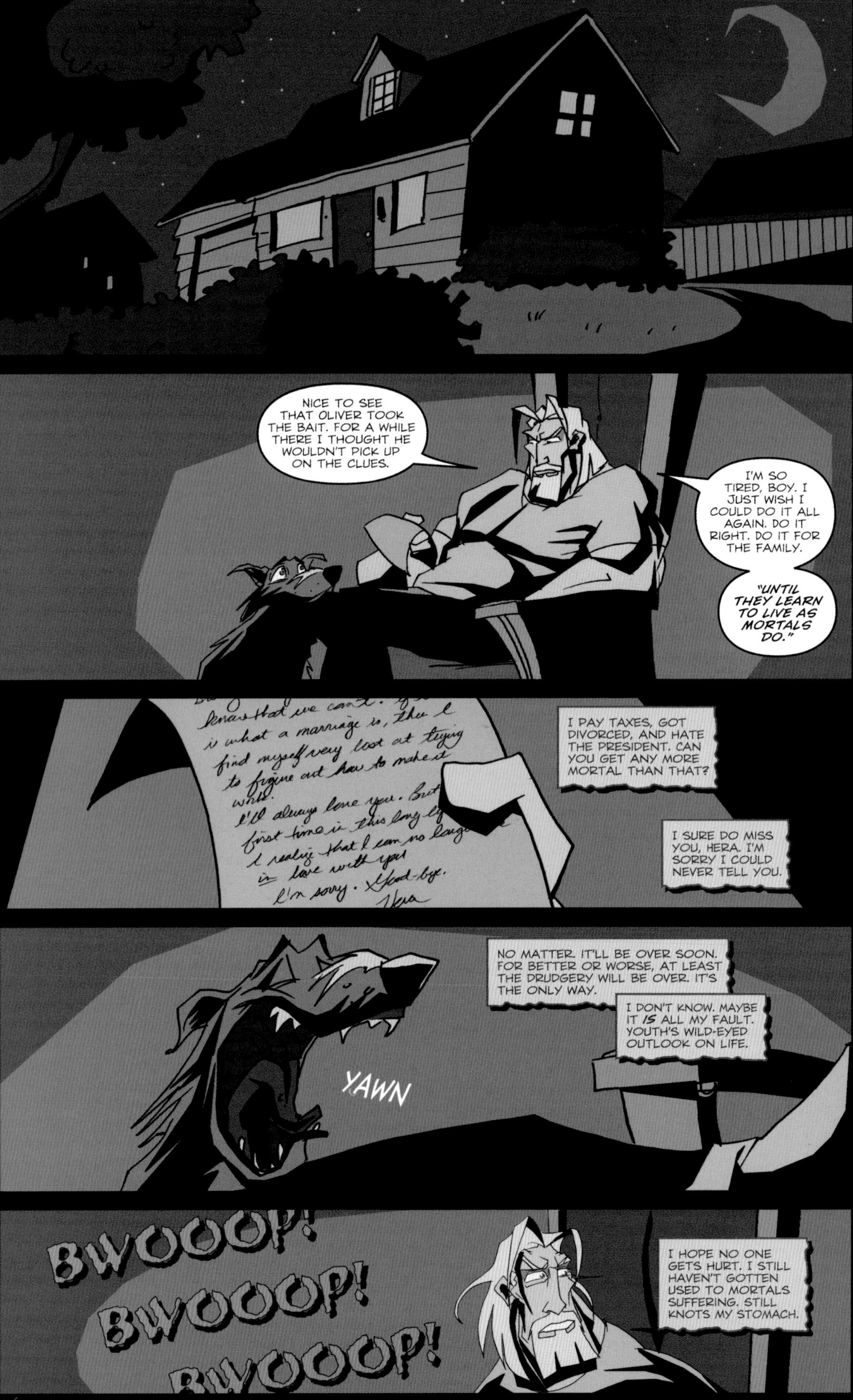
NICE TO SEE THAT OLIVER TOOK THE BAIT. FOR A WHILE THERE I THOUGHT HE WOULDN'T PICK UP ON THE CLUES.
I'M SO TIRED, BOY. I JUST WISH I COULD DO IT ALL AGAIN. DO IT RIGHT. DO IT FOR THE FAMILY.
"UNTIL THEY LEARN TO LIVE AS MORTALS DO."
is what a marriage is, then I
find myself very lost at trying
to figure out how to make it
work.
I'll always love you. But
in love with you
I'm sorry. Good-bye.
I PAY TAXES, GOT DIVORCED, AND HATE THE PRESIDENT. CAN YOU GET ANY MORE MORTAL THAN THAT?
I SURE DO MISS YOU, HERA. I'M SORRY I COULD NEVER TELL YOU.
NO MATTER. IT'LL BE OVER SOON. FOR BETTER OR WORSE, AT LEAST THE DRUDGERY WILL BE OVER. IT'S THE ONLY WAY.
I DON'T KNOW. MAYBE IT *IS* ALL MY FAULT. YOUTH'S WILD-EYED OUTLOOK ON LIFE.
YAWN
BWOOOP!
BWOOOP!
BWOOOP!
I HOPE NO ONE GETS HURT. I STILL HAVEN'T GOTTEN USED TO MORTALS SUFFERING. STILL KNOTS MY STOMACH.

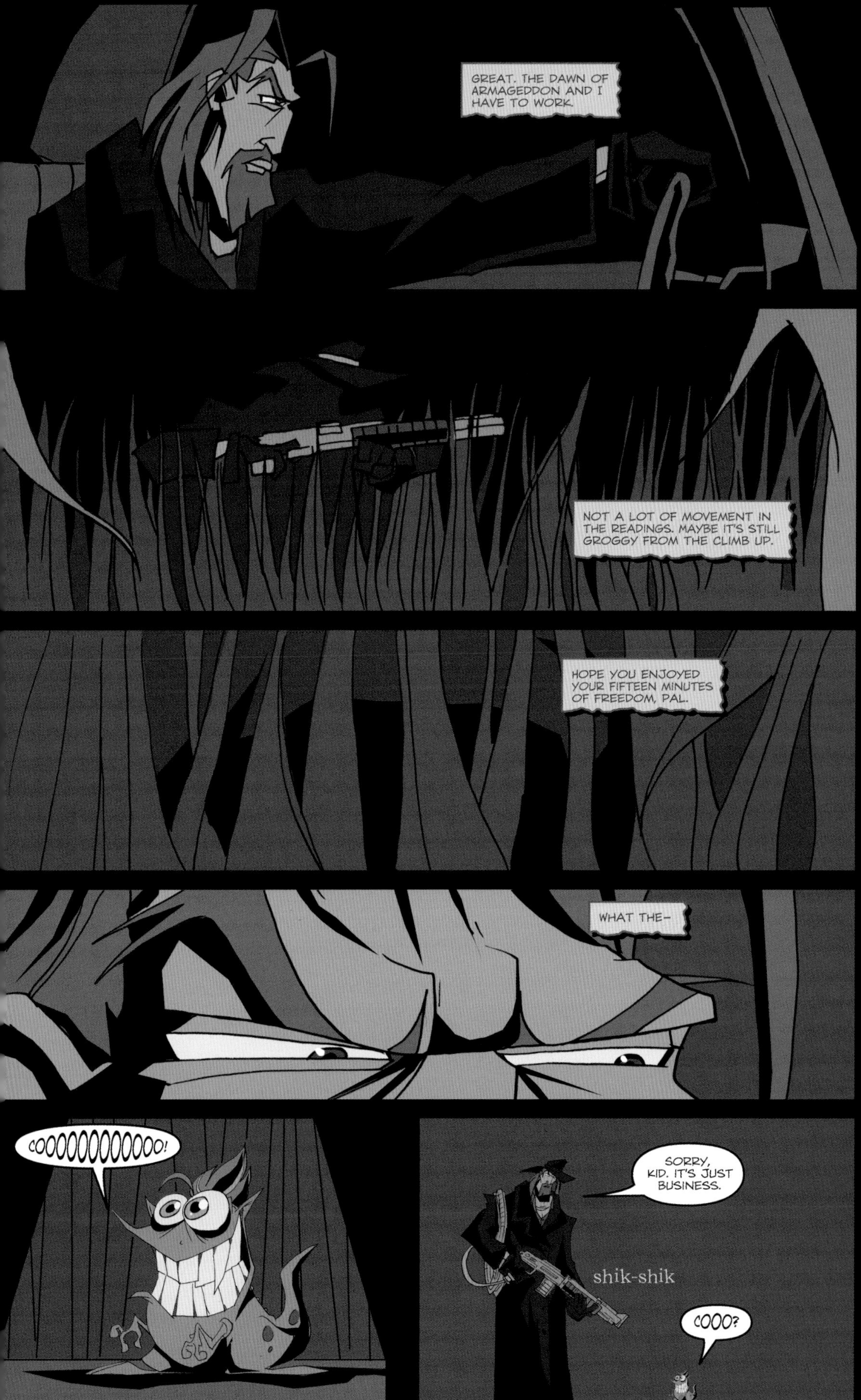
GREAT. THE DAWN OF ARMAGEDDON AND I HAVE TO WORK.
NOT A LOT OF MOVEMENT IN THE READINGS. MAYBE IT'S STILL GROGGY FROM THE CLIMB UP.
HOPE YOU ENJOYED YOUR FIFTEEN MINUTES OF FREEDOM, PAL.
WHAT THE–
COOOOOOOOOOOOO!
SORRY, KID. IT'S JUST BUSINESS.
shik-shik
COOO?

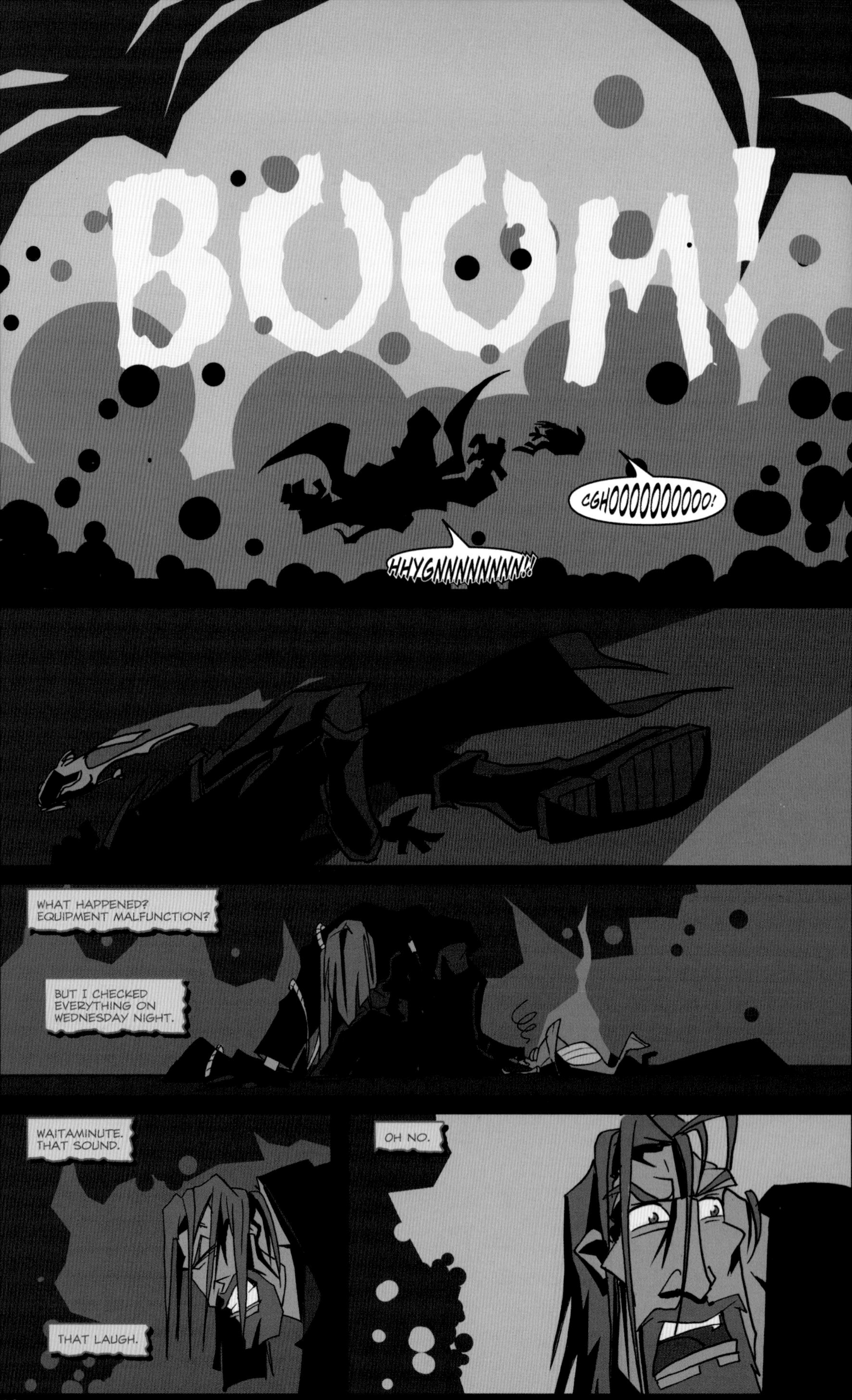
BOOM!
CGHOOOOOOOOOO!
HHYGNNNNNNNN!!
WHAT HAPPENED? EQUIPMENT MALFUNCTION?
BUT I CHECKED EVERYTHING ON WEDNESDAY NIGHT.
WAITAMINUTE. THAT SOUND.
THAT LAUGH.
OH NO.

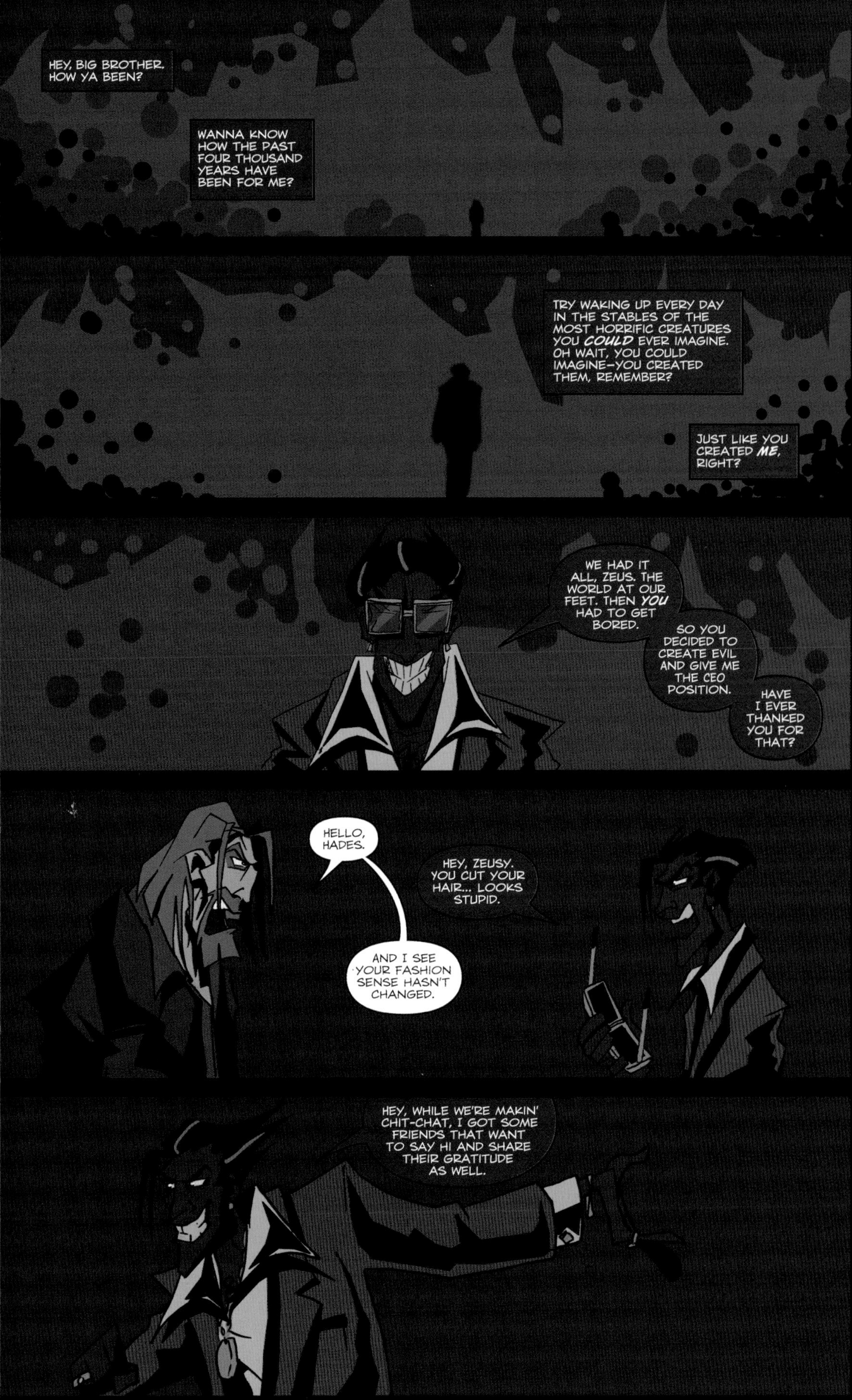
HEY, BIG BROTHER. HOW YA BEEN?
WANNA KNOW HOW THE PAST FOUR THOUSAND YEARS HAVE BEEN FOR ME?
TRY WAKING UP EVERY DAY IN THE STABLES OF THE MOST HORRIFIC CREATURES YOU *COULD* EVER IMAGINE. OH WAIT, YOU COULD IMAGINE–YOU CREATED THEM, REMEMBER?
JUST LIKE YOU CREATED *ME*, RIGHT?
WE HAD IT ALL, ZEUS. THE WORLD AT OUR FEET. THEN *YOU* HAD TO GET BORED.
SO YOU DECIDED TO CREATE EVIL AND GIVE ME THE CEO POSITION.
HAVE I EVER THANKED YOU FOR THAT?
HELLO, HADES.
HEY, ZEUSY. YOU CUT YOUR HAIR... LOOKS STUPID.
AND I SEE YOUR FASHION SENSE HASN'T CHANGED.
HEY, WHILE WE'RE MAKIN' CHIT-CHAT, I GOT SOME FRIENDS THAT WANT TO SAY HI AND SHARE THEIR GRATITUDE AS WELL.

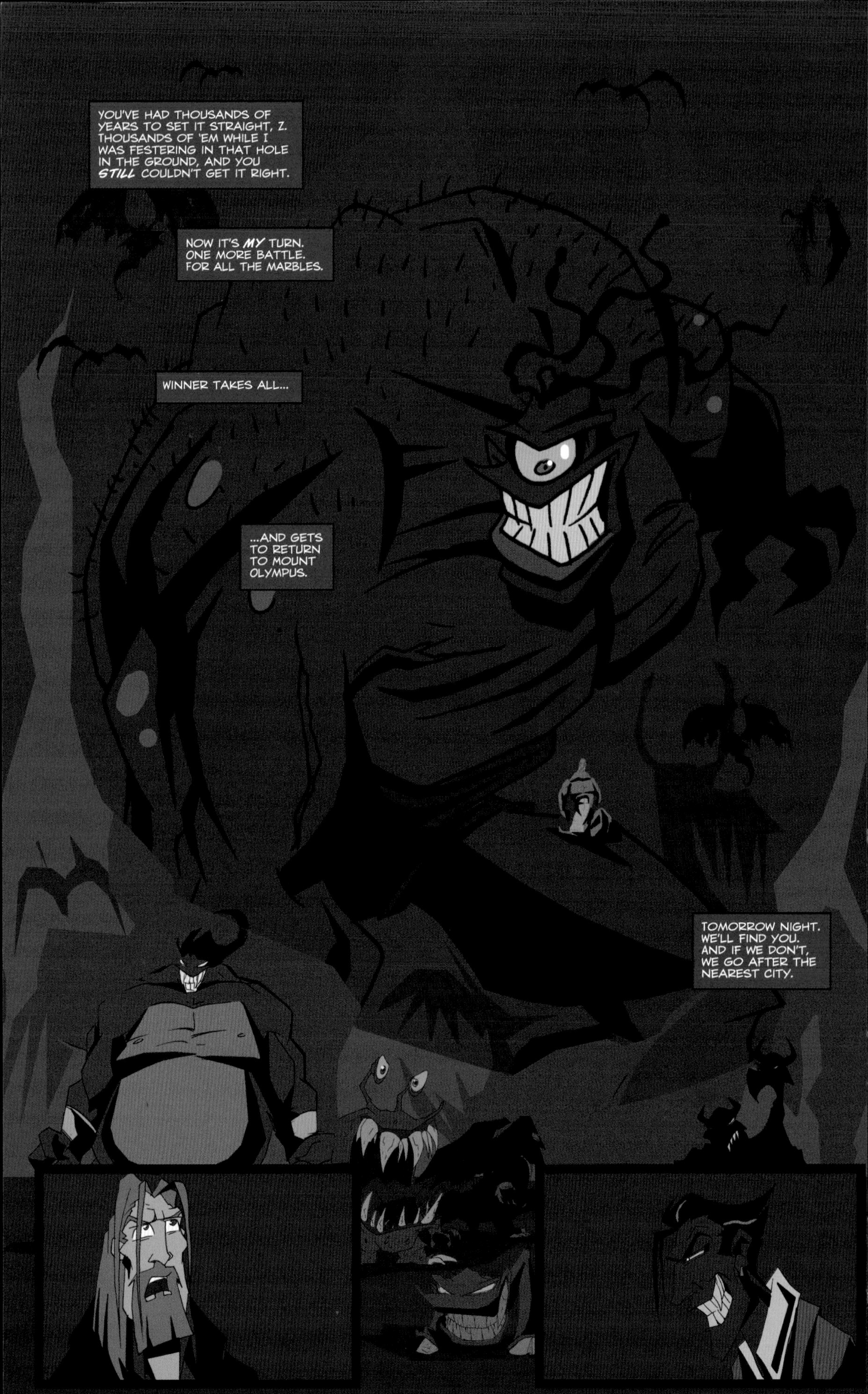
YOU'VE HAD THOUSANDS OF YEARS TO SET IT STRAIGHT, Z. THOUSANDS OF 'EM WHILE I WAS FESTERING IN THAT HOLE IN THE GROUND, AND YOU STILL COULDN'T GET IT RIGHT.
NOW IT'S MY TURN. ONE MORE BATTLE. FOR ALL THE MARBLES.
WINNER TAKES ALL...
...AND GETS TO RETURN TO MOUNT OLYMPUS.
TOMORROW NIGHT. WE'LL FIND YOU. AND IF WE DON'T, WE GO AFTER THE NEAREST CITY.

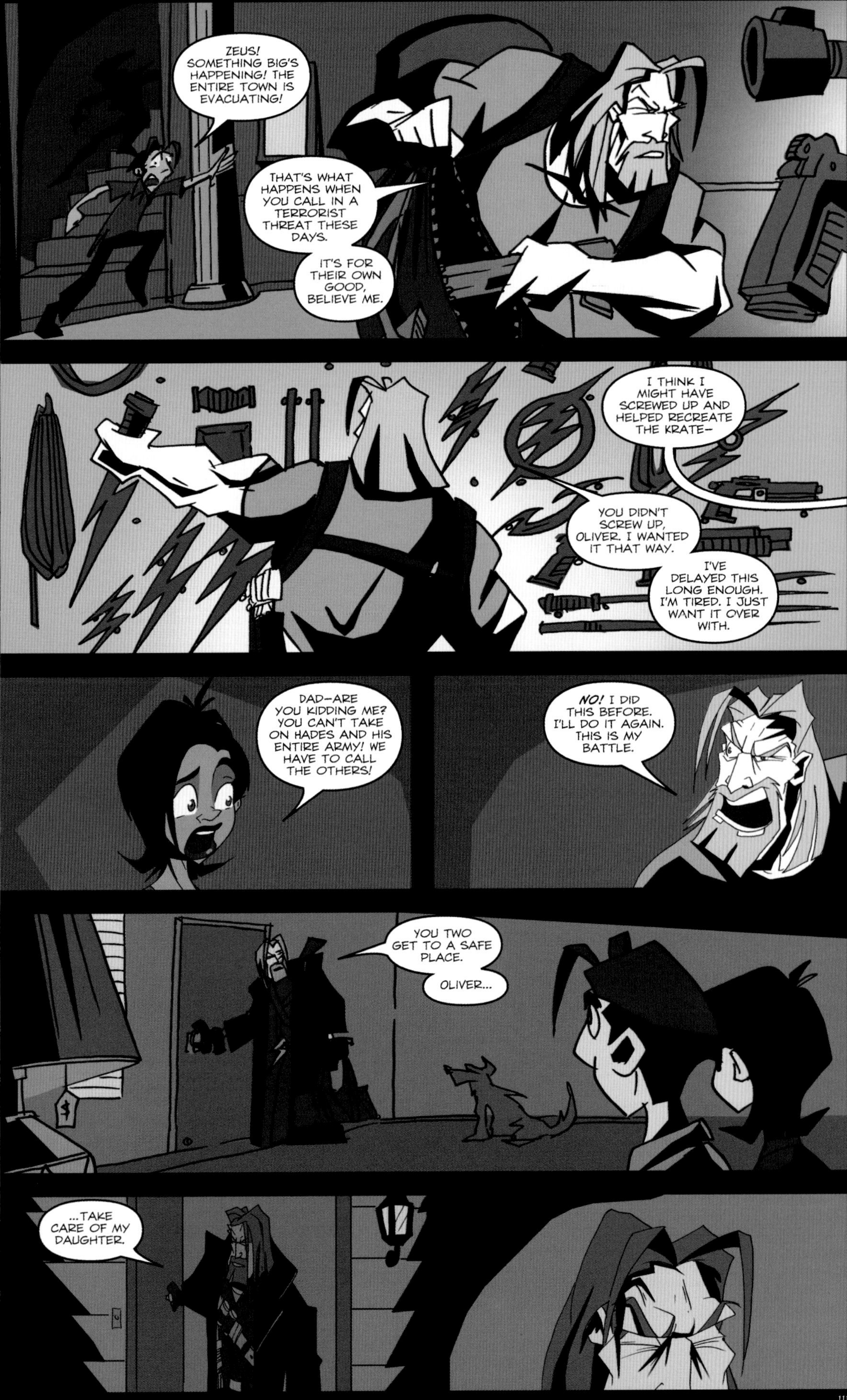
ZEUS! SOMETHING BIG'S HAPPENING! THE ENTIRE TOWN IS EVACUATING!
THAT'S WHAT HAPPENS WHEN YOU CALL IN A TERRORIST THREAT THESE DAYS.
IT'S FOR THEIR OWN GOOD, BELIEVE ME.
I THINK I MIGHT HAVE SCREWED UP AND HELPED RECREATE THE KRATE–
YOU DIDN'T SCREW UP, OLIVER. I WANTED IT THAT WAY.
I'VE DELAYED THIS LONG ENOUGH. I'M TIRED. I JUST WANT IT OVER WITH.
DAD–ARE YOU KIDDING ME? YOU CAN'T TAKE ON HADES AND HIS ENTIRE ARMY! WE HAVE TO CALL THE OTHERS!
NO! I DID THIS BEFORE. I'LL DO IT AGAIN. THIS IS MY BATTLE.
YOU TWO GET TO A SAFE PLACE.
OLIVER...
...TAKE CARE OF MY DAUGHTER.

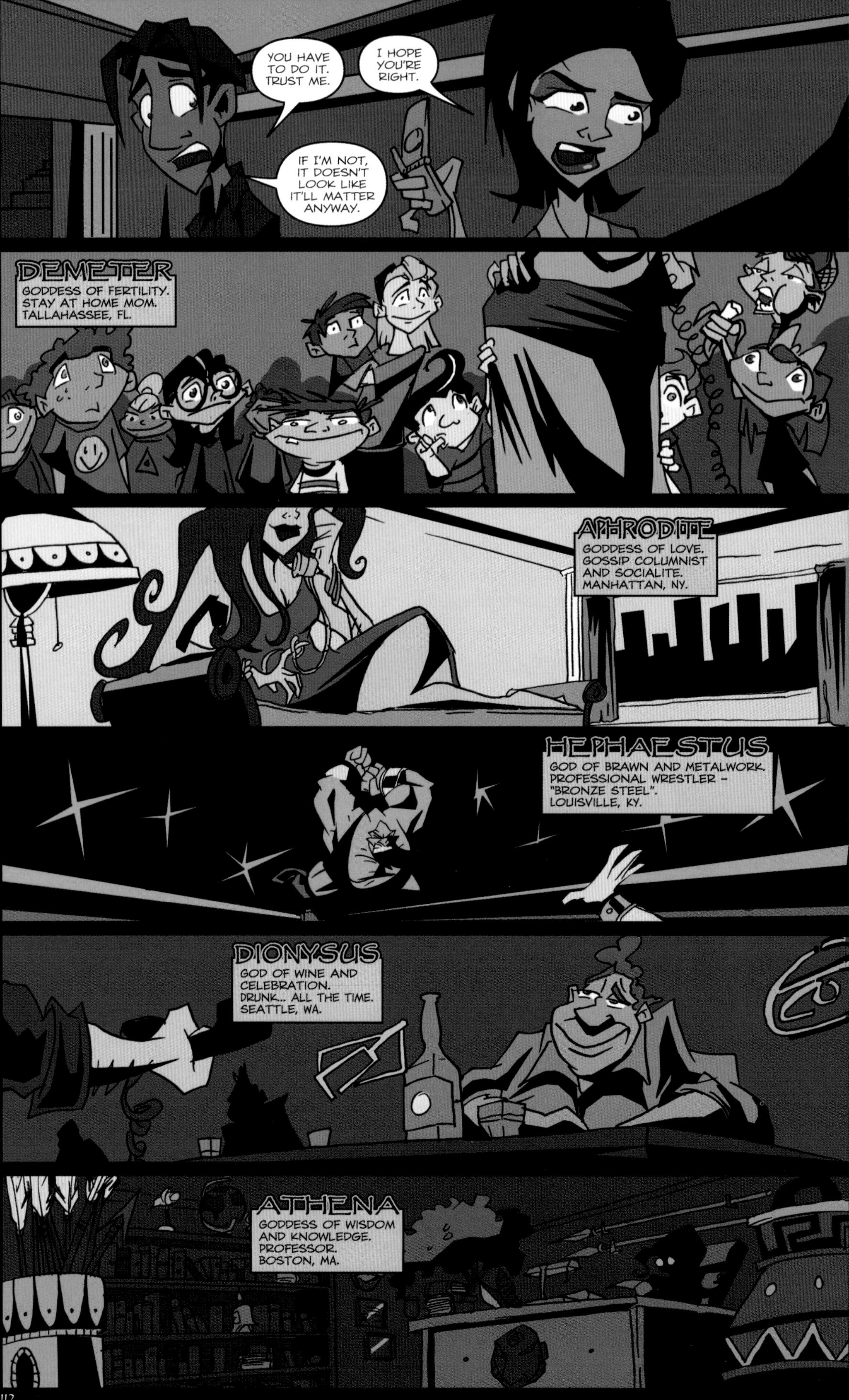
YOU HAVE TO DO IT. TRUST ME.
I HOPE YOU'RE RIGHT.
IF I'M NOT, IT DOESN'T LOOK LIKE IT'LL MATTER ANYWAY.
DEMETER
GODDESS OF FERTILITY. STAY AT HOME MOM. TALLAHASSEE, FL.
APHRODITE
GODDESS OF LOVE. GOSSIP COLUMNIST AND SOCIALITE. MANHATTAN, NY.
HEPHAESTUS
GOD OF BRAWN AND METALWORK. PROFESSIONAL WRESTLER - "BRONZE STEEL". LOUISVILLE, KY.
DIONYSUS
GOD OF WINE AND CELEBRATION. DRUNK... ALL THE TIME. SEATTLE, WA.
ATHENA
GODDESS OF WISDOM AND KNOWLEDGE. PROFESSOR. BOSTON, MA.

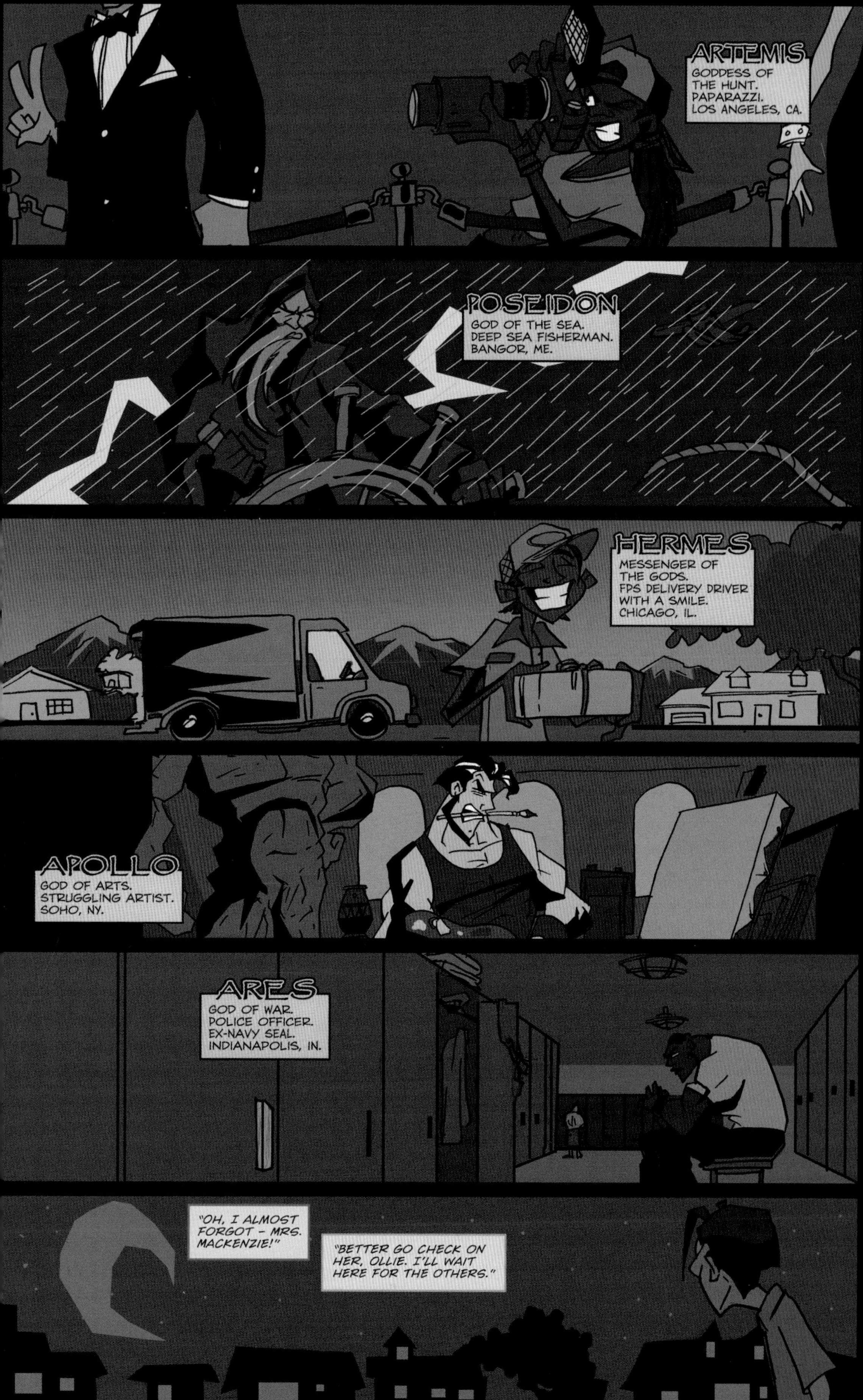
ARTEMIS
GODDESS OF THE HUNT. PAPARAZZI. LOS ANGELES, CA.
POSEIDON
GOD OF THE SEA. DEEP SEA FISHERMAN. BANGOR, ME.
HERMES
MESSENGER OF THE GODS. FPS DELIVERY DRIVER WITH A SMILE. CHICAGO, IL.
APOLLO
GOD OF ARTS. STRUGGLING ARTIST. SOHO, NY.
ARES
GOD OF WAR. POLICE OFFICER. EX-NAVY SEAL. INDIANAPOLIS, IN.
"OH, I ALMOST FORGOT – MRS. MACKENZIE!"
"BETTER GO CHECK ON HER, OLLIE. I'LL WAIT HERE FOR THE OTHERS."

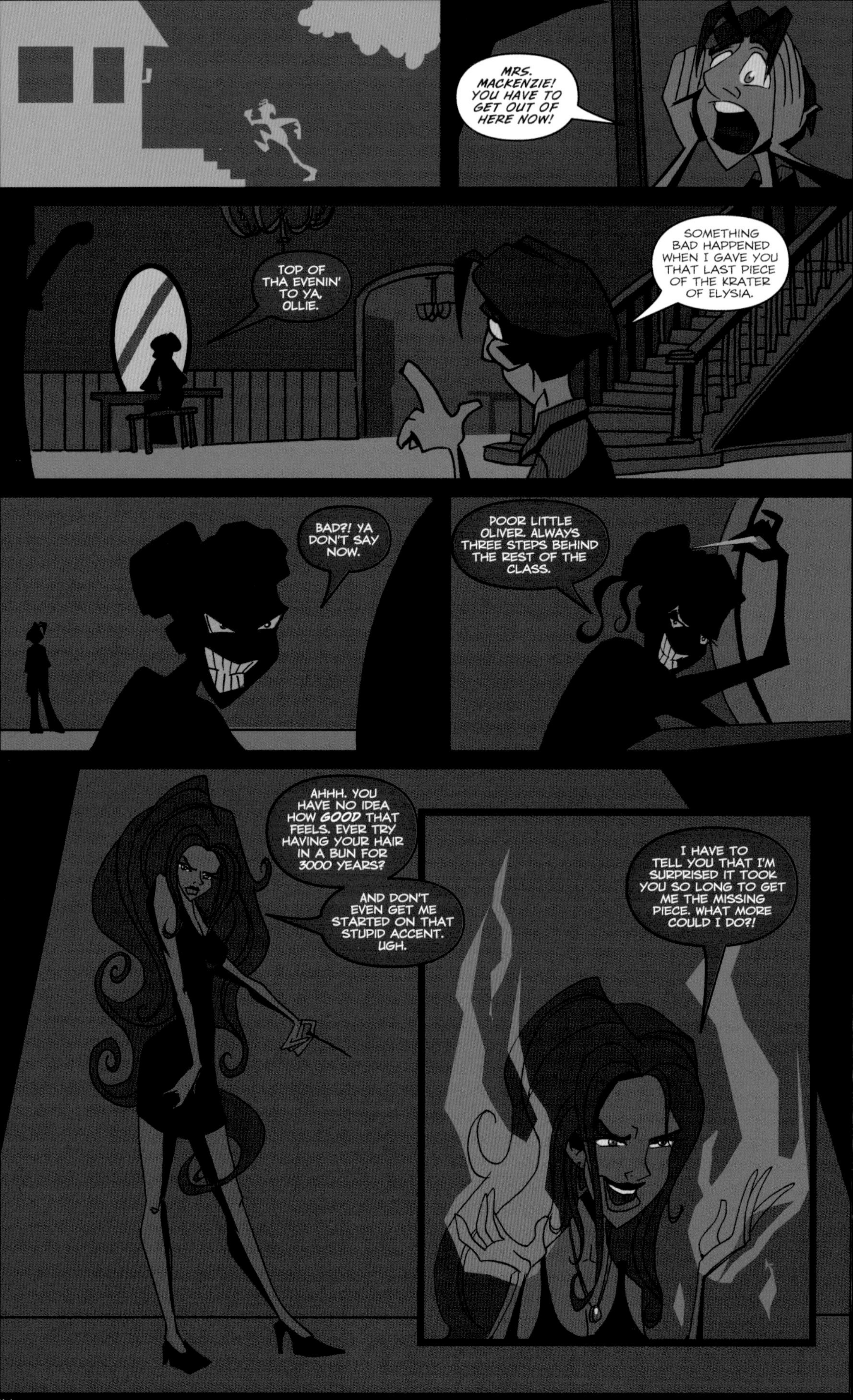
MRS. MACKENZIE! YOU HAVE TO GET OUT OF HERE NOW!
TOP OF THA EVENIN' TO YA, OLLIE.
SOMETHING BAD HAPPENED WHEN I GAVE YOU THAT LAST PIECE OF THE KRATER OF ELYSIA.
BAD?! YA DON'T SAY NOW.
POOR LITTLE OLIVER. ALWAYS THREE STEPS BEHIND THE REST OF THE CLASS.
AHHH. YOU HAVE NO IDEA HOW GOOD THAT FEELS. EVER TRY HAVING YOUR HAIR IN A BUN FOR 3000 YEARS?
AND DON'T EVEN GET ME STARTED ON THAT STUPID ACCENT. UGH.
I HAVE TO TELL YOU THAT I'M SURPRISED IT TOOK YOU SO LONG TO GET ME THE MISSING PIECE. WHAT MORE COULD I DO?!

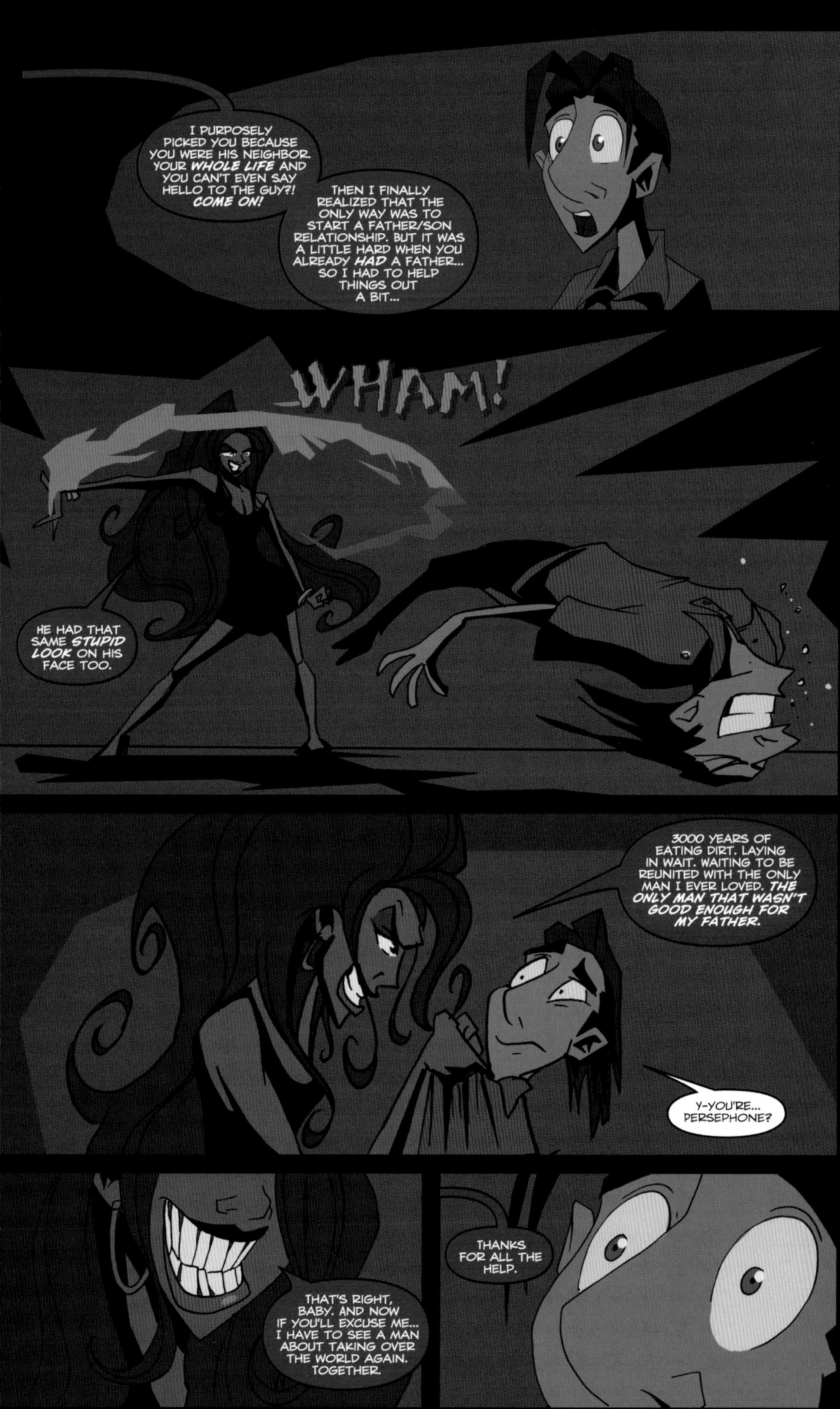

I PURPOSELY PICKED YOU BECAUSE YOU WERE HIS NEIGHBOR. YOUR WHOLE LIFE AND YOU CAN'T EVEN SAY HELLO TO THE GUY?! COME ON!
THEN I FINALLY REALIZED THAT THE ONLY WAY WAS TO START A FATHER/SON RELATIONSHIP. BUT IT WAS A LITTLE HARD WHEN YOU ALREADY HAD A FATHER... SO I HAD TO HELP THINGS OUT A BIT...
WHAM!
HE HAD THAT SAME STUPID LOOK ON HIS FACE TOO.
3000 YEARS OF EATING DIRT. LAYING IN WAIT. WAITING TO BE REUNITED WITH THE ONLY MAN I EVER LOVED. THE ONLY MAN THAT WASN'T GOOD ENOUGH FOR MY FATHER.
Y-YOU'RE... PERSEPHONE?
THAT'S RIGHT, BABY. AND NOW IF YOU'LL EXCUSE ME... I HAVE TO SEE A MAN ABOUT TAKING OVER THE WORLD AGAIN. TOGETHER.
THANKS FOR ALL THE HELP.

BACK AT ZEUS'S PALACE, THE GODS PREPARE TO LEAVE.

THALIA'S A SWEET KID, BUT THERE AIN'T NO WAY I'M STICKIN' AROUND TO LISTEN TO SOME PENCIL NECK WAX ON ABOUT MY BROTHER.

YOU'RE RIGHT. LET'S GO.

"UM... EXCUSE ME?"

OH! UH... UHHHH.

STOP BEING SUCH BULLIES. LISTEN TO WHAT THE KID HAS TO SAY. AND NO SLEEPING, DIONYSUS!

UHH...

SWALLOWING HARD, OLIVER AWKWARDLY BEGINS THE SPEECH OF HIS LIFE...

"UM... YOU DON'T KNOW ME. BUT TRUST ME WHEN I SAY I KNOW ALL OF *YOU*. I HAVE NO IDEA WHAT YOUR LIVES MUST HAVE BEEN LIKE SINCE YOU LEFT OLYMPUS, NOR WOULD I ASSUME TO.

"BUT I KNOW A LOT OF YOU HAVE PROBLEMS WITH YOUR DAD... SOME OF YOU WITH YOUR BROTHER. I'M NOT HERE TO DENY THAT.

"BUT ONE THING YOU *CAN'T* DENY IS FAMILY. FAMILY IS THE ONE BOND THAT CAN'T BE BROKEN BY TIME, DISTANCE, OR EMOTION. IT EXISTS WITHOUT EFFORT ON THE MOST BASIC OF LEVELS... EVEN WHEN YOU'RE A FAMILY LIKE THIS.

"ZEUS NEEDS YOUR HELP... EVEN IF HE CAN'T SAY SO. SO I'M GOING TO SAY IT FOR HIM. I'VE GOTTEN TO KNOW HIM OVER THE PAST FEW MONTHS, AND I'M PROUD TO CALL HIM MY FRIEND. I CAN ONLY IMAGINE HOW PROUD I WOULD BE TO CALL HIM FAMILY.

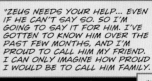

"HELP US... PLEASE."

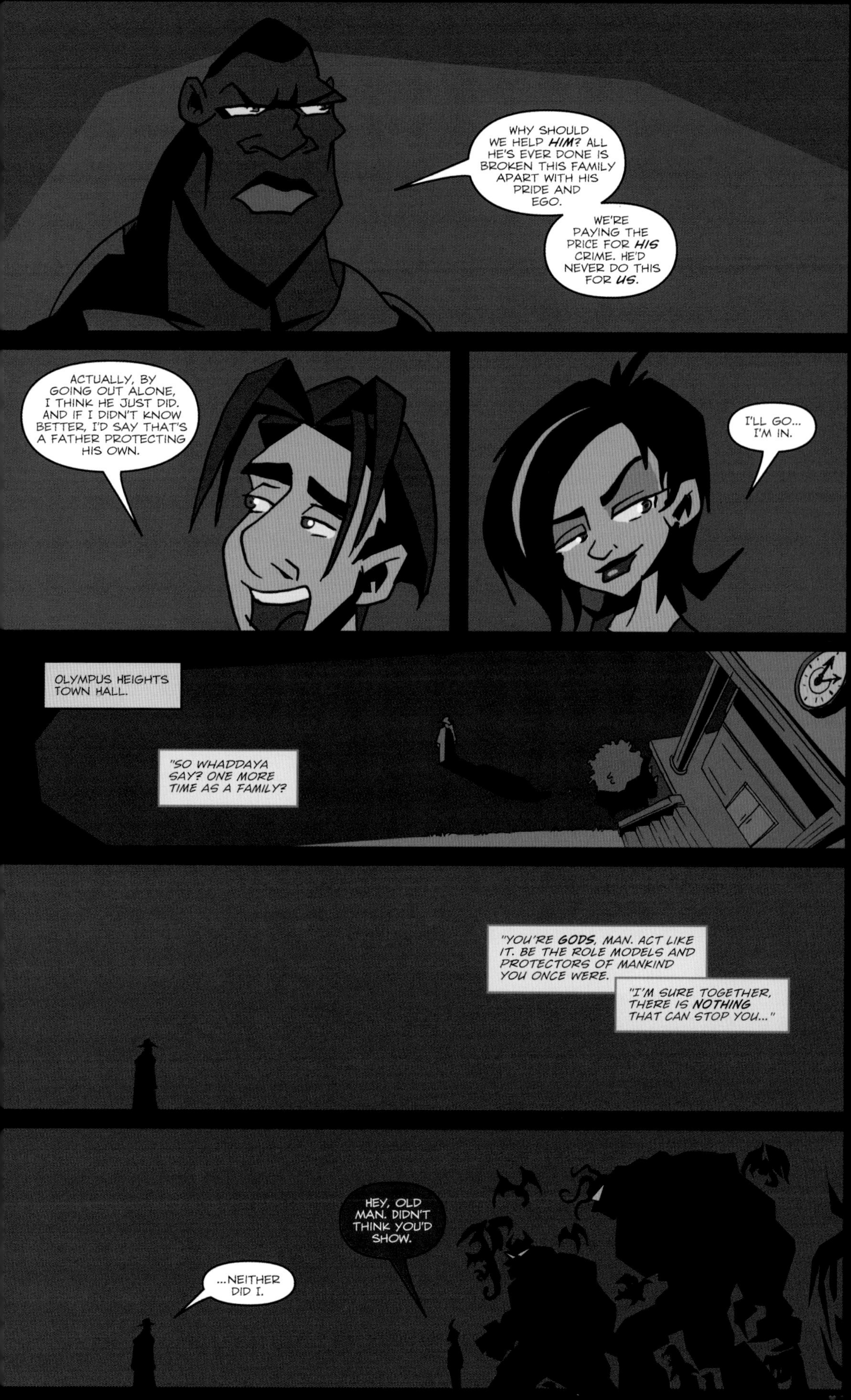
WHY SHOULD WE HELP HIM? ALL HE'S EVER DONE IS BROKEN THIS FAMILY APART WITH HIS PRIDE AND EGO.
WE'RE PAYING THE PRICE FOR HIS CRIME. HE'D NEVER DO THIS FOR US.
ACTUALLY, BY GOING OUT ALONE, I THINK HE JUST DID. AND IF I DIDN'T KNOW BETTER, I'D SAY THAT'S A FATHER PROTECTING HIS OWN.
I'LL GO... I'M IN.
OLYMPUS HEIGHTS TOWN HALL.
"SO WHADDAYA SAY? ONE MORE TIME AS A FAMILY?
"YOU'RE GODS, MAN. ACT LIKE IT. BE THE ROLE MODELS AND PROTECTORS OF MANKIND YOU ONCE WERE.
"I'M SURE TOGETHER, THERE IS NOTHING THAT CAN STOP YOU..."
HEY, OLD MAN. DIDN'T THINK YOU'D SHOW.
...NEITHER DID I.

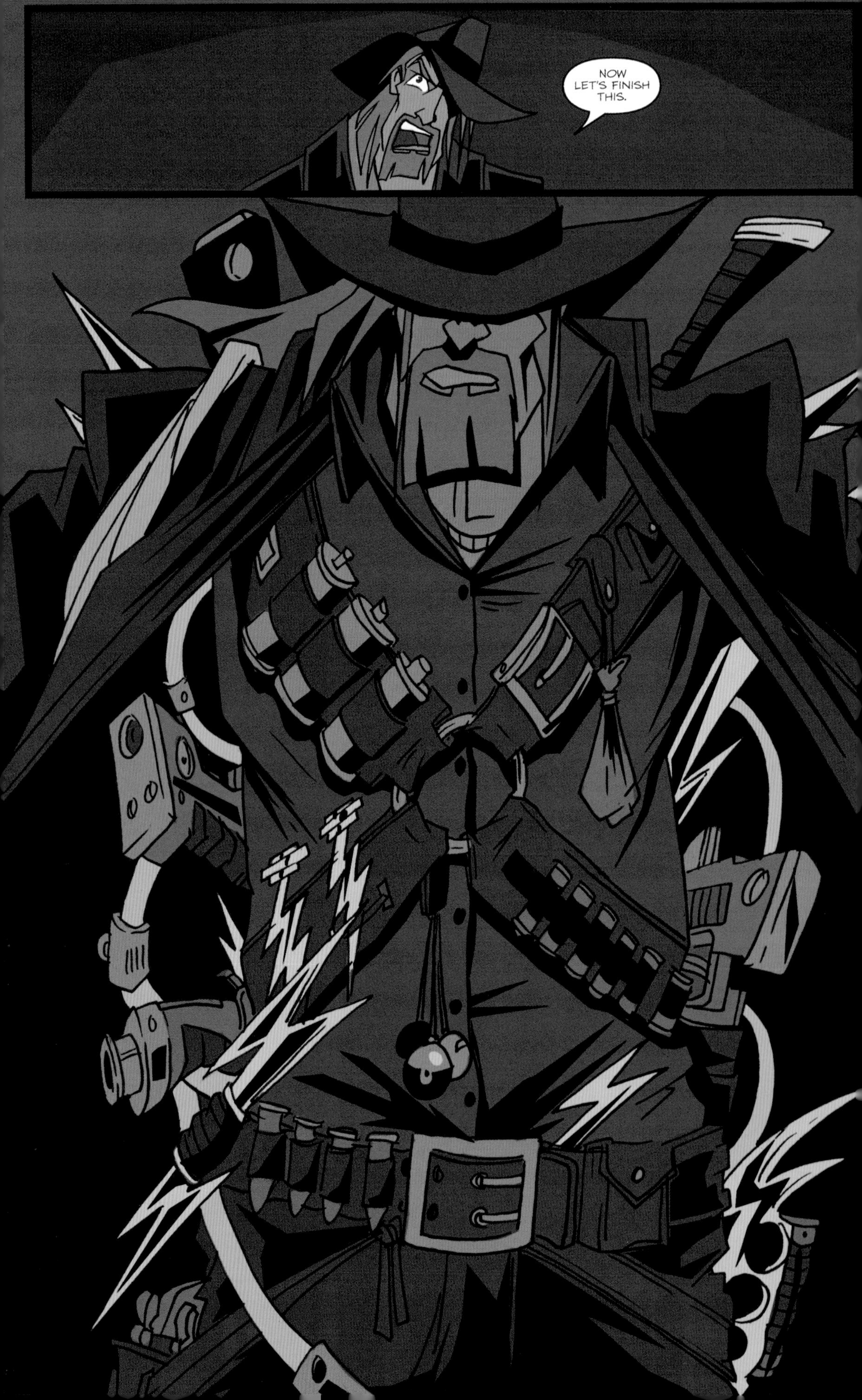
NOW LET'S FINISH THIS.

LT. GUS McSWEENY (ret.)

Gus woke up earlier than normal that Thursday morning. Couldn't really say why, but he just had one of those feelings. Either today was going to be a great day, or he would wish he had never woken up. Not that he hadn't experienced his share of those days before, mind you.

Back in Korea and even as an advisor in the Persian Gulf, Gus developed a keen sense of knowing how the day would turn out. Maybe it was the way the sun peeked in through his bedroom blinds, or the tiny slit in his Army issue pitch tent.

Was it the sounds of nature? Or maybe it was something deeper, more mysterious. Anyone who thought that, though, obviously never truly knew Angus McSweeny. Gus was a man of principle, a no-nonsense man who quickly dismissed his men's claims that the land was possessed by evil spirits when they couldn't see the enemy coming. Gus was the type of iron man who would stay on point for three days straight, just to show his men that "spirits" had nothing to do with it, and that it was merely caused by their own lack of attentiveness.

Today just felt like one of those days.

Like the day when he knew his wife Petula had given birth to their first son, even though he was stationed halfway around the world; like the day when his platoon was ambushed and he managed to crawl with his shrapnel-ridden left leg into a hollow tree stump and wait out the enemy.

And a day like today. A day where he would realize that maybe, after seventy-two years of life, he hadn't seen it all...

After finally appeasing his wife and leaving the service, breakfast had become a series of rituals. Half a grapefruit, a dozen vitamin supplements, and a short glass of non-fat milk. And though

Petula never noticed Gus's gagging on the food each day, she would always read off the day's menu to him, just to drive home the point that he was going to one day get his cholesterol in check.

With the same peck and hug each day, she would send Gus off to work with his metal lunch pail filled with carrot sticks, a piece of rye bread, and a juice box with some godforsaken cartoon character on it. Gus never understood the juice box. Maybe she thought it made him feel young. Little did she know that Gus's inability to figure out the appeal of a talking sea sponge actually made him feel older. And just like he did every day, Gus emptied the box's contents into a trash bin, anxiously awaiting the abundance of fatty foods in the brown bag that Oliver brought every day.

It was business as usual at the Olympus Heights Museum that day except that Mrs. Mackenzie, Oliver, and that Seymour putz weren't anywhere to be found. So Gus decided to leave the doors locked until someone came in that could show the visitors around. But just as it had been for the past eight years of Gus's employment, the only visitor was a family in a minivan needing a pee break. Gus naturally obliged, as always.

The sun eventually set. Gus held his stomach as it groaned in protest of missing Oliver's mother's cooking. He could sure go for some brightly colored purple liquid with 10% real juice in it right about now. Heck, even a carrot stick.

Suddenly, the room began to shake! Intermittent large poundings dropped a few works of art onto the floor. Gus frantically looked around to see what was happening. He ran to the large upstairs window, beside the Mythology Wing. Gus's jaw dropped. He squinted to see better, but didn't believe his eyes. If he didn't know better, he'd swear he saw the silhouettes of giant HEADS moving along the horizon, above the tree line!

Petula. He had to get home.

Gus spun around only to find himself face-to-face with a strange sight... dozens of the museum statues coming to life! One by one, their stone shells fell to the floor as the snarling and drooling monsters spied Gus, alone and silhouetted by the large window behind him.

Gus's panic soon turned into a grin. He remembered the hunting shotgun he had in his locker. He remembered the tire iron by the loading dock. And he remembered being a young soldier again.

He made the dash to the stairs, headed for his locker. The monsters sprang into action, clamoring after him. It would be struggle. Not only because of his bum left leg, but also due to the fact that he was so dang hungry.

...and thus, Gus vowed to eat his carrots and drink his unnaturally colored juice every day.

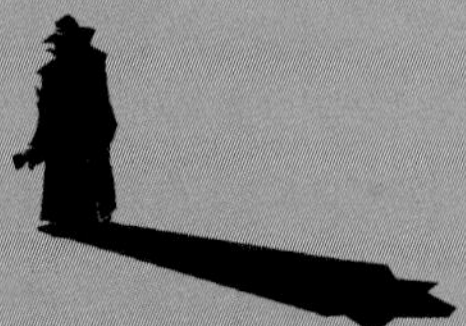

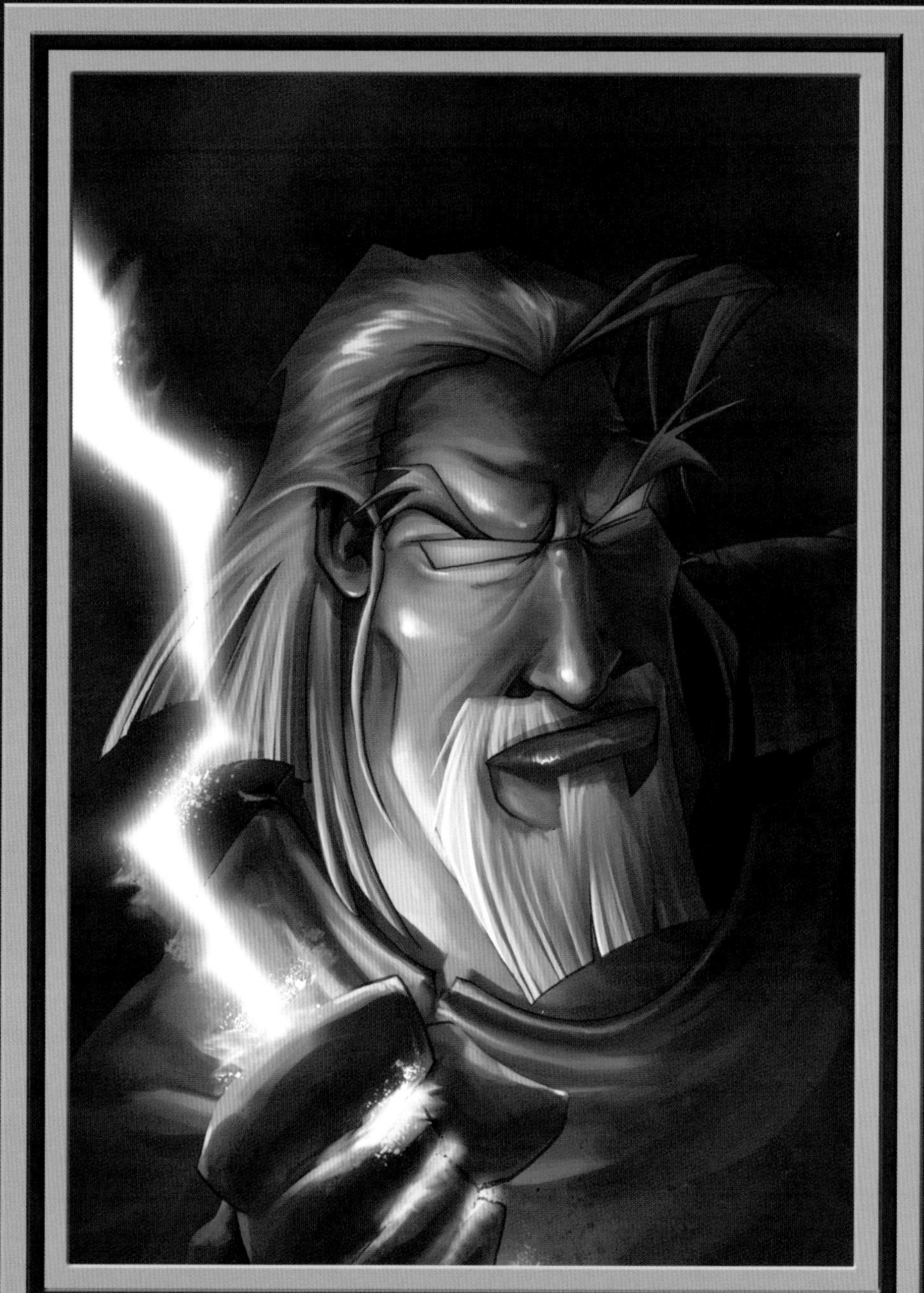

Chapter Five

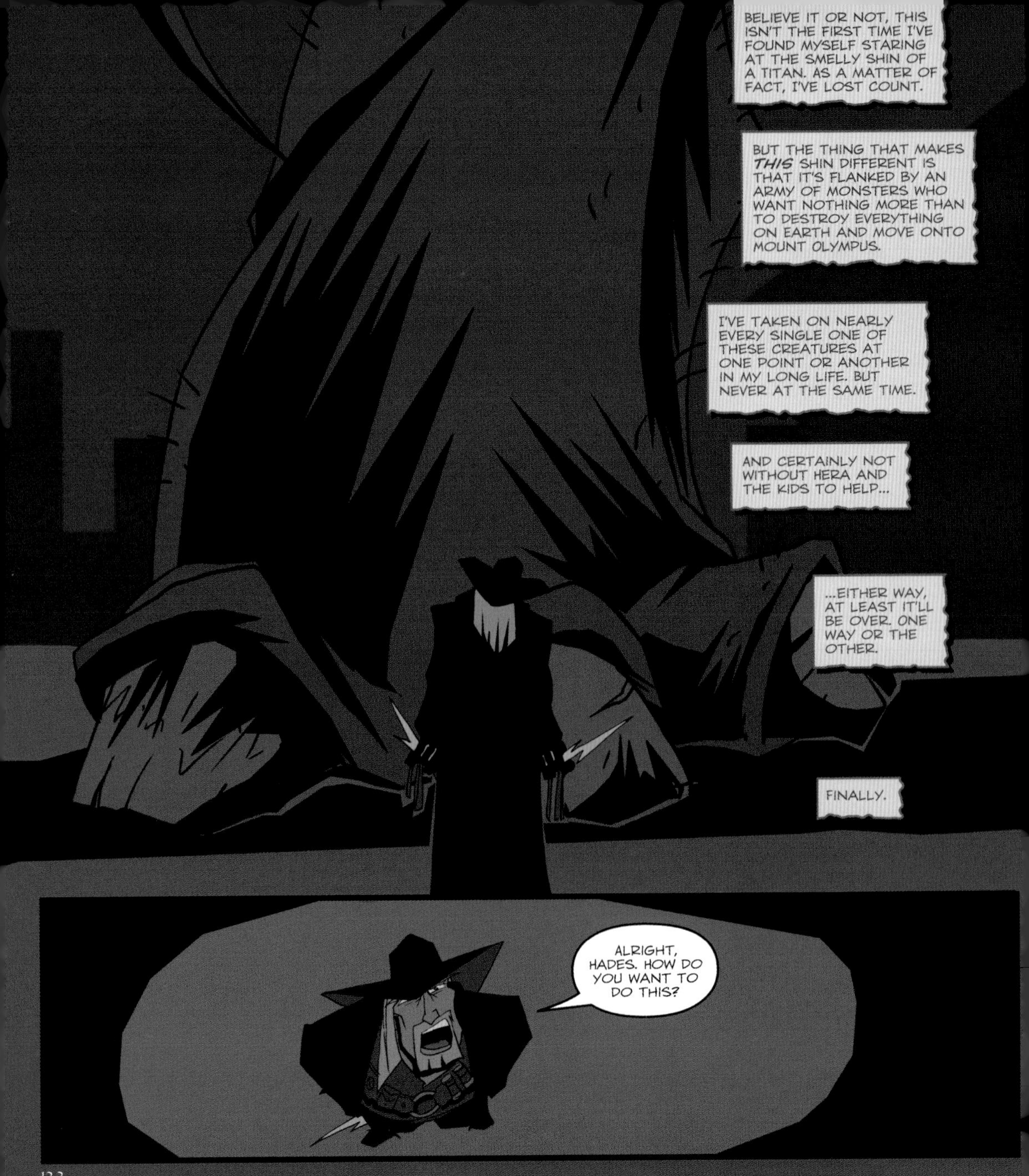
BELIEVE IT OR NOT, THIS ISN'T THE FIRST TIME I'VE FOUND MYSELF STARING AT THE SMELLY SHIN OF A TITAN. AS A MATTER OF FACT, I'VE LOST COUNT.
BUT THE THING THAT MAKES *THIS* SHIN DIFFERENT IS THAT IT'S FLANKED BY AN ARMY OF MONSTERS WHO WANT NOTHING MORE THAN TO DESTROY EVERYTHING ON EARTH AND MOVE ONTO MOUNT OLYMPUS.
I'VE TAKEN ON NEARLY EVERY SINGLE ONE OF THESE CREATURES AT ONE POINT OR ANOTHER IN MY LONG LIFE. BUT NEVER AT THE SAME TIME.
AND CERTAINLY NOT WITHOUT HERA AND THE KIDS TO HELP...
...EITHER WAY, AT LEAST IT'LL BE OVER. ONE WAY OR THE OTHER.
FINALLY.
ALRIGHT, HADES. HOW DO YOU WANT TO DO THIS?

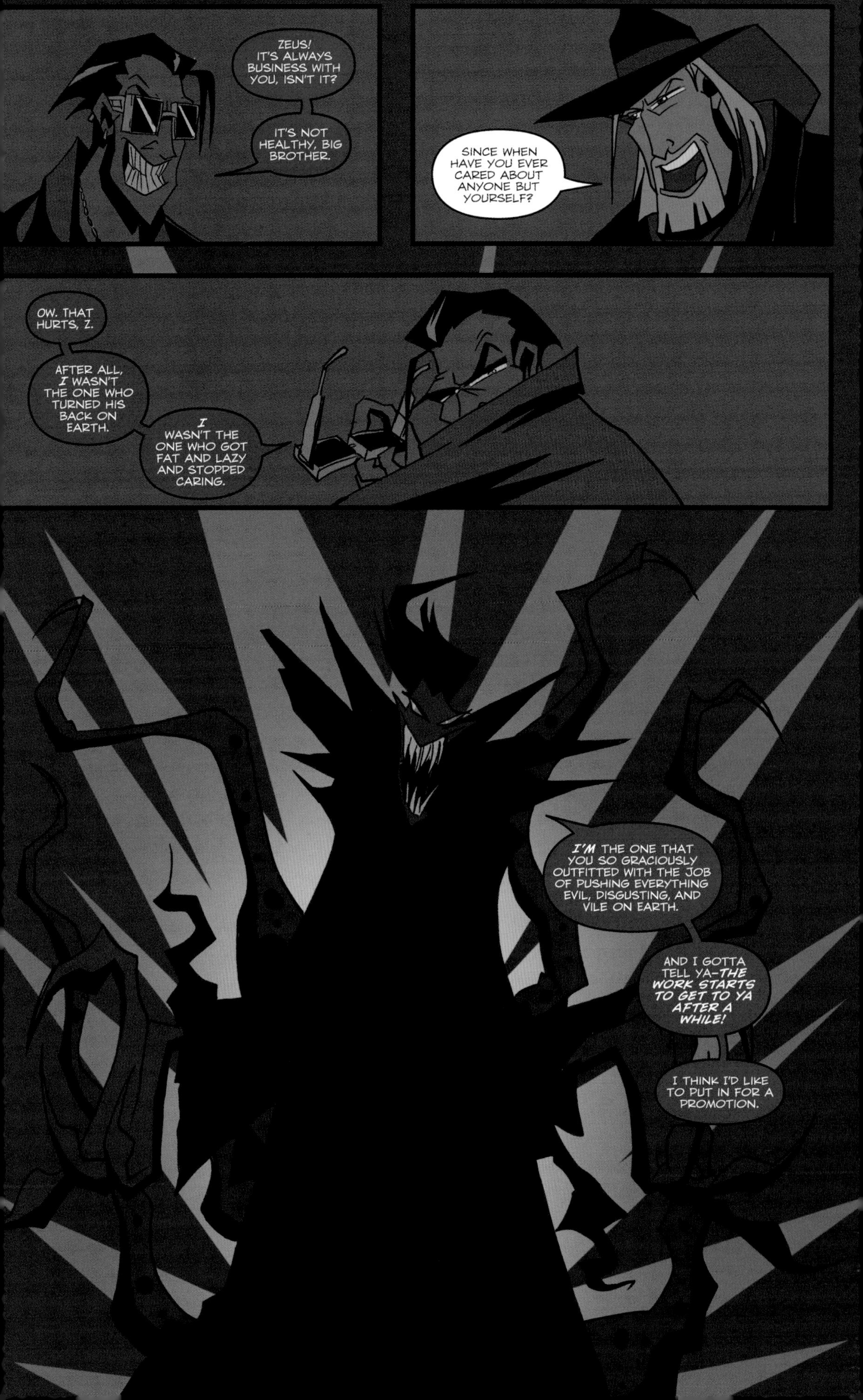
ZEUS! IT'S ALWAYS BUSINESS WITH YOU, ISN'T IT?
IT'S NOT HEALTHY, BIG BROTHER.
SINCE WHEN HAVE YOU EVER CARED ABOUT ANYONE BUT YOURSELF?
OW. THAT HURTS, Z.
AFTER ALL, *I* WASN'T THE ONE WHO TURNED HIS BACK ON EARTH.
I WASN'T THE ONE WHO GOT FAT AND LAZY AND STOPPED CARING.
I'M THE ONE THAT YOU SO GRACIOUSLY OUTFITTED WITH THE JOB OF PUSHING EVERYTHING EVIL, DISGUSTING, AND VILE ON EARTH.
AND I GOTTA TELL YA--*THE WORK STARTS TO GET TO YA AFTER A WHILE!*
I THINK I'D LIKE TO PUT IN FOR A PROMOTION.

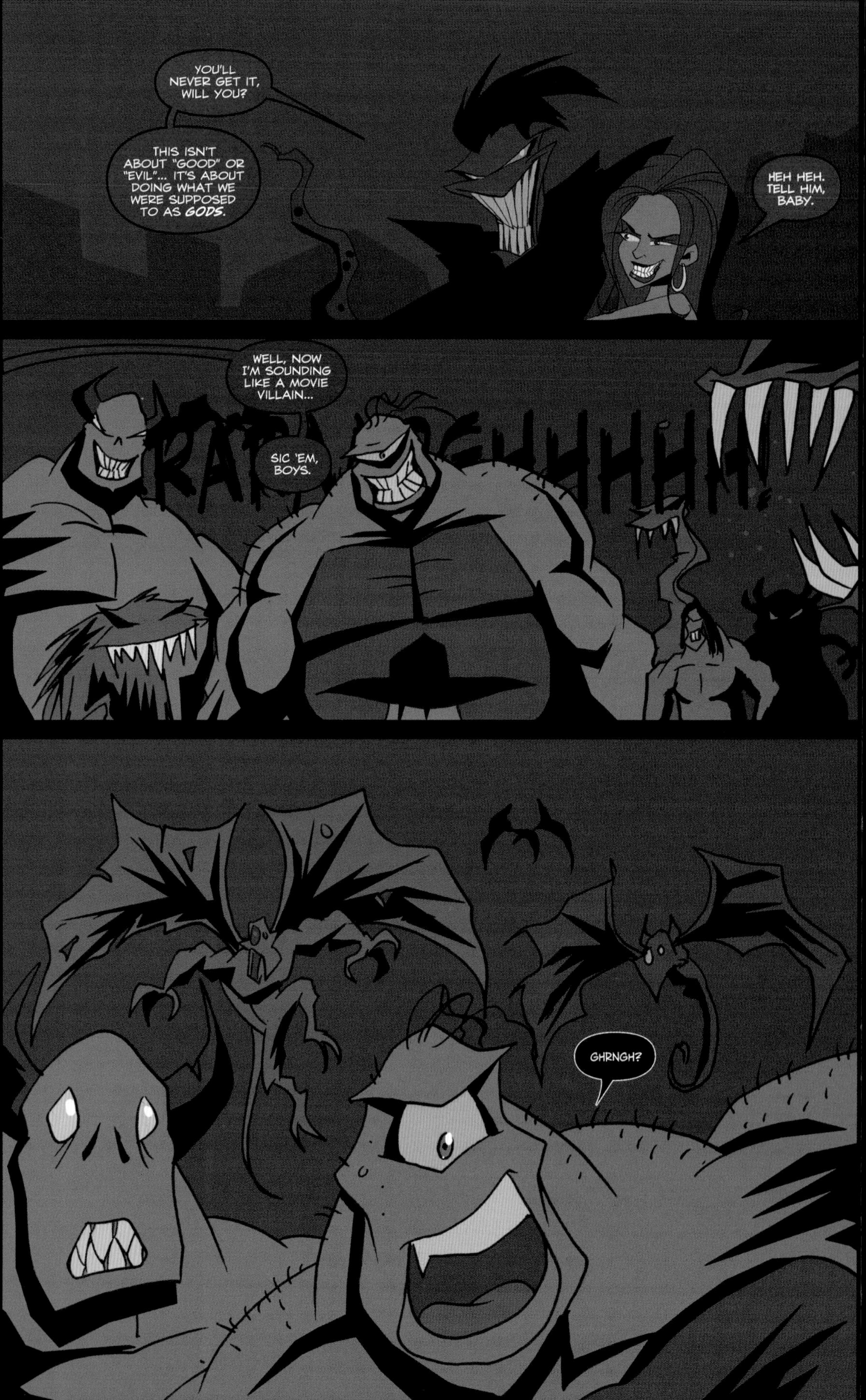
YOU'LL NEVER GET IT, WILL YOU?
THIS ISN'T ABOUT "GOOD" OR "EVIL"... IT'S ABOUT DOING WHAT WE WERE SUPPOSED TO AS GODS.
HEH HEH. TELL HIM, BABY.
WELL, NOW I'M SOUNDING LIKE A MOVIE VILLAIN...
SIC 'EM, BOYS.
GHRNGH?

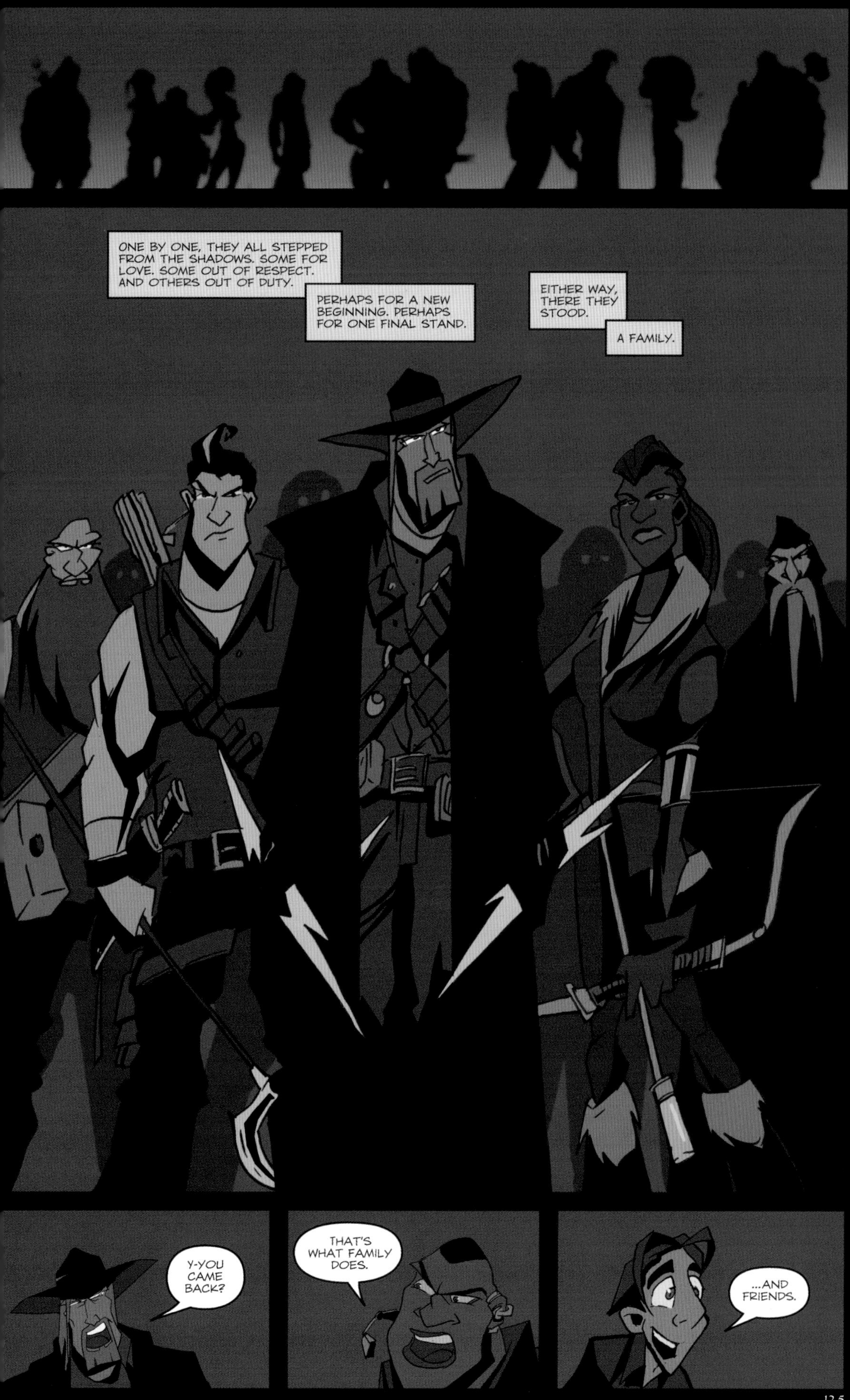

ONE BY ONE, THEY ALL STEPPED FROM THE SHADOWS. SOME FOR LOVE. SOME OUT OF RESPECT. AND OTHERS OUT OF DUTY.
PERHAPS FOR A NEW BEGINNING. PERHAPS FOR ONE FINAL STAND.
EITHER WAY, THERE THEY STOOD.
A FAMILY.
Y-YOU CAME BACK?
THAT'S WHAT FAMILY DOES.
...AND FRIENDS.

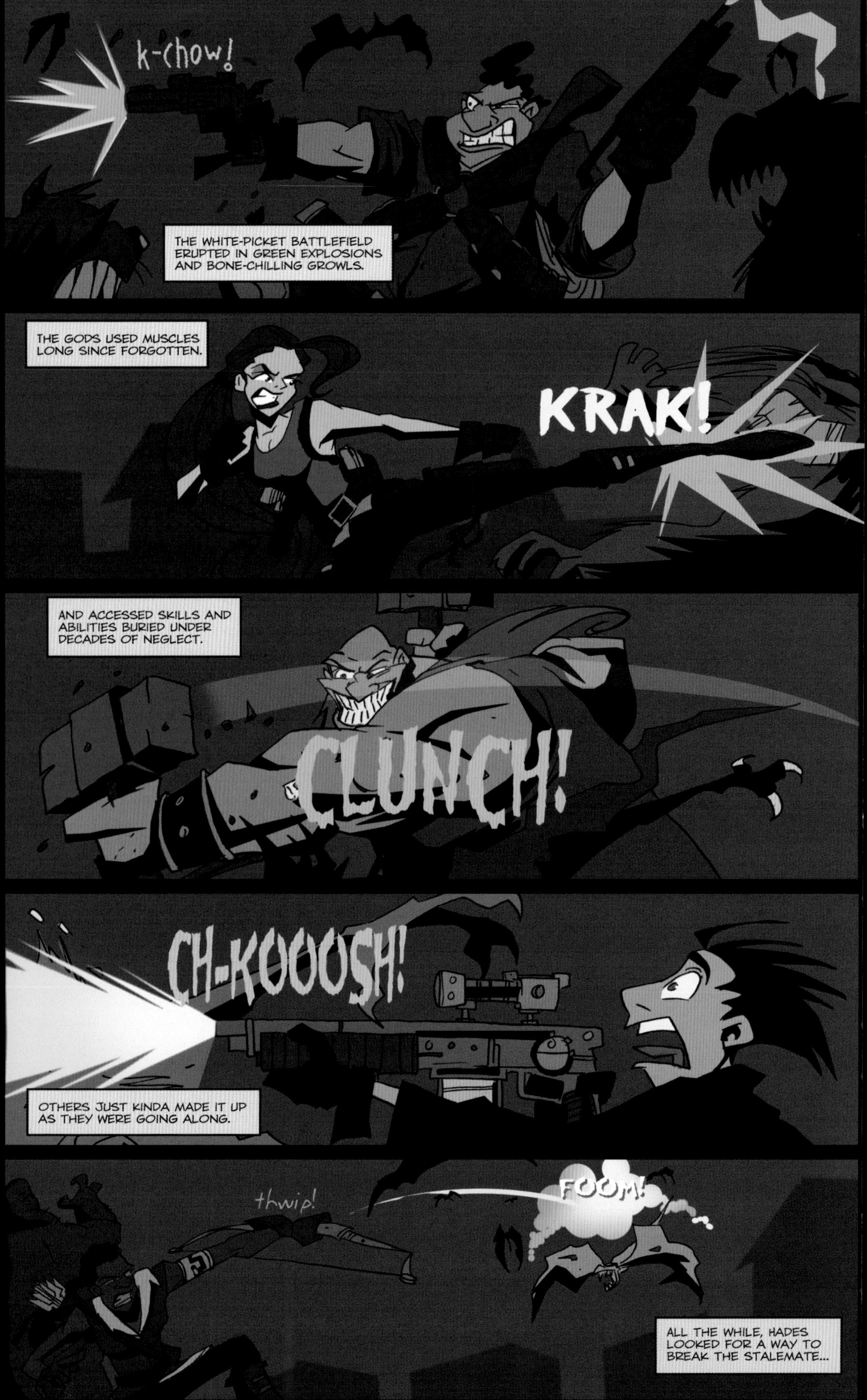
k-chow!
THE WHITE-PICKET BATTLEFIELD ERUPTED IN GREEN EXPLOSIONS AND BONE-CHILLING GROWLS.
THE GODS USED MUSCLES LONG SINCE FORGOTTEN.
KRAK!
AND ACCESSED SKILLS AND ABILITIES BURIED UNDER DECADES OF NEGLECT.
CLUNCH!
CH-KOOOSH!
OTHERS JUST KINDA MADE IT UP AS THEY WERE GOING ALONG.
thwip!
FOOM!
ALL THE WHILE, HADES LOOKED FOR A WAY TO BREAK THE STALEMATE...

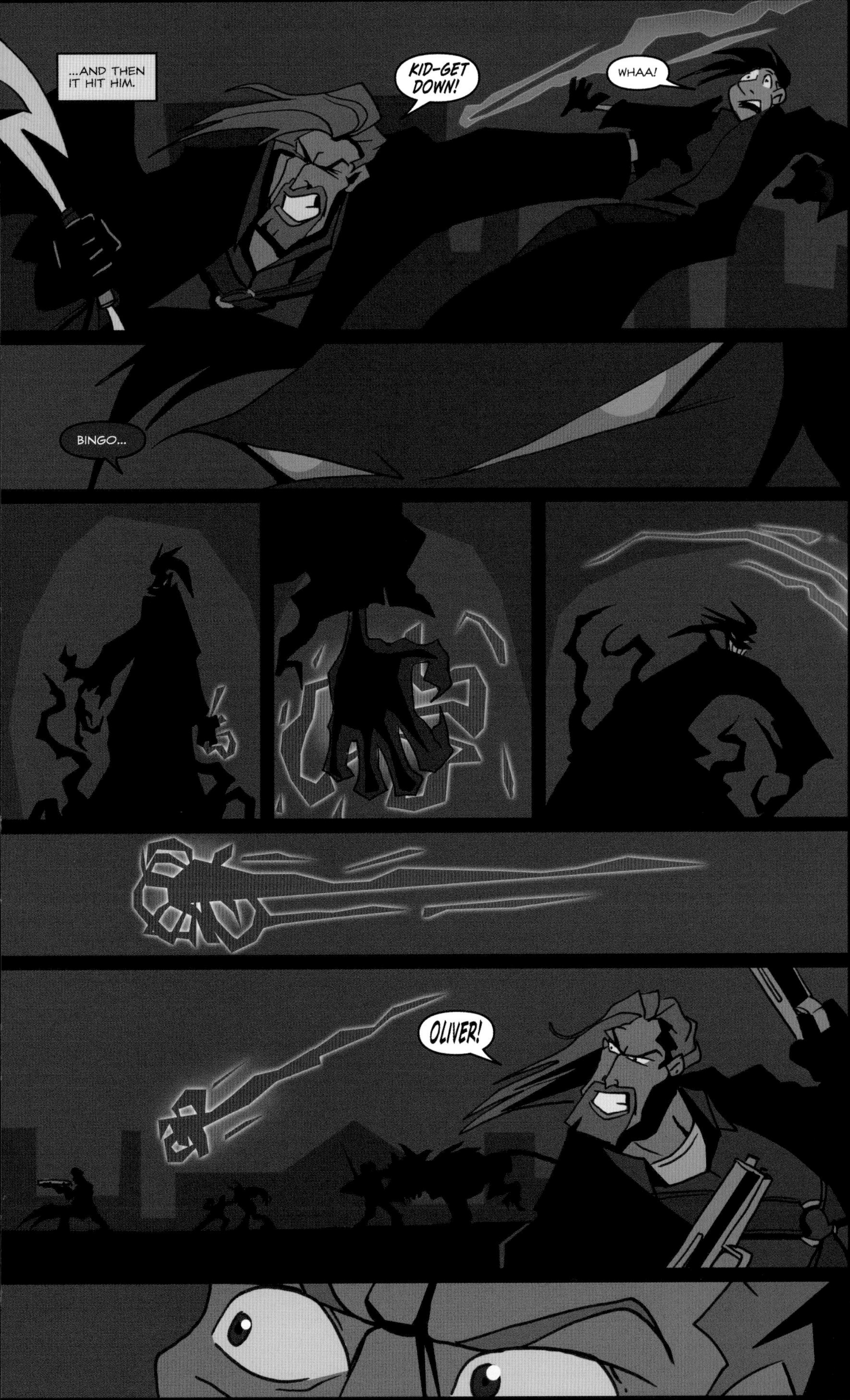
...AND THEN IT HIT HIM.
KID-GET DOWN!
WHAA!
BINGO...
OLIVER!

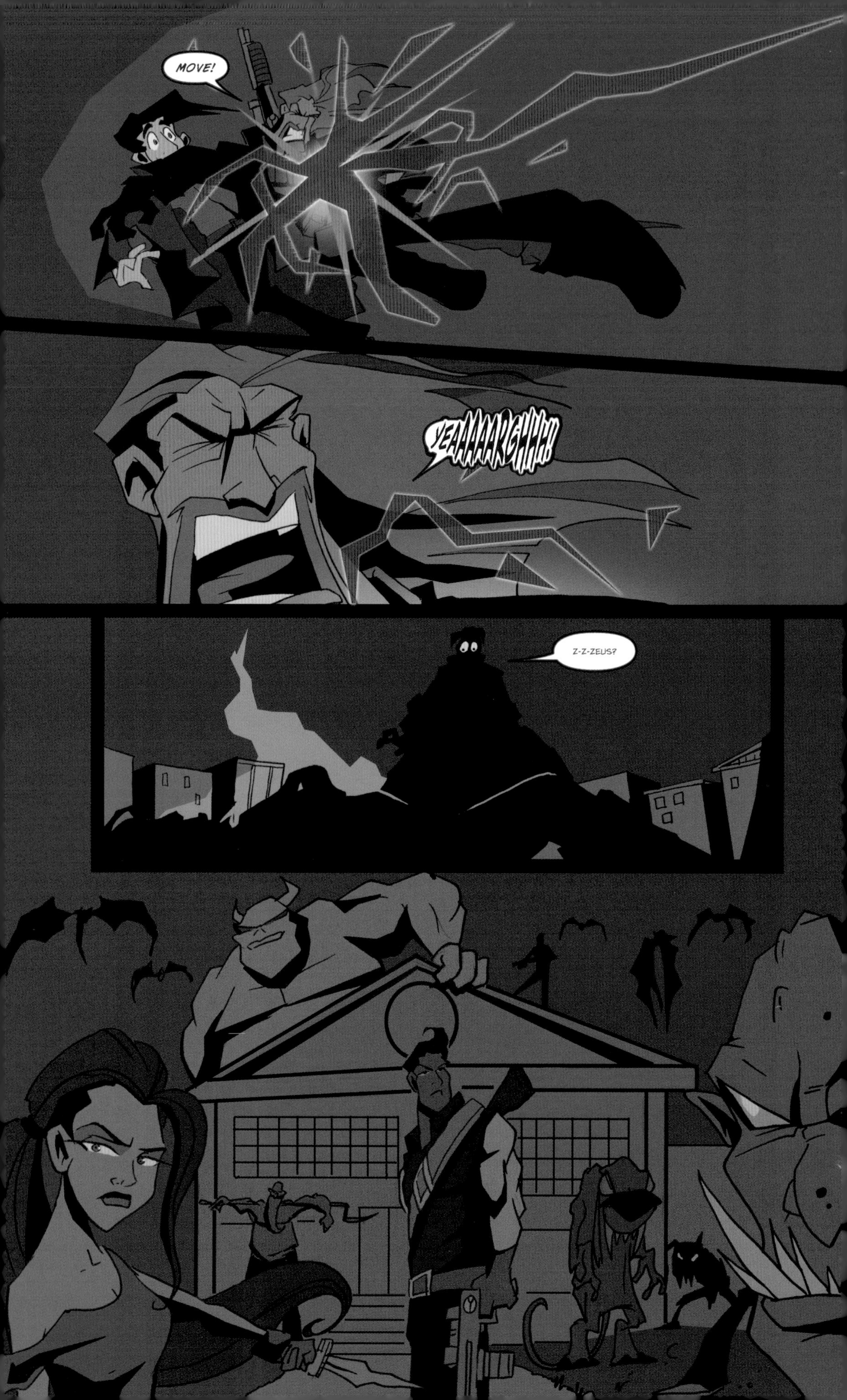
MOVE!
YEAAAAARGHHH!!
Z-Z-ZEUS?

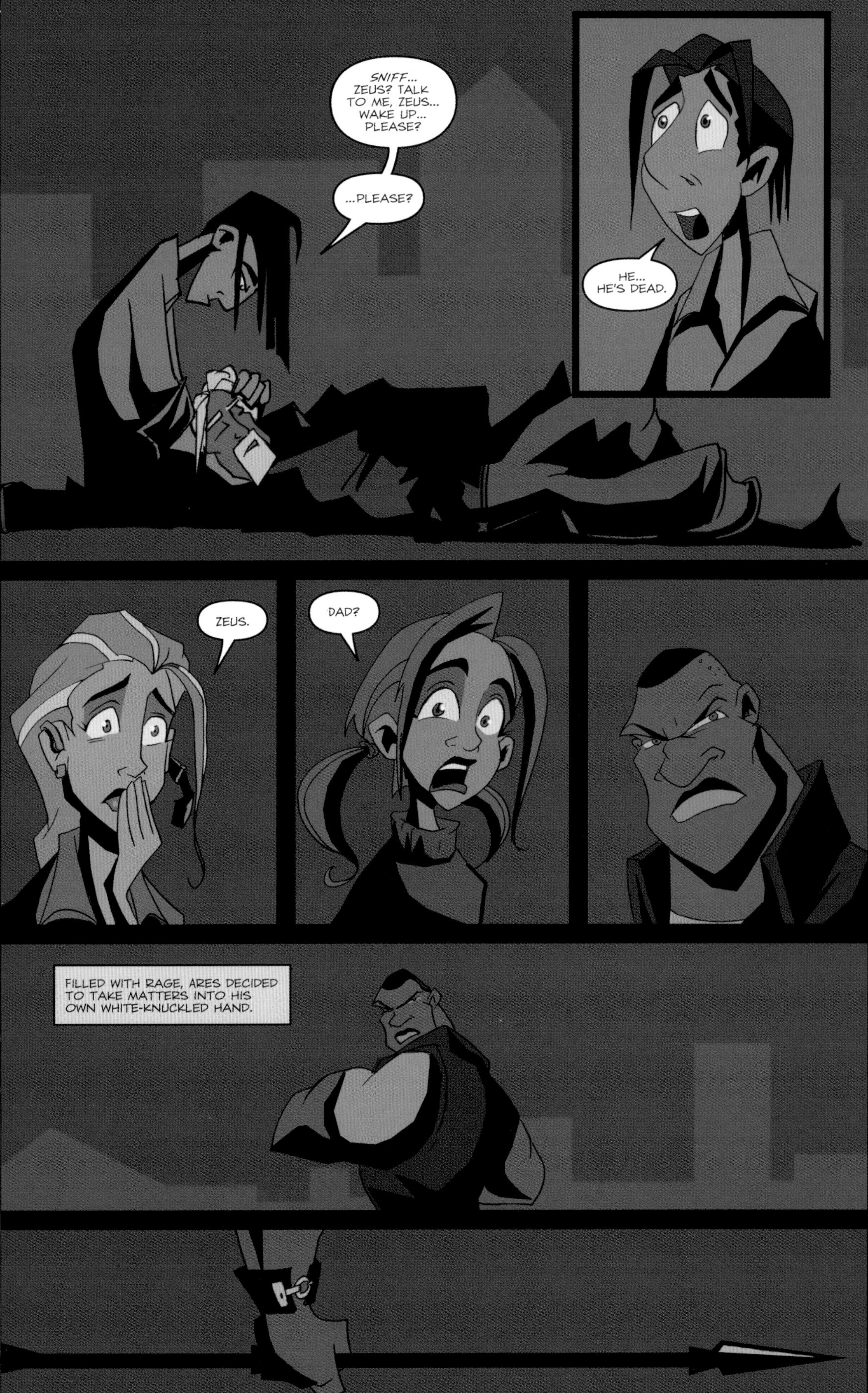
SNIFF... ZEUS? TALK TO ME, ZEUS... WAKE UP... PLEASE?
...PLEASE?
HE... HE'S DEAD.
ZEUS.
DAD?
FILLED WITH RAGE, ARES DECIDED TO TAKE MATTERS INTO HIS OWN WHITE-KNUCKLED HAND.

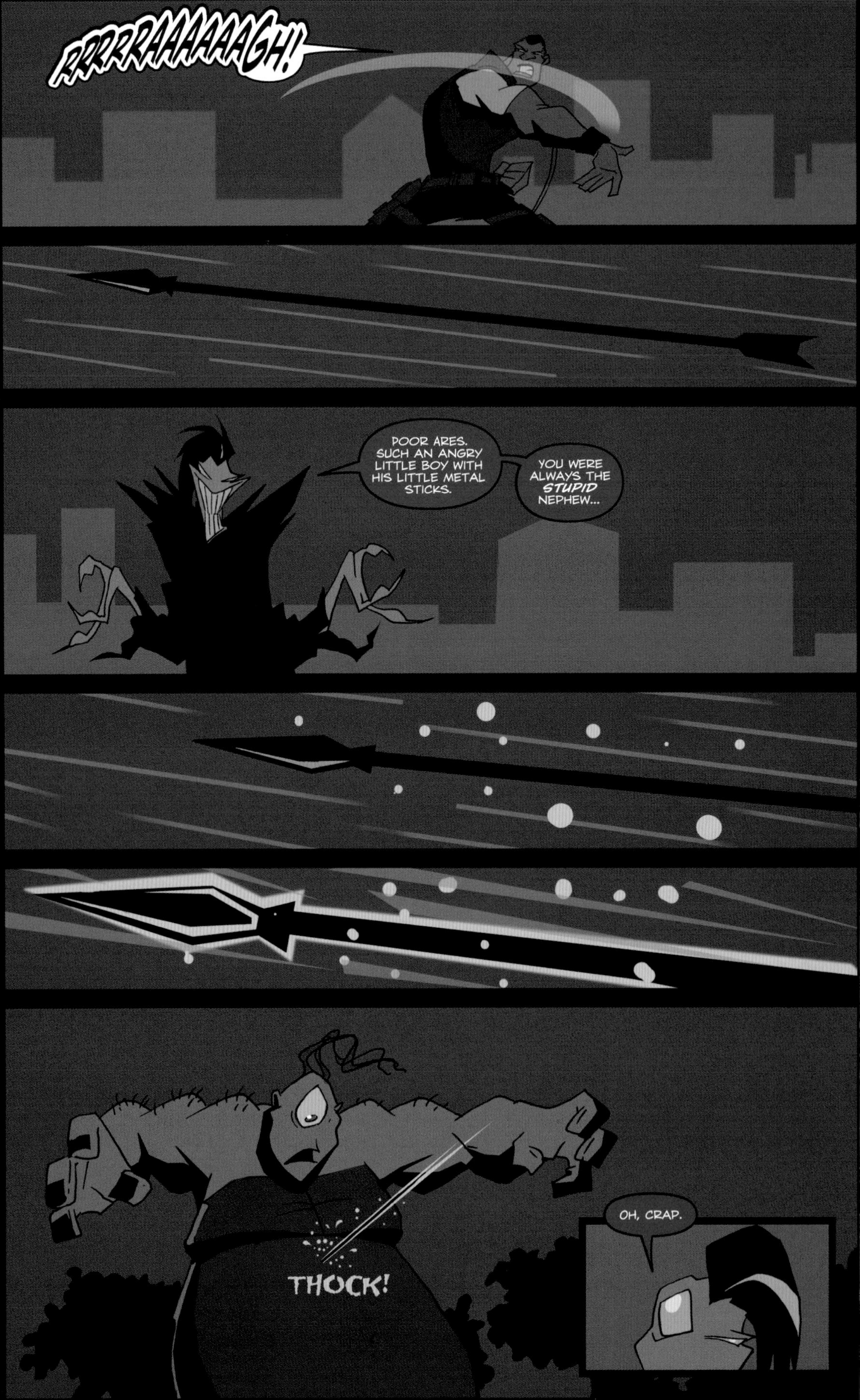

RRRRRAAAAAAGH!
POOR ARES. SUCH AN ANGRY LITTLE BOY WITH HIS LITTLE METAL STICKS.
YOU WERE ALWAYS THE STUPID NEPHEW...
THOCK!
OH, CRAP.

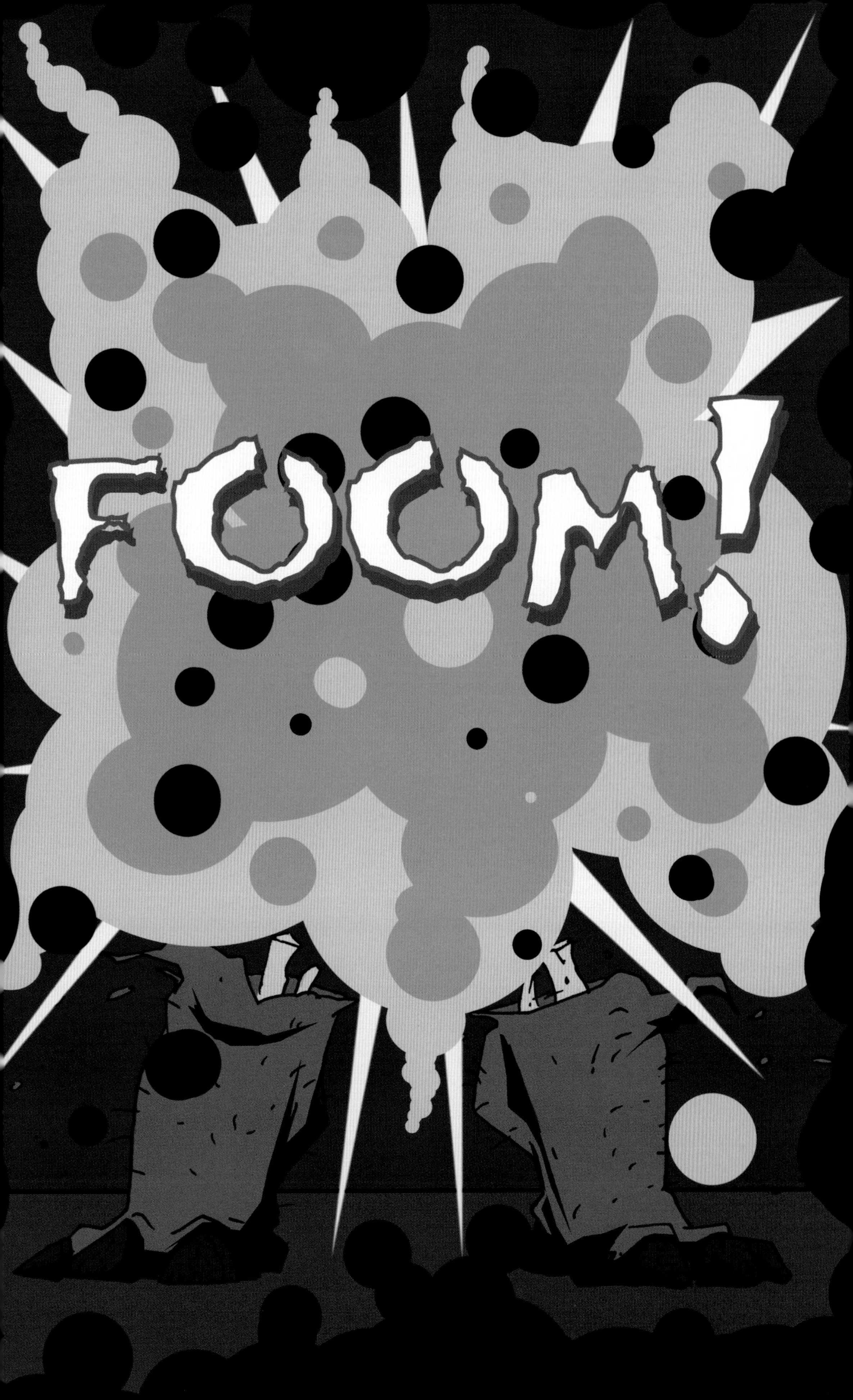
FOOM!

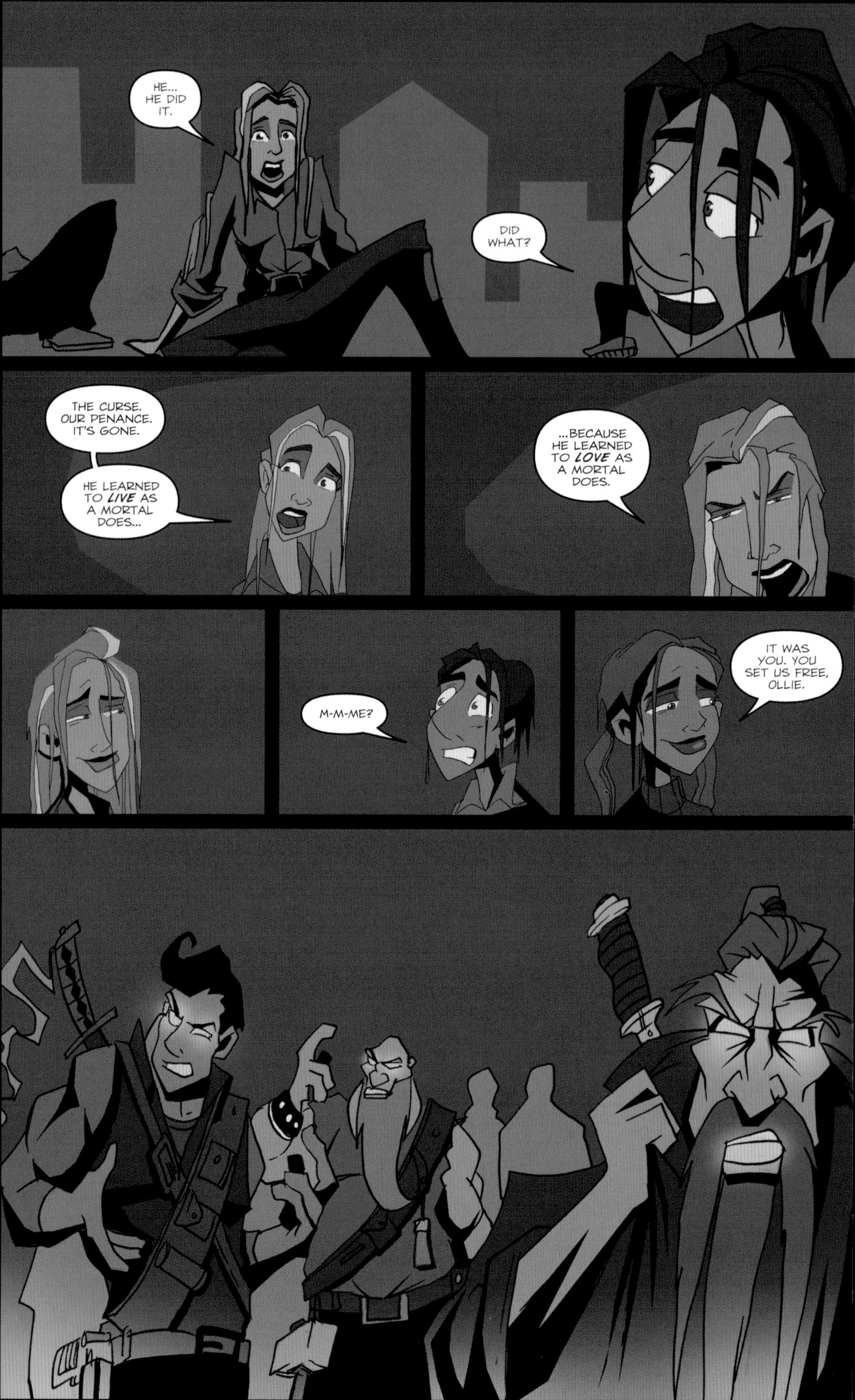
HE... HE DID IT.
DID WHAT?
THE CURSE. OUR PENANCE. IT'S GONE.
HE LEARNED TO *LIVE* AS A MORTAL DOES...
...BECAUSE HE LEARNED TO *LOVE* AS A MORTAL DOES.
M-M-ME?
IT WAS YOU. YOU SET US FREE, OLLIE.

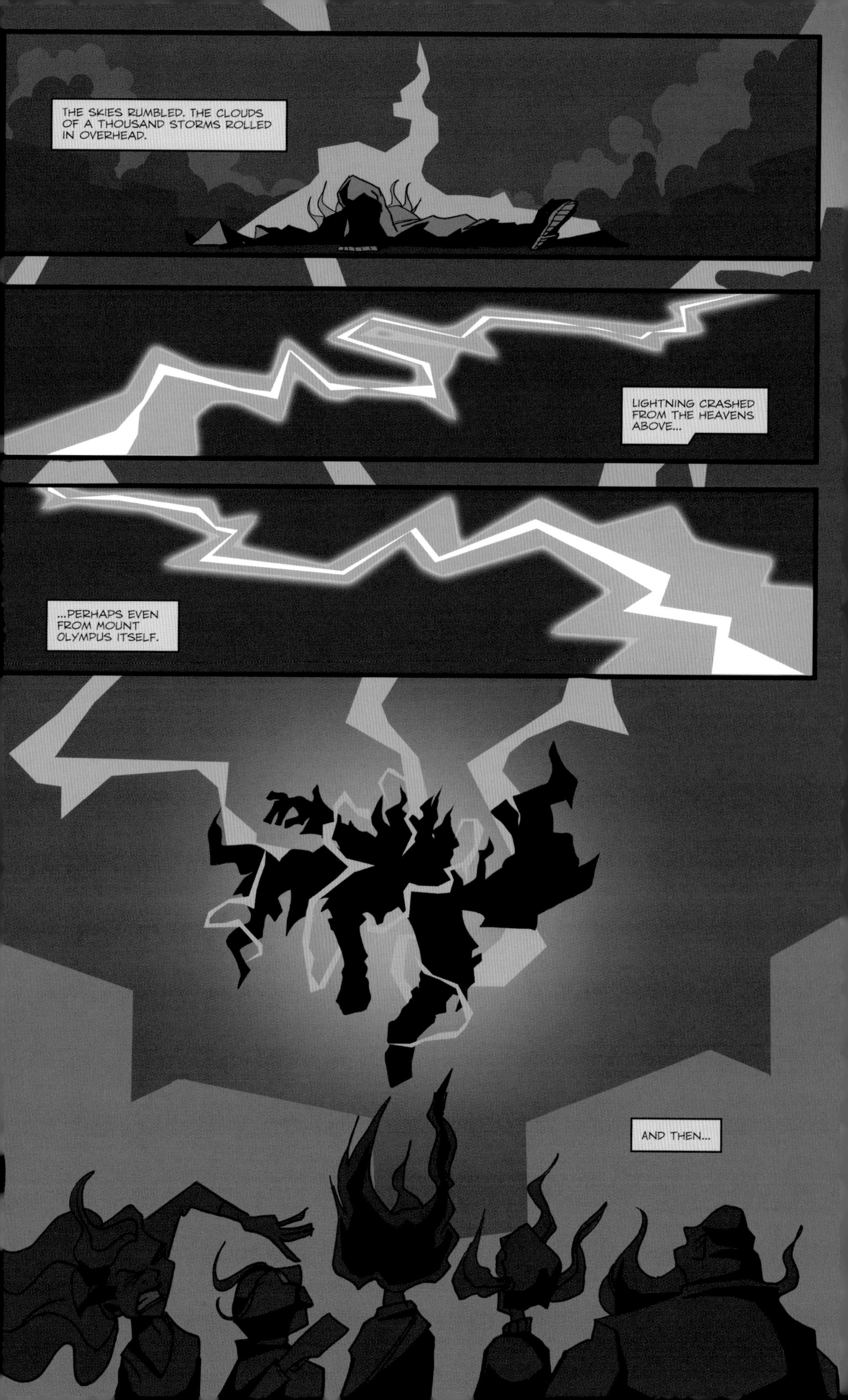
THE SKIES RUMBLED. THE CLOUDS OF A THOUSAND STORMS ROLLED IN OVERHEAD.
LIGHTNING CRASHED FROM THE HEAVENS ABOVE...
...PERHAPS EVEN FROM MOUNT OLYMPUS ITSELF.
AND THEN...

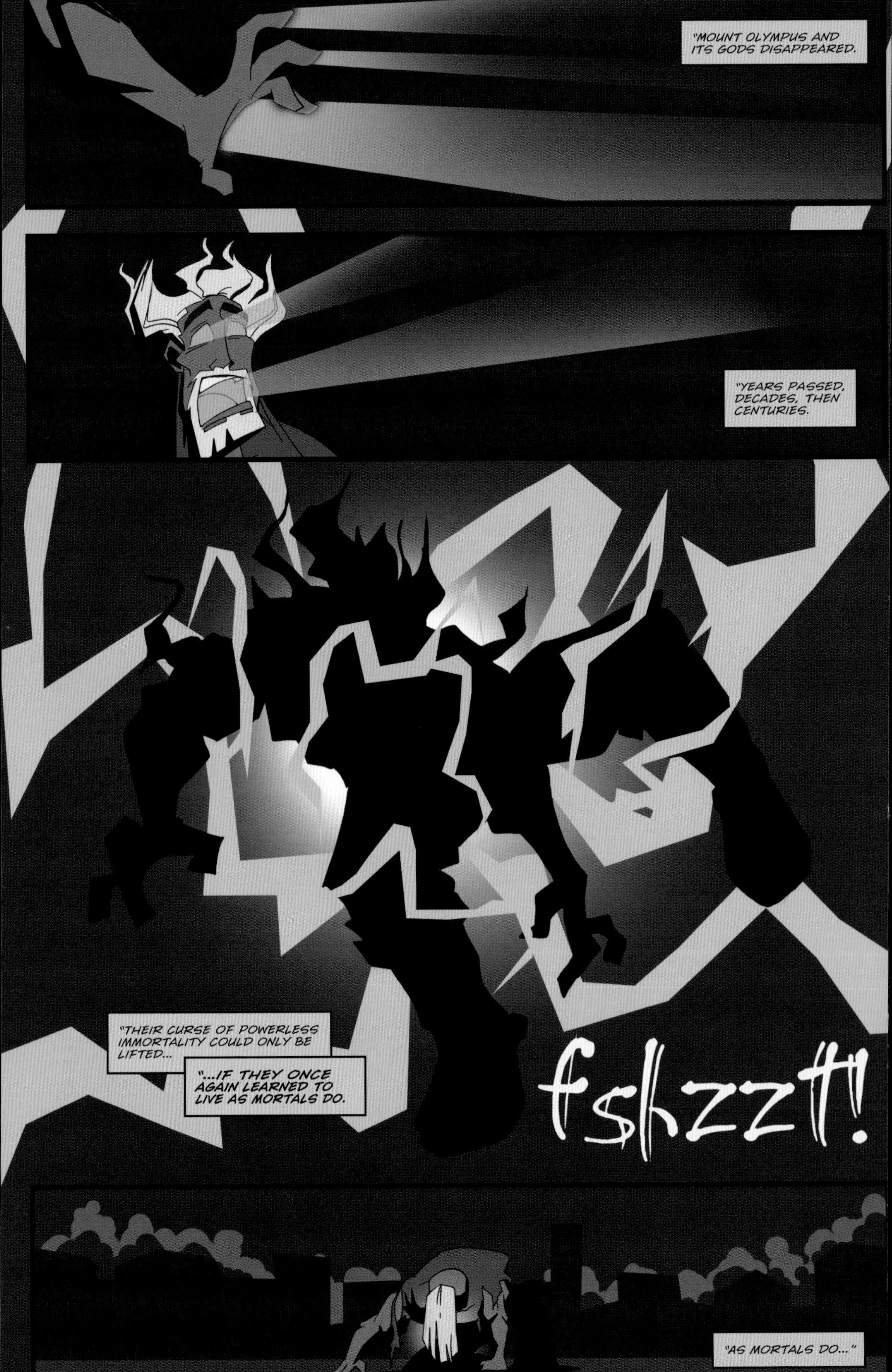
"MOUNT OLYMPUS AND ITS GODS DISAPPEARED.
"YEARS PASSED, DECADES, THEN CENTURIES.
"THEIR CURSE OF POWERLESS IMMORTALITY COULD ONLY BE LIFTED...
"...IF THEY ONCE AGAIN LEARNED TO LIVE AS MORTALS DO.
fshzzt!
"AS MORTALS DO..."

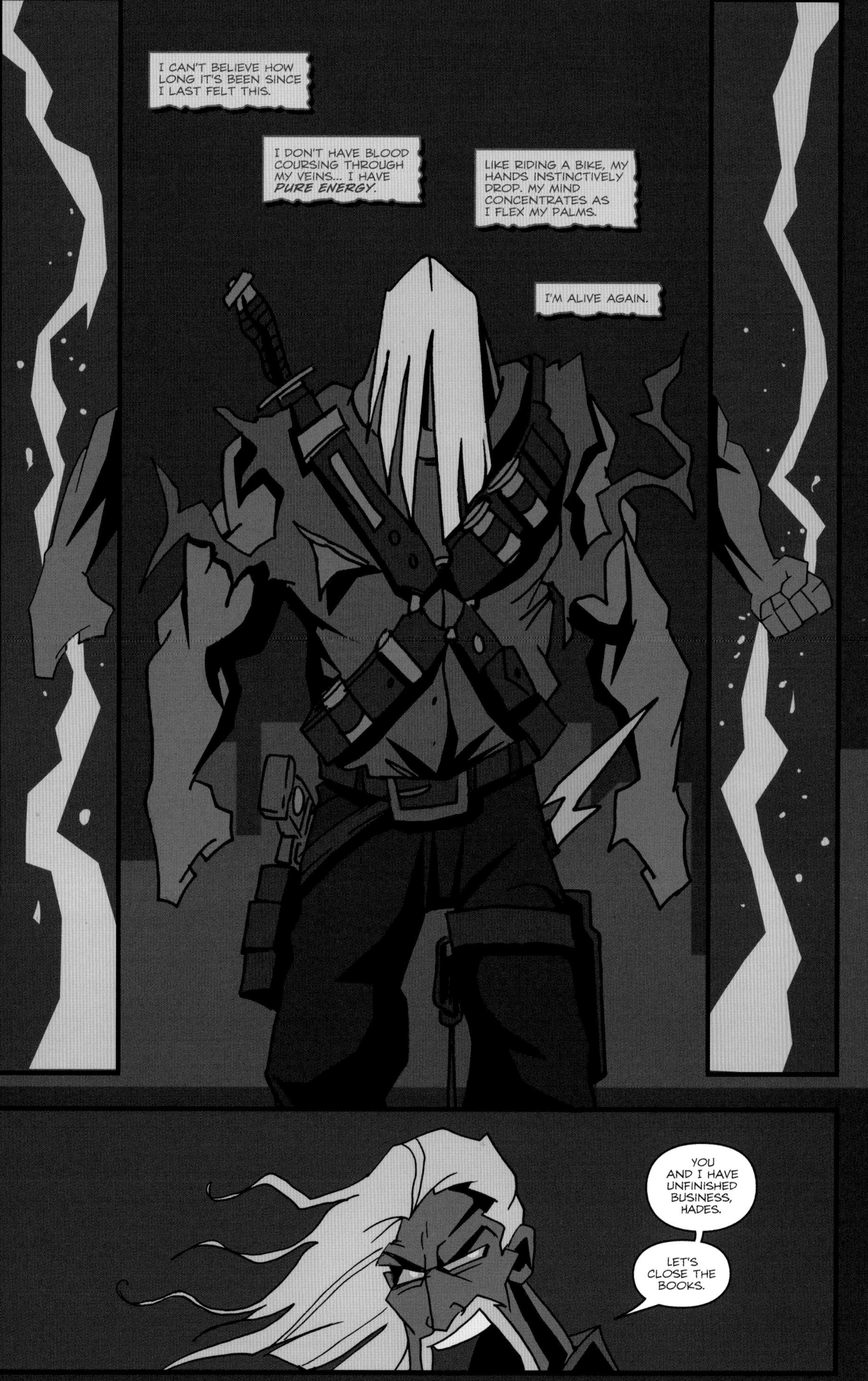
I CAN'T BELIEVE HOW LONG IT'S BEEN SINCE I LAST FELT THIS.
I DON'T HAVE BLOOD COURSING THROUGH MY VEINS... I HAVE *PURE ENERGY*.
LIKE RIDING A BIKE, MY HANDS INSTINCTIVELY DROP. MY MIND CONCENTRATES AS I FLEX MY PALMS.
I'M ALIVE AGAIN.
YOU AND I HAVE UNFINISHED BUSINESS, HADES.
LET'S CLOSE THE BOOKS.

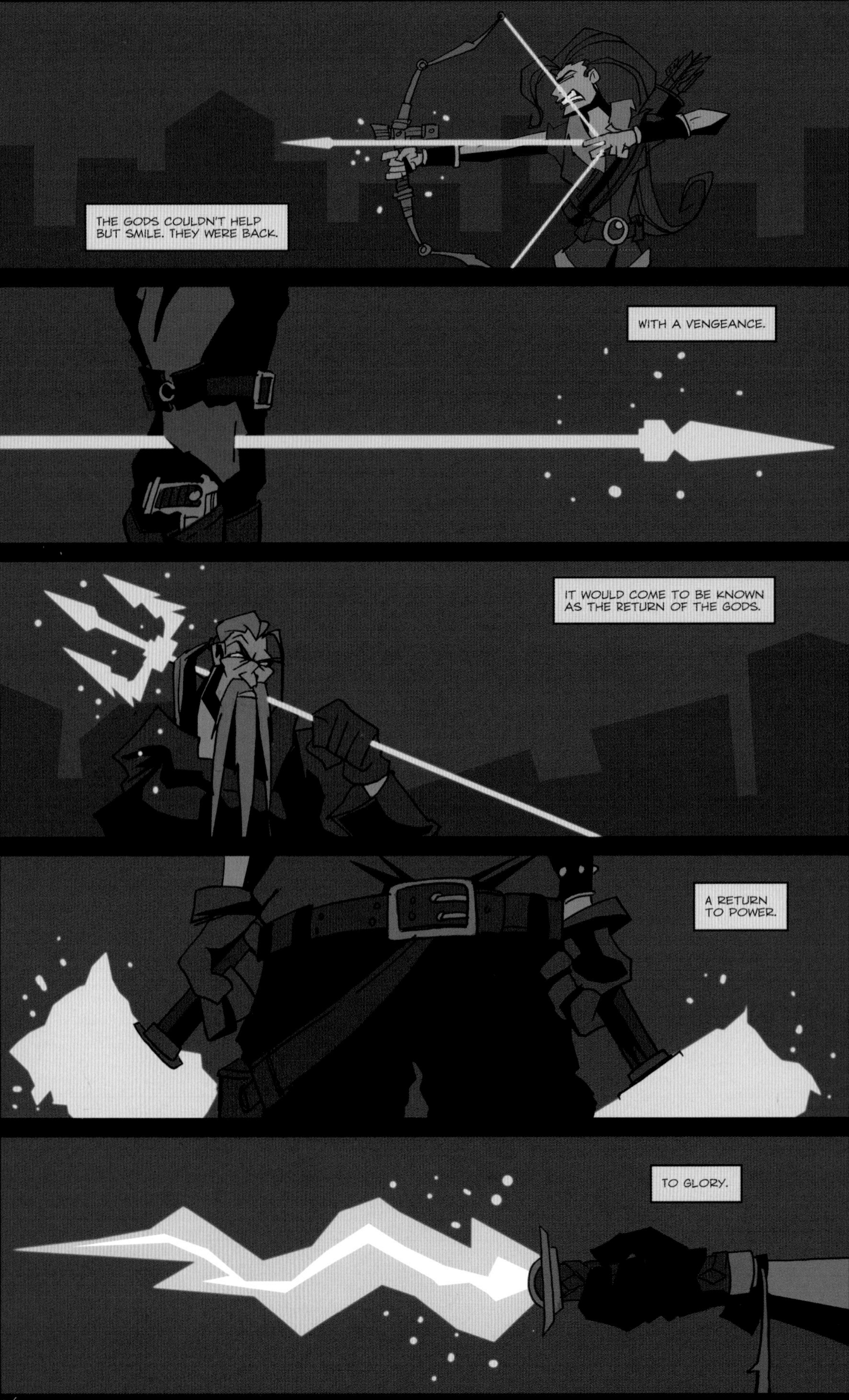
THE GODS COULDN'T HELP BUT SMILE. THEY WERE BACK.
WITH A VENGEANCE.
IT WOULD COME TO BE KNOWN AS THE RETURN OF THE GODS.
A RETURN TO POWER.
TO GLORY.

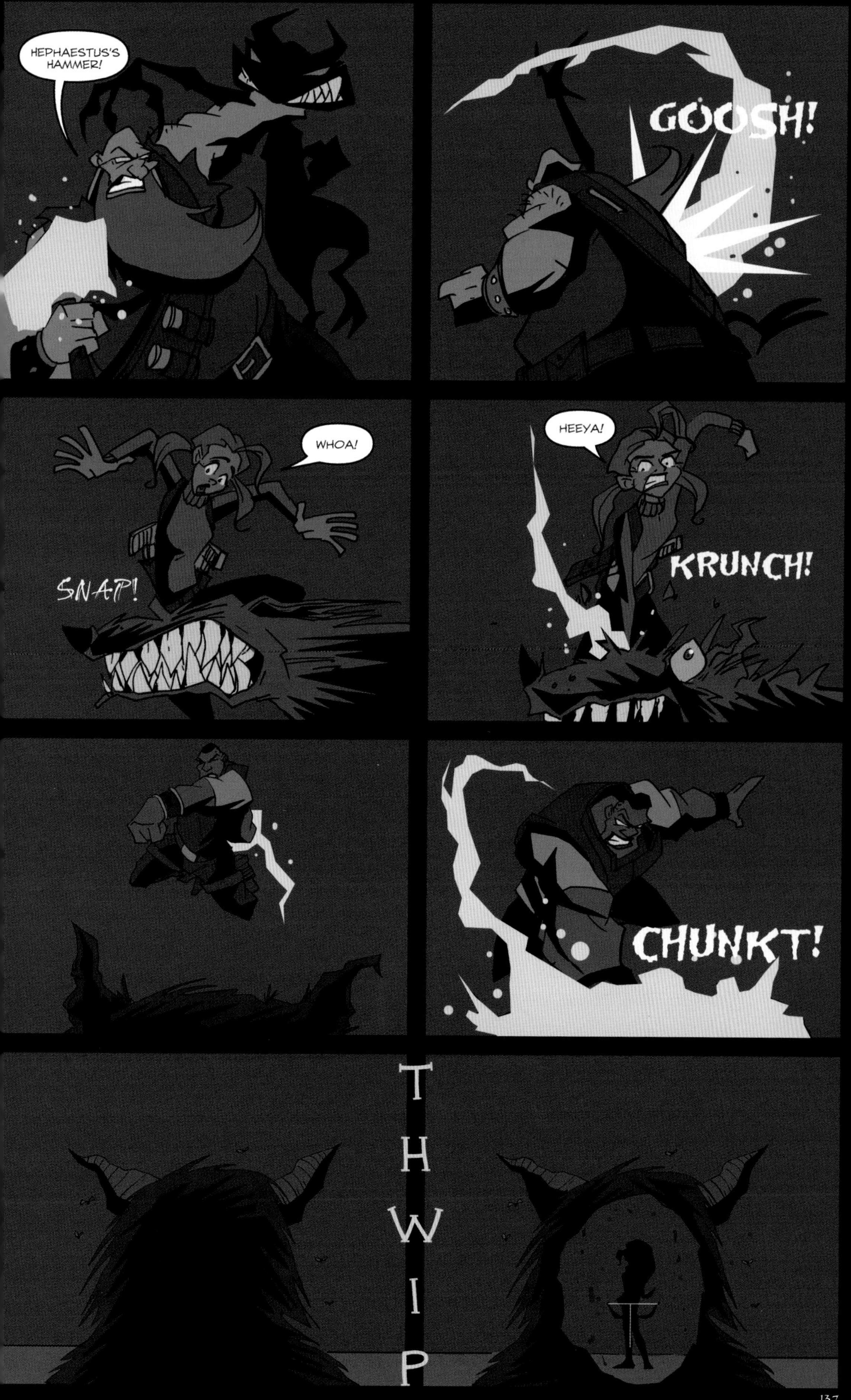
HEPHAESTUS'S HAMMER!
GOOSH!
WHOA!
SNAP!
HEEYA!
KRUNCH!
CHUNKT!
THWIP

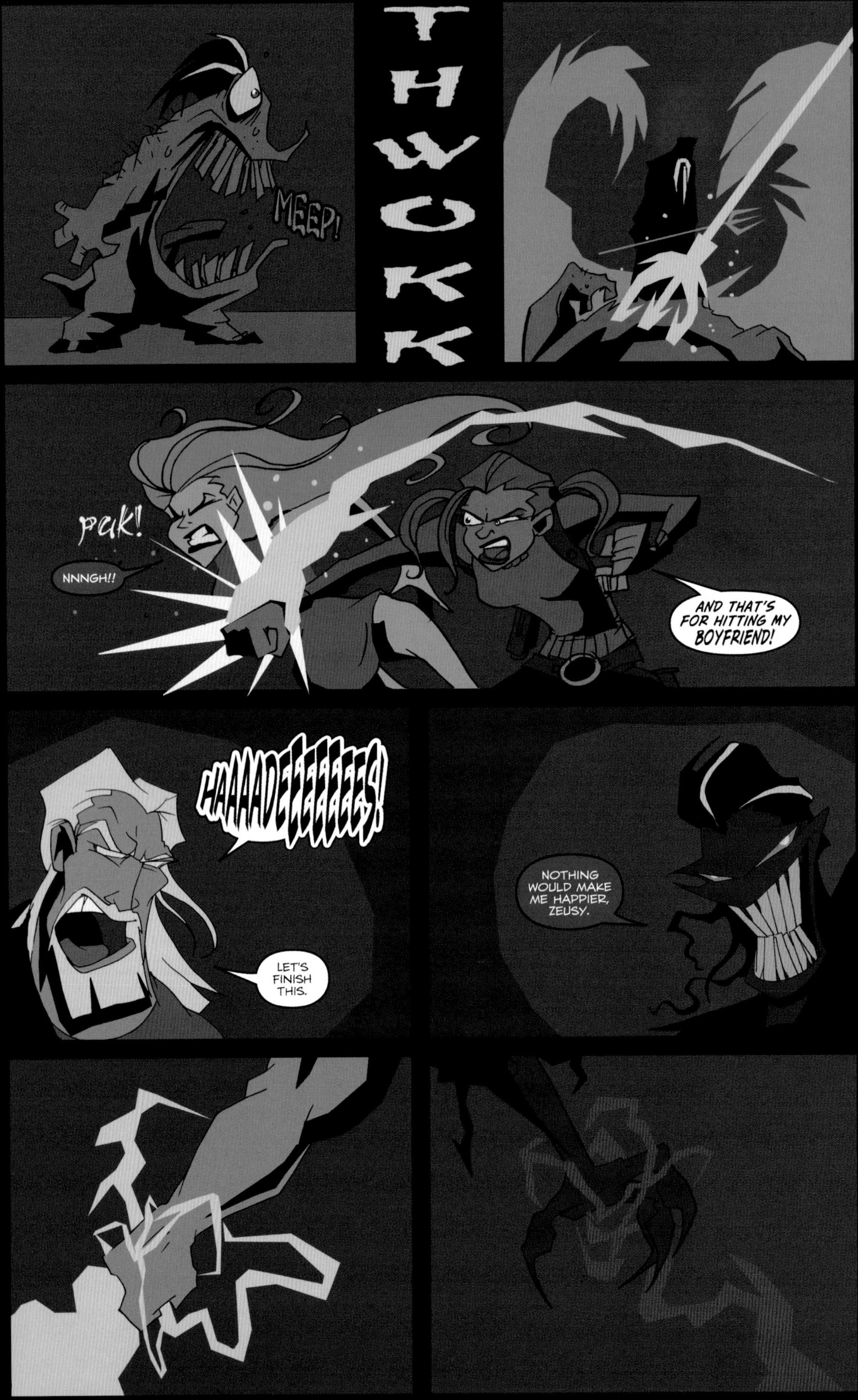
MEEP!
THWOKK
PAK!
NNNGH!!
AND THAT'S FOR HITTING MY BOYFRIEND!
HAAAADEEEEEEES!
LET'S FINISH THIS.
NOTHING WOULD MAKE ME HAPPIER, ZEUSY.

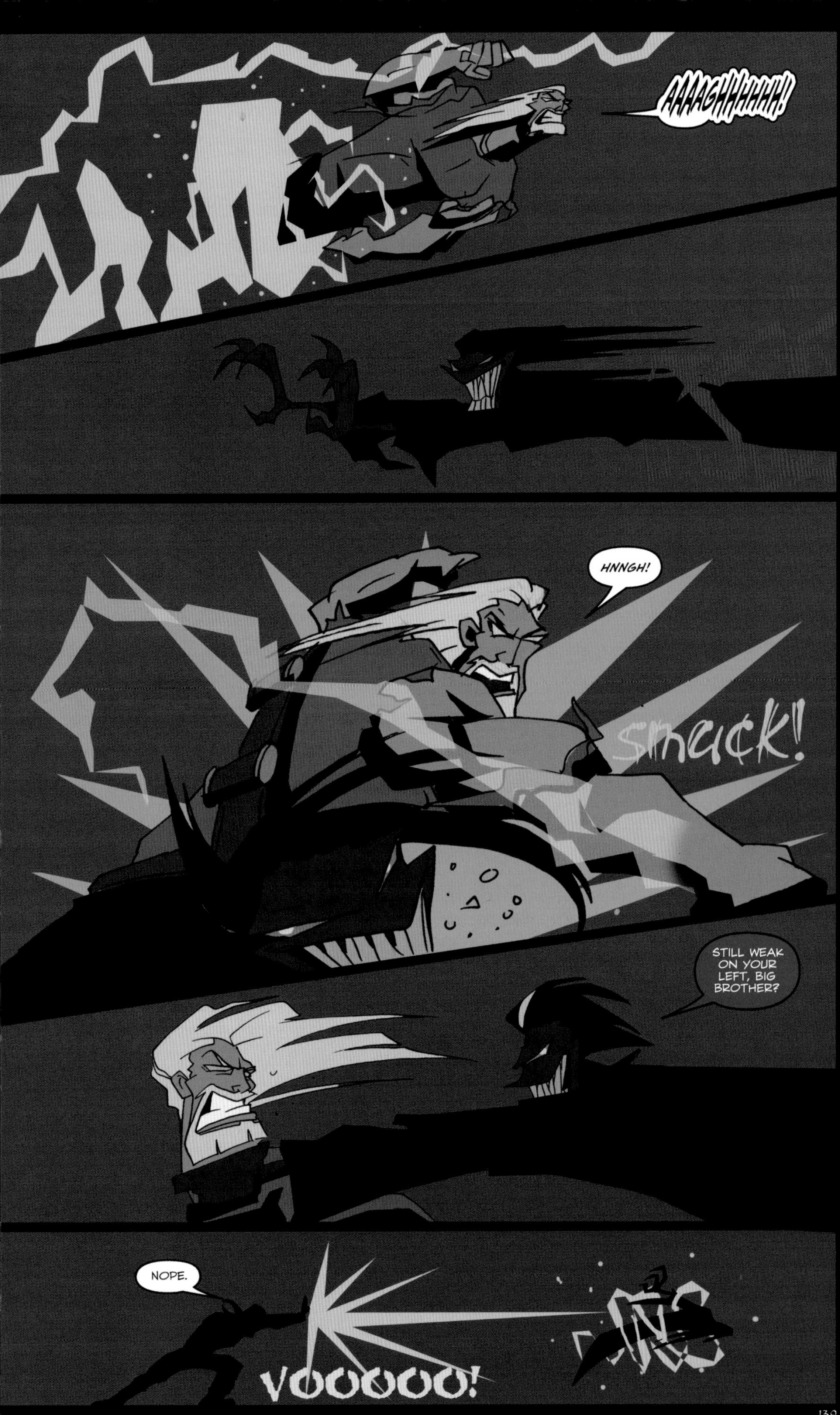
AAAAGHHHHHH!
HNNGH!
SMACK!
STILL WEAK ON YOUR LEFT, BIG BROTHER?
NOPE.
VOOOOOO!

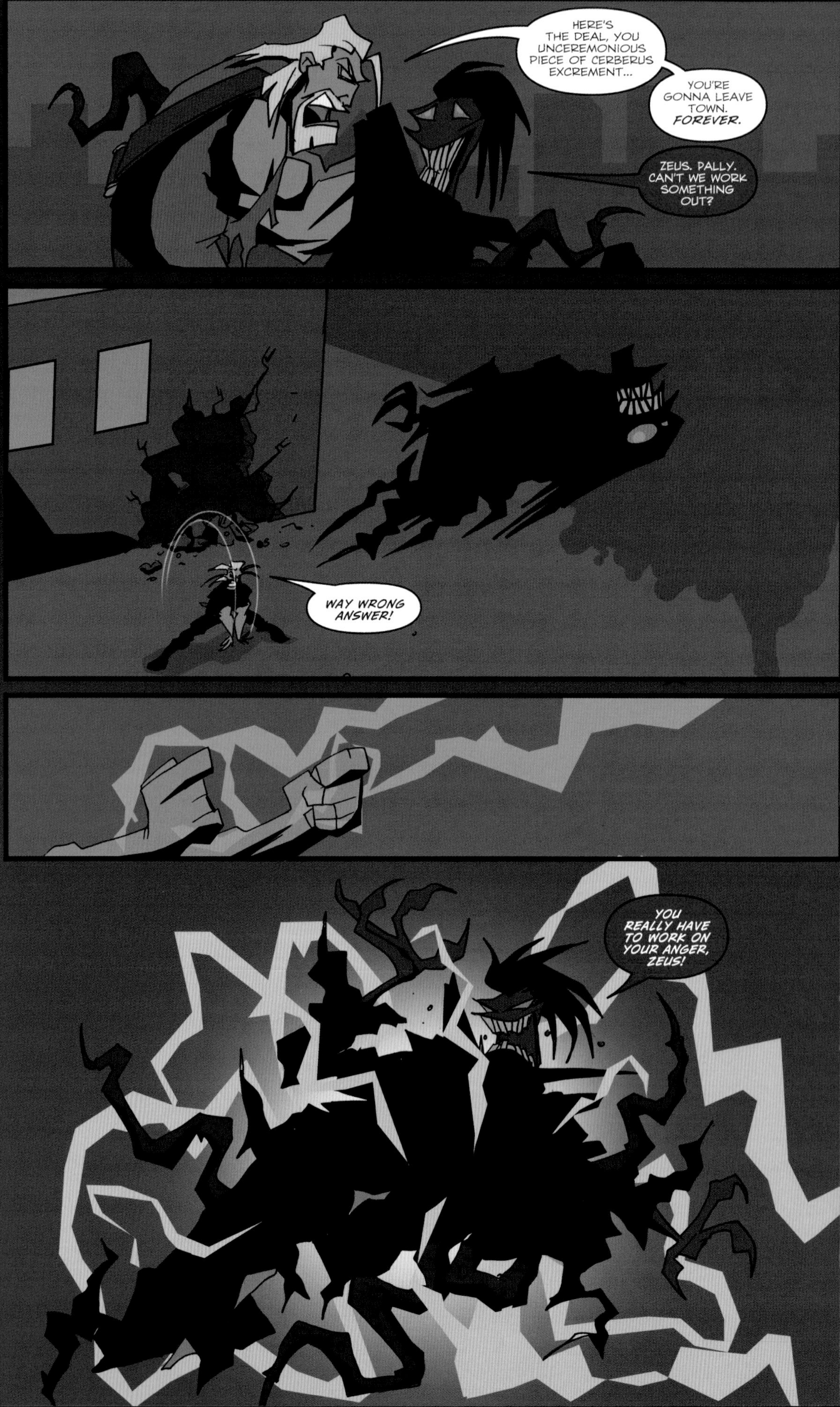
HERE'S THE DEAL, YOU UNCEREMONIOUS PIECE OF CERBERUS EXCREMENT...
YOU'RE GONNA LEAVE TOWN. *FOREVER.*
ZEUS. PALLY. CAN'T WE WORK SOMETHING OUT?
WAY WRONG ANSWER!
YOU REALLY HAVE TO WORK ON YOUR ANGER, ZEUS!

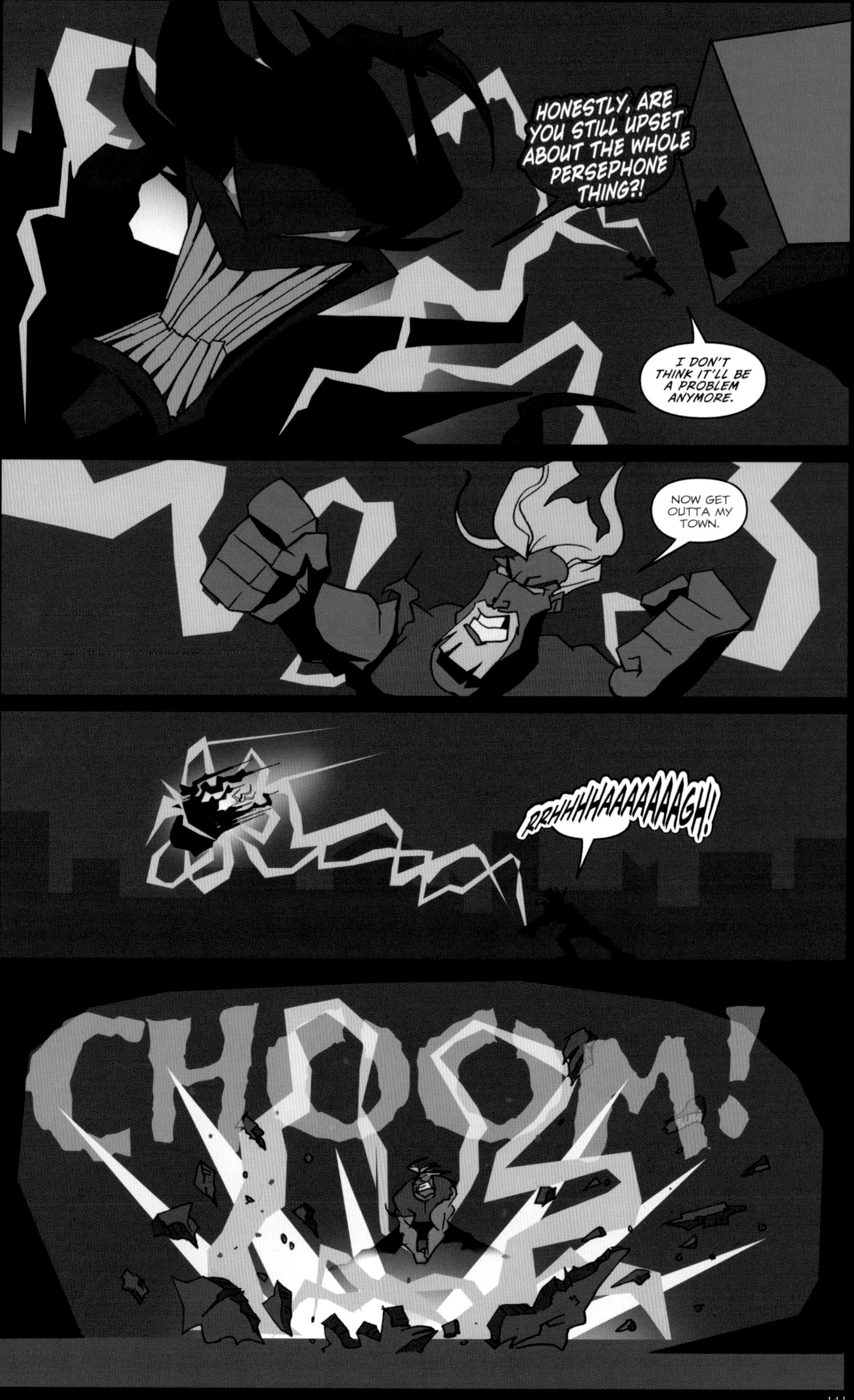
HONESTLY, ARE YOU STILL UPSET ABOUT THE WHOLE PERSEPHONE THING?!
I DON'T THINK IT'LL BE A PROBLEM ANYMORE.
NOW GET OUTTA MY TOWN.
RRHHHHAAAAAAAGH!
CHOOM!

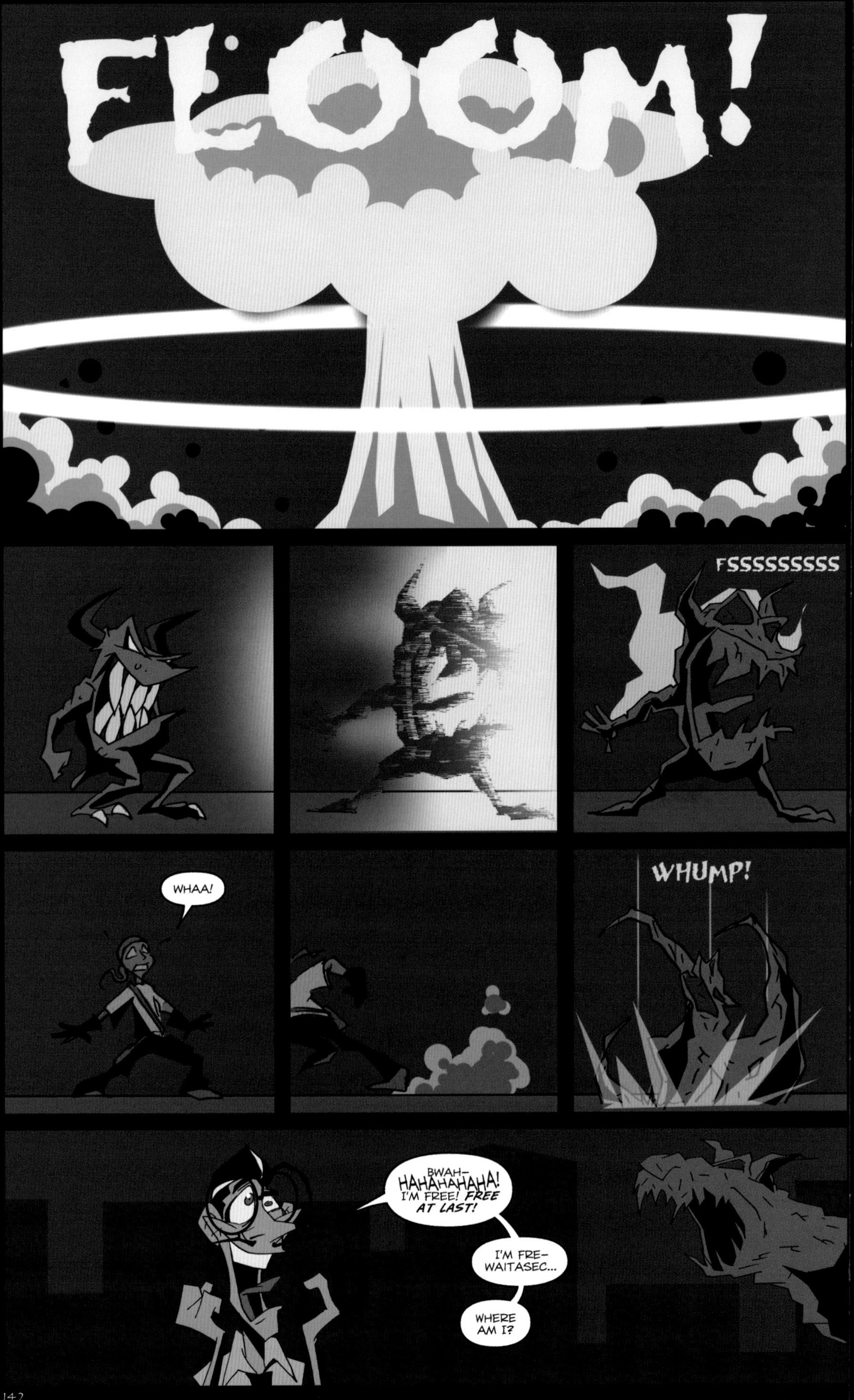
FLOOM!
FSSSSSSSSS
WHAA!
WHUMP!
BWAH-HAHAHAHAHA! I'M FREE! FREE AT LAST!
I'M FRE- WAITASEC...
WHERE AM I?

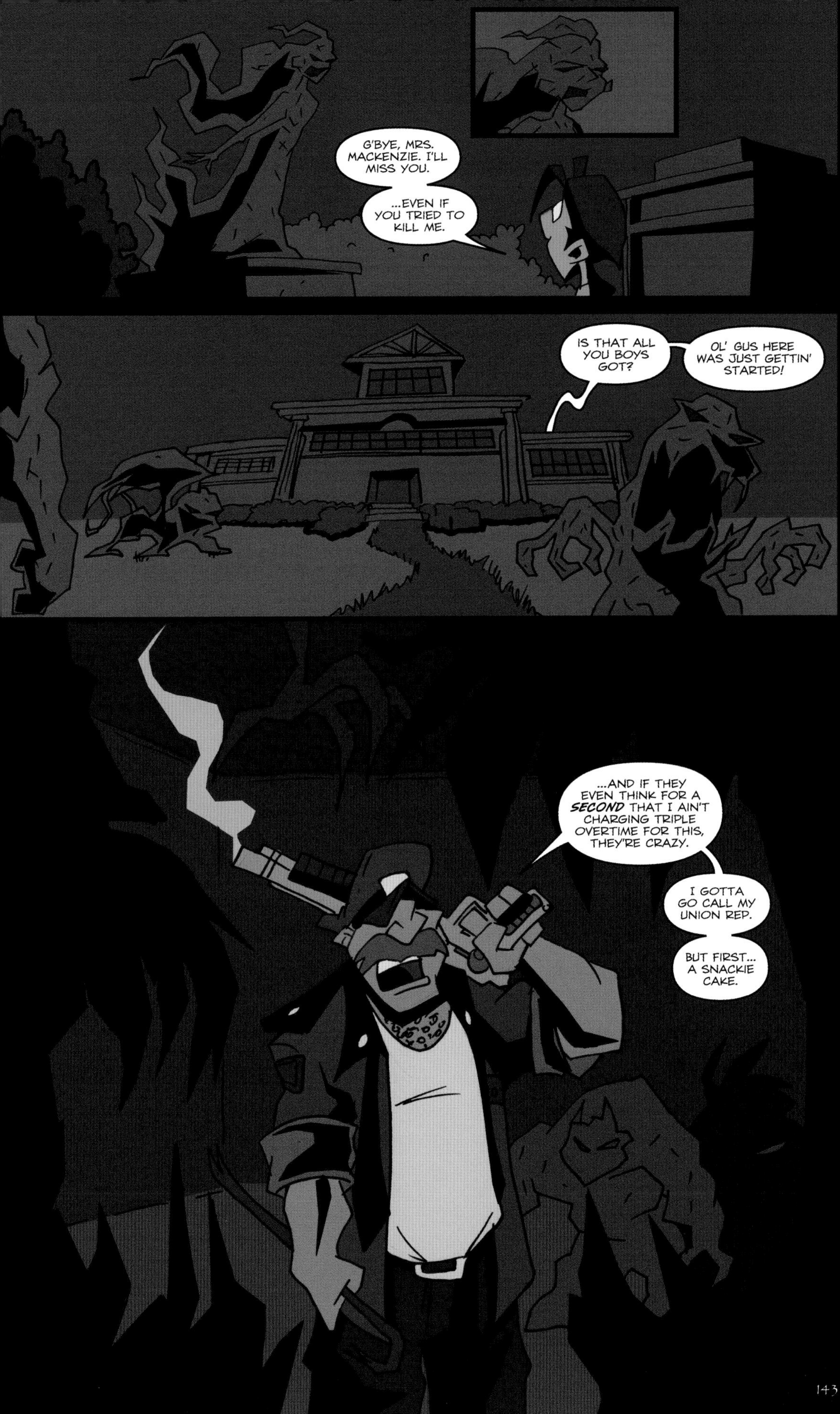
G'BYE, MRS. MACKENZIE. I'LL MISS YOU.
...EVEN IF YOU TRIED TO KILL ME.
IS THAT ALL YOU BOYS GOT?
OL' GUS HERE WAS JUST GETTIN' STARTED!
...AND IF THEY EVEN THINK FOR A **SECOND** THAT I AIN'T CHARGING TRIPLE OVERTIME FOR THIS, THEY'RE CRAZY.
I GOTTA GO CALL MY UNION REP.
BUT FIRST... A SNACKIE CAKE.

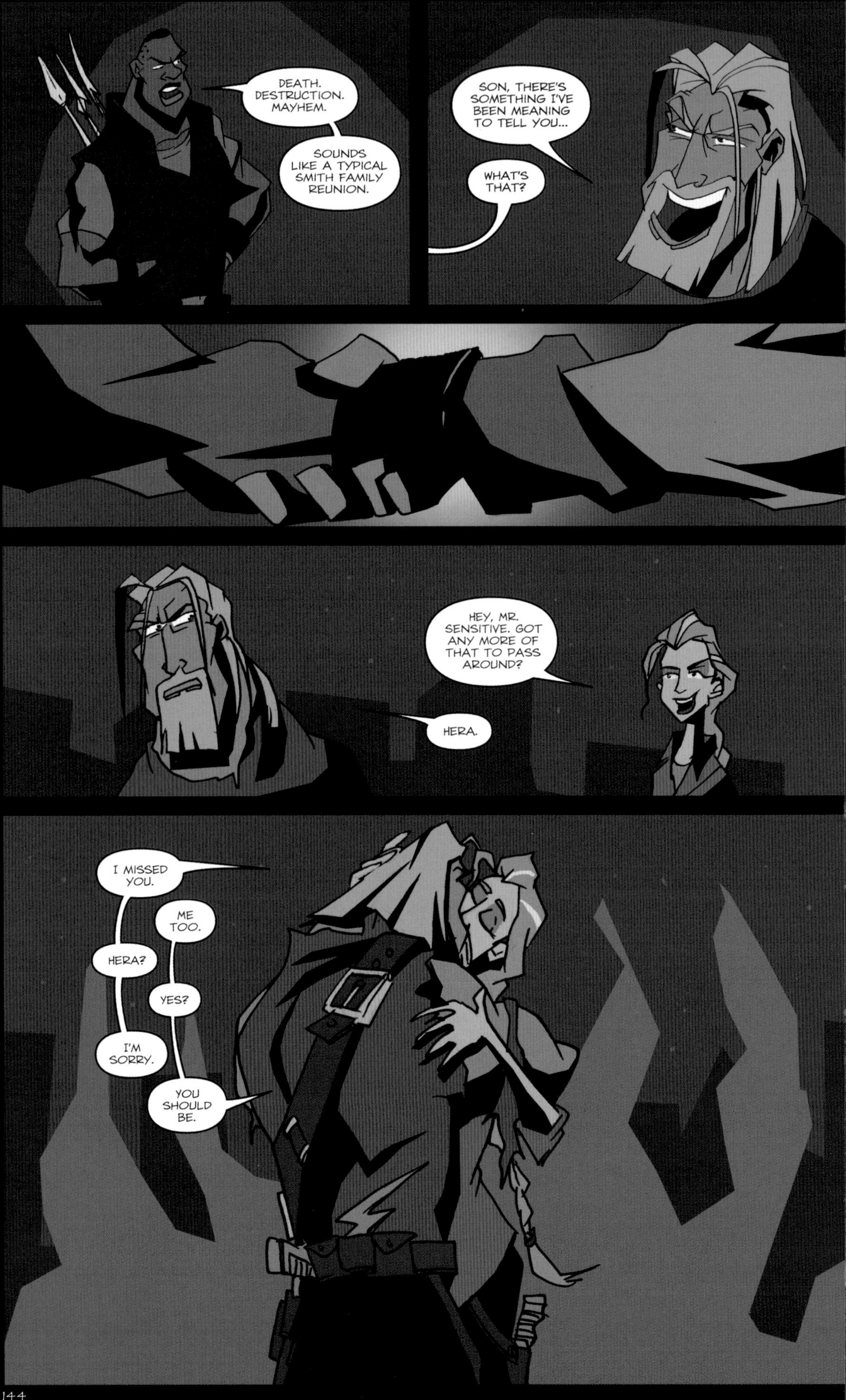
DEATH. DESTRUCTION. MAYHEM.
SOUNDS LIKE A TYPICAL SMITH FAMILY REUNION.
SON, THERE'S SOMETHING I'VE BEEN MEANING TO TELL YOU...
WHAT'S THAT?
HEY, MR. SENSITIVE. GOT ANY MORE OF THAT TO PASS AROUND?
HERA.
I MISSED YOU.
ME TOO.
HERA?
YES?
I'M SORRY.
YOU SHOULD BE.

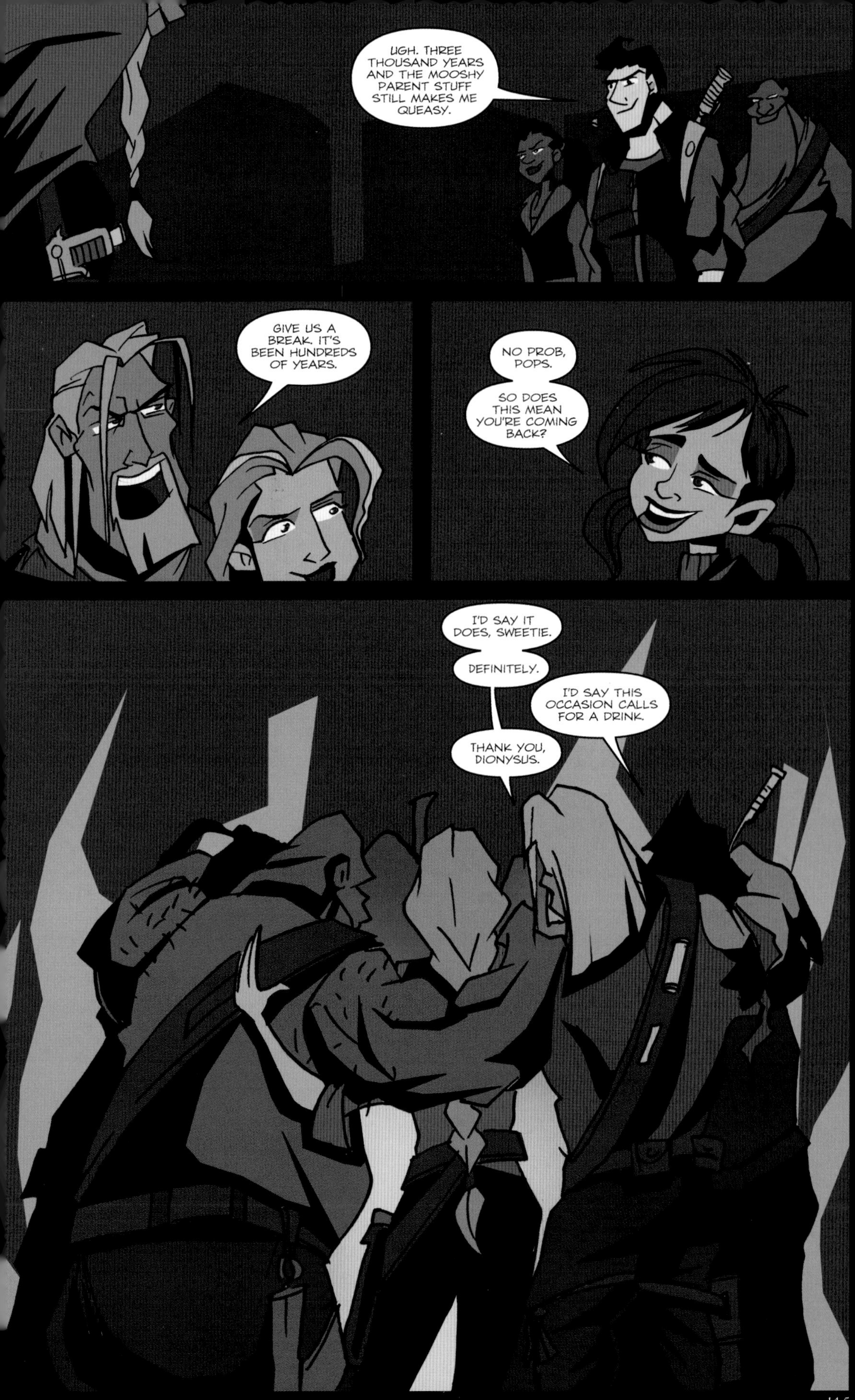
UGH. THREE THOUSAND YEARS AND THE MOOSHY PARENT STUFF STILL MAKES ME QUEASY.
GIVE US A BREAK. IT'S BEEN HUNDREDS OF YEARS.
NO PROB, POPS.
SO DOES THIS MEAN YOU'RE COMING BACK?
I'D SAY IT DOES, SWEETIE.
DEFINITELY.
I'D SAY THIS OCCASION CALLS FOR A DRINK.
THANK YOU, DIONYSUS.

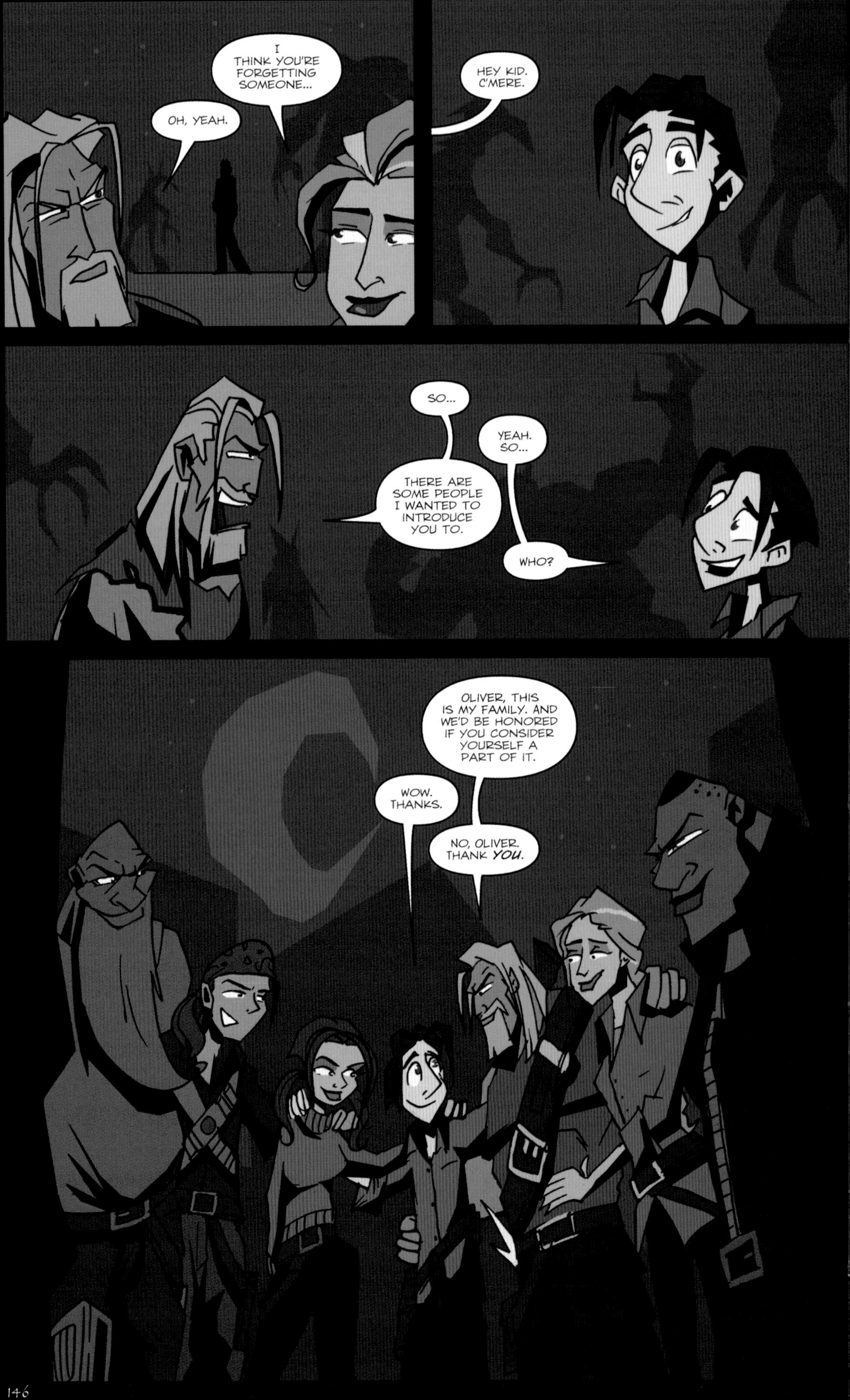
OH, YEAH.
I THINK YOU'RE FORGETTING SOMEONE...
HEY KID. C'MERE.
SO...
THERE ARE SOME PEOPLE I WANTED TO INTRODUCE YOU TO.
YEAH. SO...
WHO?
OLIVER, THIS IS MY FAMILY. AND WE'D BE HONORED IF YOU CONSIDER YOURSELF A PART OF IT.
WOW. THANKS.
NO, OLIVER. THANK *YOU*.

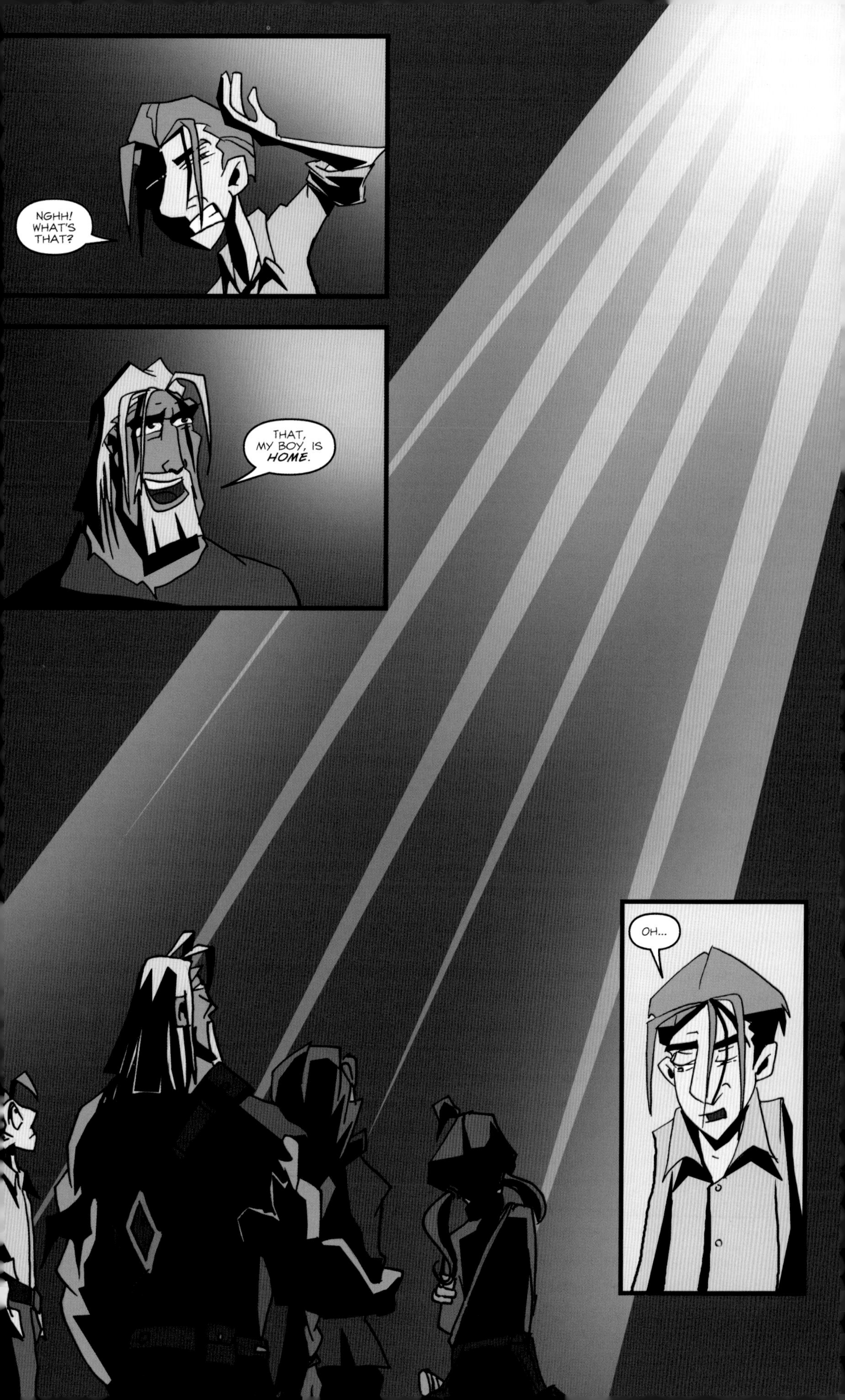
NGHH! WHAT'S THAT?
THAT, MY BOY, IS **HOME**.
OH...

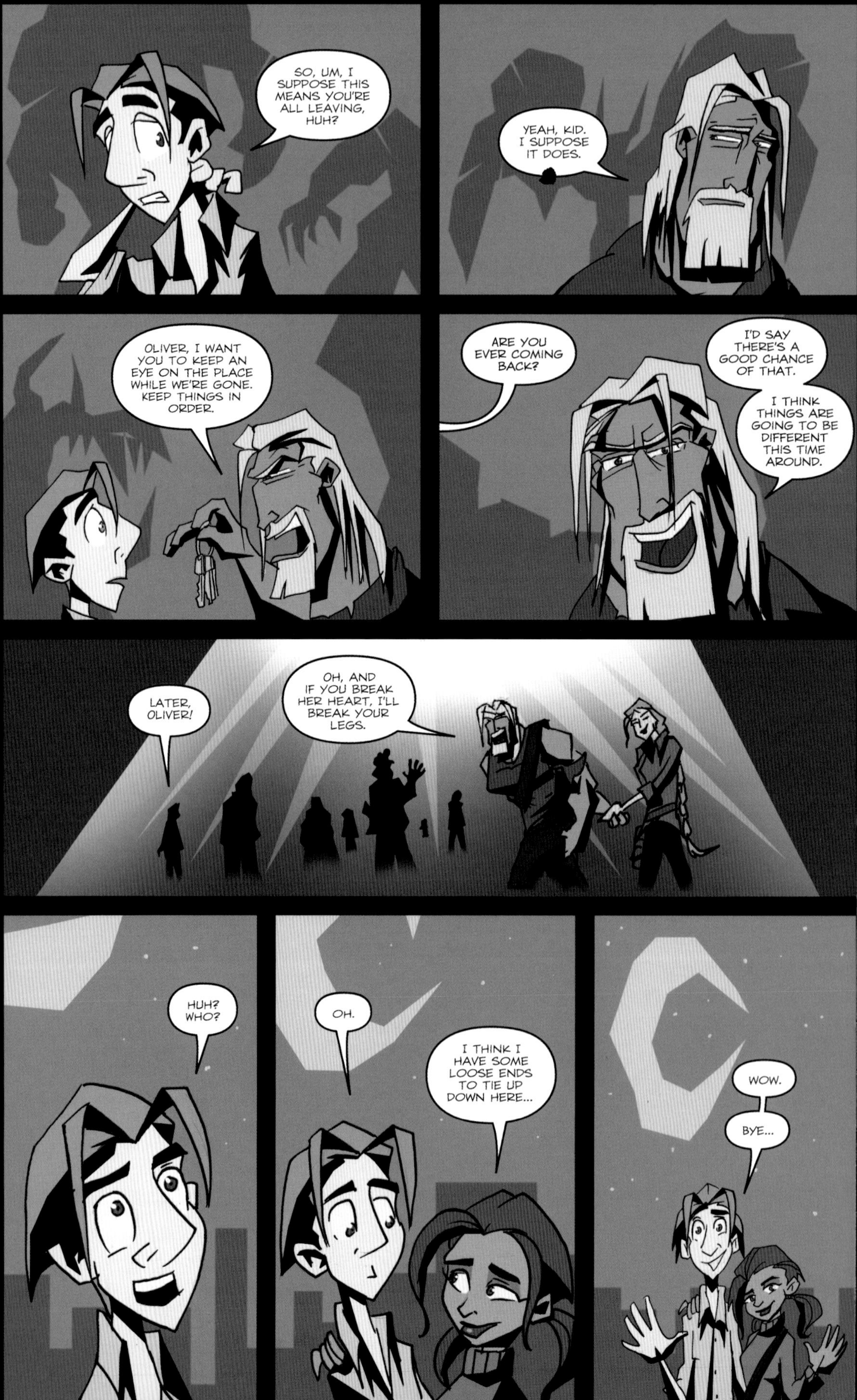
SO, UM, I SUPPOSE THIS MEANS YOU'RE ALL LEAVING, HUH?
YEAH, KID. I SUPPOSE IT DOES.
OLIVER, I WANT YOU TO KEEP AN EYE ON THE PLACE WHILE WE'RE GONE. KEEP THINGS IN ORDER.
ARE YOU EVER COMING BACK?
I'D SAY THERE'S A GOOD CHANCE OF THAT.
I THINK THINGS ARE GOING TO BE DIFFERENT THIS TIME AROUND.
LATER, OLIVER!
OH, AND IF YOU BREAK HER HEART, I'LL BREAK YOUR LEGS.
HUH? WHO?
OH.
I THINK I HAVE SOME LOOSE ENDS TO TIE UP DOWN HERE...
WOW.
BYE...

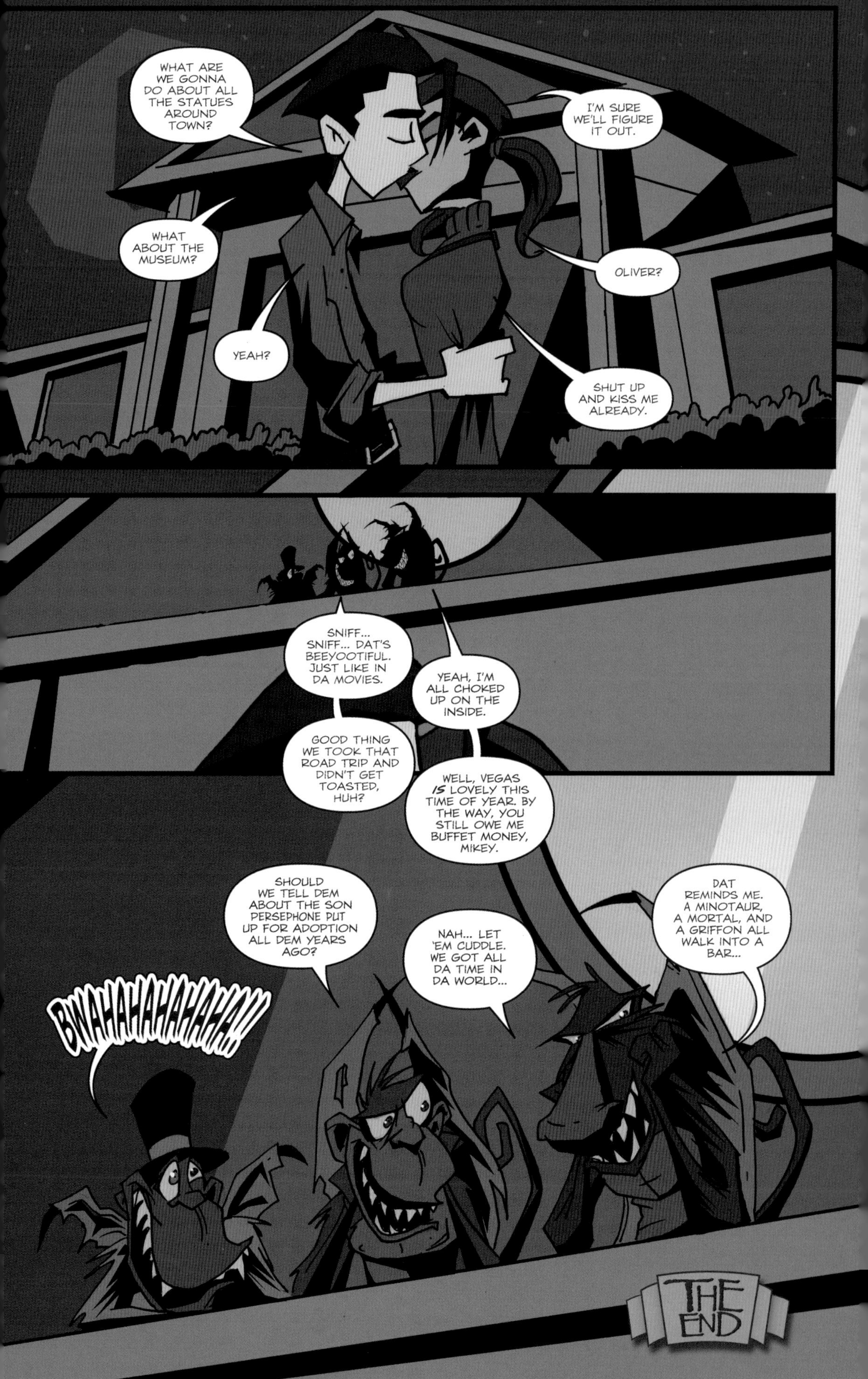
WHAT ARE WE GONNA DO ABOUT ALL THE STATUES AROUND TOWN?
I'M SURE WE'LL FIGURE IT OUT.
WHAT ABOUT THE MUSEUM?
OLIVER?
YEAH?
SHUT UP AND KISS ME ALREADY.
SNIFF... SNIFF... DAT'S BEEYOOTIFUL. JUST LIKE IN DA MOVIES.
YEAH, I'M ALL CHOKED UP ON THE INSIDE.
GOOD THING WE TOOK THAT ROAD TRIP AND DIDN'T GET TOASTED, HUH?
WELL, VEGAS *IS* LOVELY THIS TIME OF YEAR. BY THE WAY, YOU STILL OWE ME BUFFET MONEY, MIKEY.
SHOULD WE TELL DEM ABOUT THE SON PERSEPHONE PUT UP FOR ADOPTION ALL DEM YEARS AGO?
NAH... LET 'EM CUDDLE. WE GOT ALL DA TIME IN DA WORLD...
DAT REMINDS ME. A MINOTAUR, A MORTAL, AND A GRIFFON ALL WALK INTO A BAR...
BWAHAHAHAHAHAHA!!
THE END

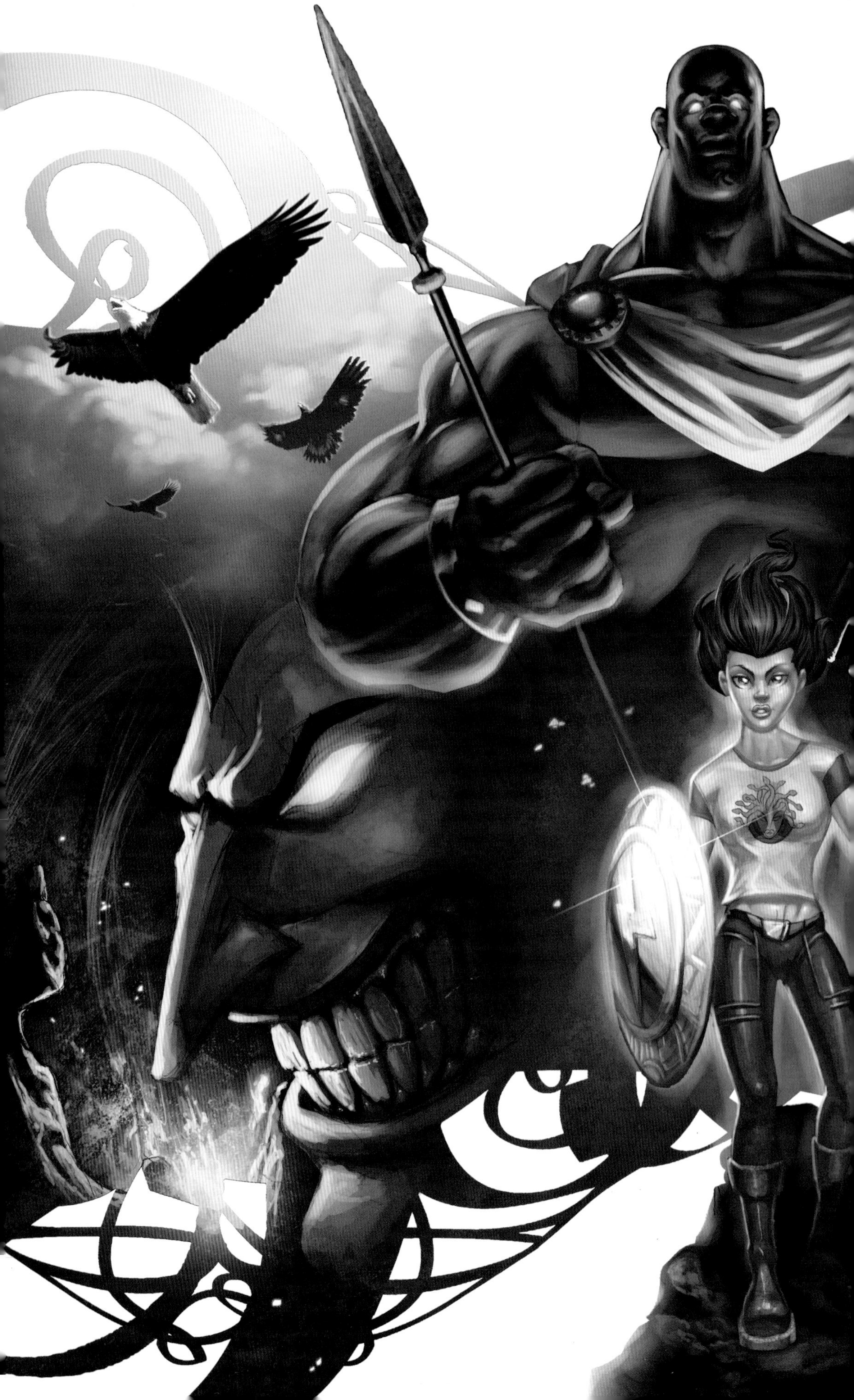

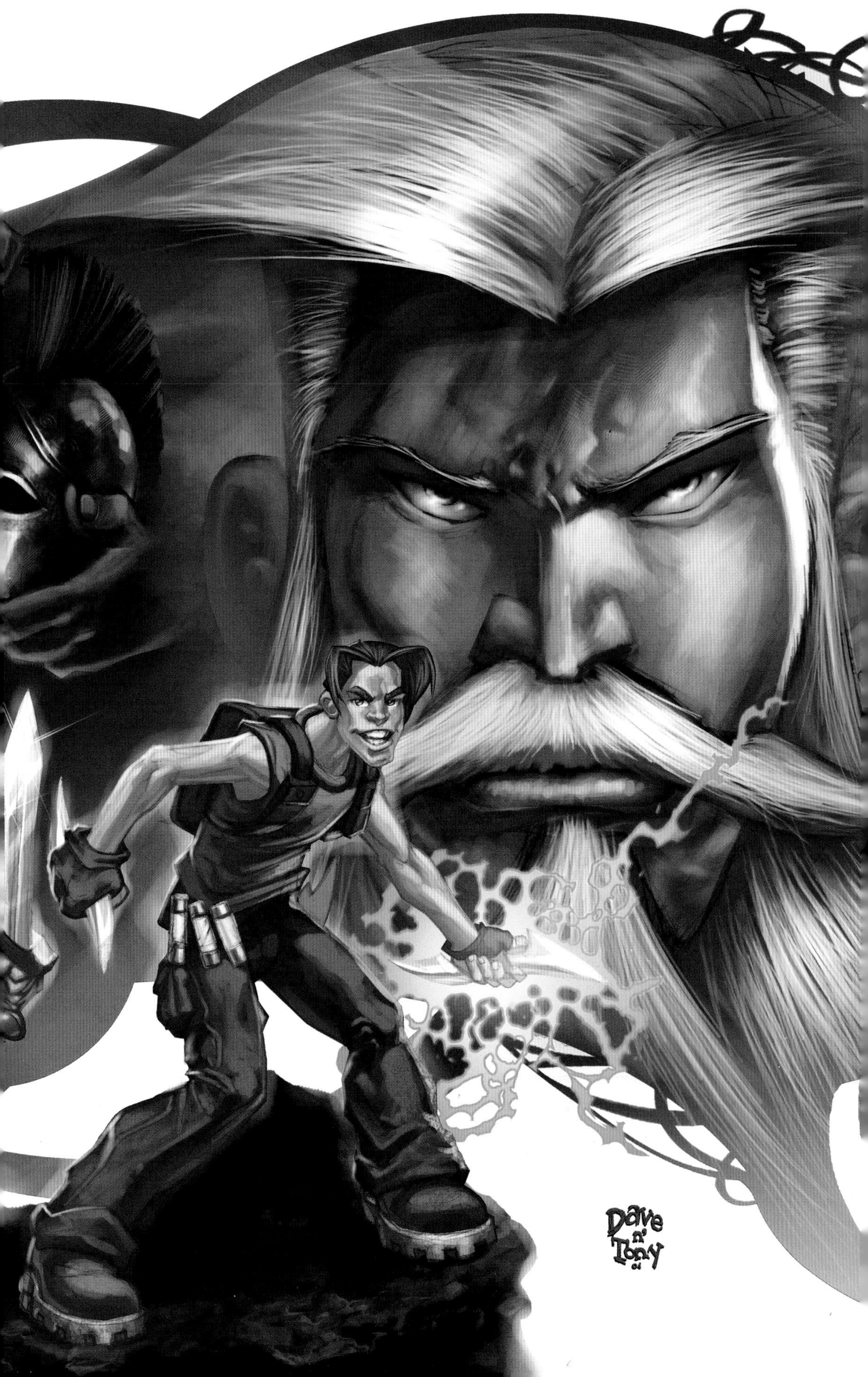
Dave n' Tony

Kevin Munroe is the creator of the CGI TV Christmas special *Donner*. He has also developed and sold TV and film projects to Disney, Warner Bros., Paramount/Nickelodeon, and many others. In addition to working in video games, Kevin has co-created and written *El Zombo Fantasma* for Dark Horse Comics. *Olympus Heights* is the first comic completely written and illustrated by Kevin, and certainly won't be his last. He is currently writing and directing his first CGI film for theatrical release in 2007.

Previous Pages: art by Dave Wilkins and Tony Washington